Emilyn, my friend with love! Hugs Catherine

Preaching the Big Questions

Doctrine Isn't Dusty

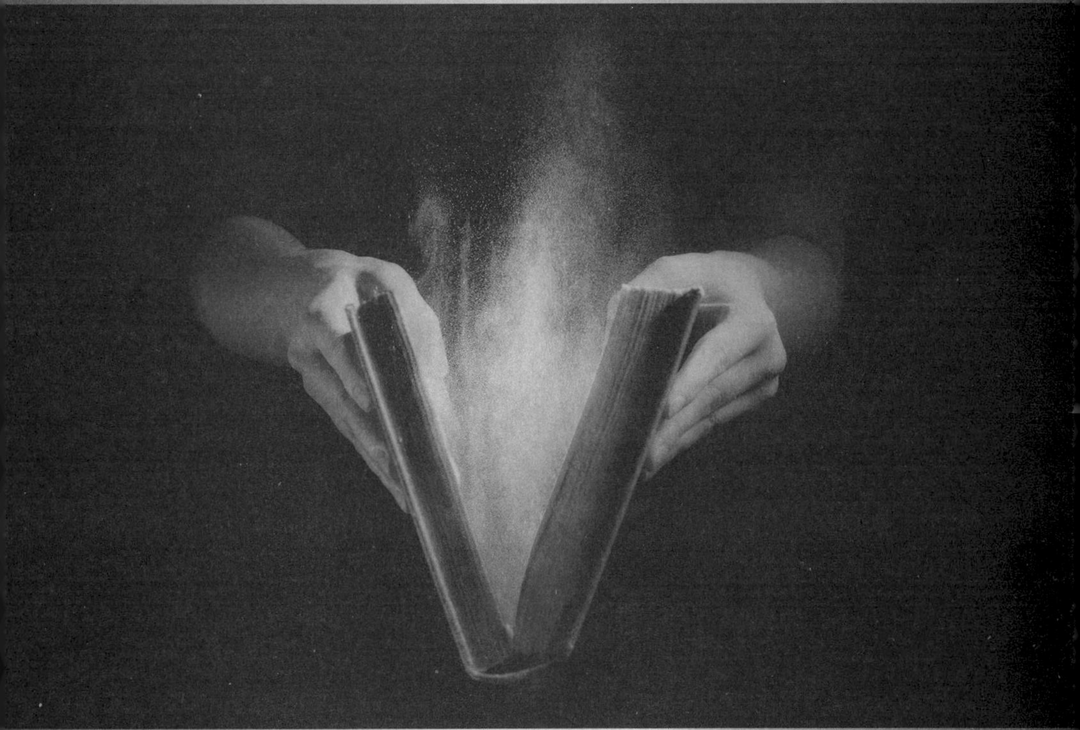

Catherine Faith MacLean and John H. Young

UNITED CHURCH
PUBLISHING HOUSE

Preaching the Big Questions
Doctrine Isn't Dusty
Catherine Faith MacLean and John H. Young

Copyright © 2015
The United Church of Canada
L'Église Unie du Canada

All rights reserved. No part of this book may be photocopied, reproduced, stored in a retrieval system, or transmitted in any form or by any means, electronic, mechanical, or otherwise, without the written permission of The United Church of Canada.

All biblical quotations, unless otherwise noted, are from the *New Revised Standard Version Bible*, copyright © 1989 National Council of the Churches of Christ in the United States of America. Used by permission. All rights reserved. Specified biblical quotations from *Good News Bible* © ABS 1995.

Care has been taken to trace ownership of copyright material contained in this text. The publisher will gratefully accept any information that will enable it to rectify any reference or credit in subsequent printings.

Library and Archives Canada Cataloguing in Publication
MacLean, Catherine Faith, 1958–, author
    Preaching the big questions : doctrine isn't dusty / Catherine Faith MacLean and John H. Young.

Issued in print and electronic formats.
ISBN 978-1-55134-231-3 (paperback).—ISBN 978-1-55134-232-0 (html)

    1. United Church of Canada—Doctrines. 2. Christian life—United Church of Canada authors. I. Young, John H., 1952–, author II. Title.

BX9881.M34 2015   287.9'2   C2015-905296-3
                                       C2015-905297-1

United Church Publishing House
3250 Bloor St. West, Suite 300
Toronto, ON
Canada M8X 2Y4
1-800-268-3781

bookpub@united-church.ca
www.ucrdstore.ca/ucph

UCPH is a ministry of
The United Church of Canada,
supported by Mission & Service
and readers like you.

Design/layout: Carina Cruz Domingues, mjgraphik, Graphics and Print
Cover Photo: Lightstock

Printed in Canada
5 4 3 2 1   19 18 17 16 15

Also available
as an

UCRDstore.ca

♻ 150107

Contents

Foreword v

Acknowledgements ix

Introduction 1

1. Sovereignty of God: Between a Rock and a Hard Place 21
2. Christology: "Who Do You Say That I Am?" 35
3. Atonement: Two Wrongs Don't Make a Right 51
4. The Authority of Scripture: The Word of God? 77
5. Sin and Regeneration: There's an Elephant in the Room 95
6. Human Depravity: Talking about Our Shadow Side 117
7. Grace and Salvation: Water to Our Thirst 135
8. The Church: God's Gift to the World? 153
9. Vocation: Called in Our Post-Christendom Society 169
10. Ministry: Equipping the Saints 187
11. Baptism: "We Want to Get Her Done" 207
12. Holy Communion:
    "What Should We Do with the Leftover Elements?" 225
13. Last Things: The Destination and the Journey 241

For Further Reading 257

Notes 259

Foreword

A popular adage has been making the rounds in church (and other) circles: "You've got to walk the talk." This saying has to do with integrity, with practising what you preach. It is about congruity between what you say and how you act and live. For a number of years now I have flipped this adage around, saying we need to "talk the walk." On a personal level, this means that you need to be able to understand and articulate why you act and live in a particular way. In communal terms, as people of the Christian faith, it means being able to articulate the reasons that inform our practice of ministry, including our ethical commitments and our work for justice, healing, and transformation. To use biblical language, you need to "always be ready to make your defense to anyone who demands from you an accounting for the hope that is in you; yet do it with gentleness and reverence" (1 Peter 3:15–16).

In our post-modern context, our testimony must be current to be accepted as credible in our social market of ideas. People are interested in believability and authenticity. We are interested to know the *why* behind a person's actions, convictions, and activism. Folks want to know the reason for your hope and for the passion that animates your commitments.

Simon Sinek's book *Start with Why: How Great Leaders Inspire Everyone to Take Action* argues that most people connect with the *why* behind what you do, more than the what and the how. What, they want to know, is the deep purpose, belief, or conviction behind what you do?

Preaching the Big Questions: Doctrine Isn't Dusty takes on 13 of the key historical doctrines of the Christian church. It is a compelling, necessary, and accessible excursion into the *why* of our faith, our theological statements, and our pastoral undertakings. The authors, Catherine and John, acknowledge that there is an unpopular stereotype attached to the word *doctrine*. For many of their colleagues in ministry—and for many of those both within and outside of the church—the word conjures up images of dusty, boring, stuffy, bygone theological articulations that are pretty much irrelevant for today.

Catherine and John—both of whom I have known for many, many years through conferences, conversations, and the wider work of the church—would beg to differ. They contend that preaching doctrine is a "crucial issue for the contemporary United Church." They suggest that doctrine "addresses the big questions of our lives, our relationships, and our understandings of God. Faithful and questioning people have brought their best energies to these questions over the centuries.... We are a living part of doctrine as we sift inherited wisdom and bring fresh ideas." Doctrine, they argue, "is less about attempting to be correct and more about exploring possibility."

Both Catherine and John believe that doctrine is not only important but even fun and stimulating to engage with. Now some of you may be a little incredulous about the latter part of that statement. Well, in the words of Mother Teresa: "Come and see." Take the plunge and read through this book. You will quickly discern that their passion and enjoyment comes through in every chapter. Why? Because they write as those who have sat intentionally and reflectively—for a long time—with questions of faith and practice, and they have been wrestled with them in scripture and in the long and storied theological tradition of the historic Christian church. They also care deeply for the world and for those who comprise the church.

The authors are enjoining us to "think critically, live faithfully"— to borrow a motto from *The Christian Century* magazine. Many of us in paid accountable ministry have huge ministry pressures. It is often difficult to feel that we can take the time to engage in what seems like the luxury of reading theology and studying and reflecting on historic articulations of the Christian faith. And yet, what is helpful in this book is the legitimate connection that is drawn between such an undertaking and the qualitative contribution that it makes to our faith, preaching, pastoral care, ethical practice, and worship leadership, as well as to the lives and faith of the ones we are privileged to serve in our pastoral charges and venues of ministry.

In reflecting on the doctrine of grace, Catherine writes: "Doctrine doesn't constrict the preacher—it gives us adventure." And in John's chapter on the doctrine of the church, he talks about the need to strengthen, and perhaps recover "the sense of the church as a place where God can be, and is, active, and the related understanding of the church as an 'instrument of the loving Spirit of Christ.'" They are excited about not only the importance of doctrine but its applicability and its capacity to liberate and inspire.

It is worth noting that this book arose from presentations that John and Catherine made at Worship Matters and Queen's Annual Theology Conference. An overwhelming number of attendees at each of these events asked John and Catherine to put their presentations into book form. Sensitive to this request and the context out of which it came, they have structured each chapter in a way that explores a particular doctrine while attending to possible pastoral concerns that may arise. As well, they propose liturgical settings in which the doctrine may be addressed and provide a sample sermon with a biblical text or two.

I appreciate the generous hospitality of both these authors in a particular way. While stating their preferred way of understanding each doctrine there is a grace that allows for a diversity of interpretations. We are a big tented church after all.

Catherine and John are well suited for this project. Catherine is an academic who is fully ensconced in all the joy and complexity of pastoral ministry, and John is an academic who is vocationally dedicated to teaching and participating in the formation of critically thinking individuals for the tasks of ministry. Together, they are able to reflect on and write about the continuum of formation in the practice of preaching, intentional theological reflection, pastoral and spiritual care, the crafting of liturgy, and engagement in social justice.

I am writing this foreword near the beginning of the Muslim holy month of Ramadan. Our son came home the other night and engaged me in a conversation that reminded me of the importance of this book. He was working out at the gym with a Muslim acquaintance who was articulating not only why he was a Muslim, but why Islam was superior to Christianity and all other faiths. He proceeded to tell our son that "Jesus isn't really very special because he didn't do anything new." He said, "Mohammed actually recorded the words of Allah, directly." Standing there in the kitchen, our son and I had a wonderful conversation, for all intents and purposes, about the doctrines of God, Jesus, the church, sin, atonement, grace, scripture, and ministry. We spoke about respecting other faiths and traditions while not being afraid or shy about lovingly articulating our Christian faith and being proud of it. As well, we spoke about how we can work together with others for justice and the common good. Afterwards, he felt a lot more prepared, clear, and encouraged to articulate the *why* of his faith; the Christian faith. Doctrine matters!

The Rev. Dr. Anthony D. Bailey
Parkdale United Church
Ottawa, Ontario

Acknowledgements

As much as every word in this book has come through our eyes and our fingertips, they would not be in this form without the interest, encouragement, and support of others.

We deeply appreciate the churches we have served, who valued theology and preaching. They affirmed in us the pastoral significance of wrestling with doctrinal concepts, and they called us to precision in speaking theologically. They valued sermon preparation, listened actively, sent us to professional development events, and supported our writing time. We hope the people of these pastoral charges see themselves reflected with warmth and respect in these pages: Rawdon, Nova Scotia; Harrowsmith-Verona, Ontario; Restigouche, New Brunswick; Yellowknife, Northwest Territories; Canmore in the Rocky Mountains; and St. Paul's in Edmonton.

We are grateful to Mark MacLean and the working group who created the Worship Matters events in The United Church of Canada and, in particular, the team responsible for the 2007 gathering in London, Ontario. We offer thanks to Jean Stairs, Principal, and the participants at the Queen's Annual Theology Conference in 2010. Colleagues in ministry encouraged us to say more beyond the conferences; we appreciate those conversations. When we were deep into the material, students and teachers in our denomination and abroad gave us confidence that the project was worthwhile: we are grateful.

We offer thanks to Emmanuel College in Toronto for its hospitality when we managed to get to the same city at the same time, and to Queen's School of Religion for allowing us to integrate the seminary experience with pastoral formation. United Church Publishing House said yes, and the team there has been attentive and creative: thank you.

At early ages, we learned from our families the pleasure of wondering where ideas come from and why. Catherine learned the power of preaching from her father, George. In these recent years of writing together, our home lives have sustained us with patience and encouragement. Caroline has been a source of strength for John and, happily, a willing conversation partner about the book. Catherine's children, Andrew and Hannah, wrote university essays alongside her during reading weeks and cheered her progress. Earl never doubted her, or the project; his confidence and humour mean more than he can know. Many thanks, and deep love to you all.

Our collegial work has developed into friendship, and we want to acknowledge our deep appreciation for each other's stamina, imagination, and commitment.

Introduction

Faith Speaking Understanding

The bicycle was borrowed from a faculty member and the backpack was heavy. I navigated narrow streets and back lanes every day, from residence to class and home again, the weight of the books heavy on my shoulders. I secured the bike against theft with an enormous lock, and returned the books on time to avoid fines. I was careful. Evenings found me in the residence, at an oak table that seated 12, heavy into debate. Original sin and grace, Origen and Augustine, Christology and the faces of Buddha: rich, enriching conversations.

In those seminary days, I had lots of time to discuss God and to ponder theology. I loved it: the leisurely conversations as I chopped lettuce in the residence kitchen, the lively arguments as students walked across well-tended lawns, the curiosity about books we borrowed from the library, the questions we posed as we sipped espressos or cheap red wine in Harvard Square. The topics mattered. I learned about the roots of justice, the trajectories of contemplation, the issues of relationships, and the influence of social location. The study of God's presence in human history and experience gave me a reliable lens through which to see the world.

Now I chop vegetables for my children, dash along the expressway to a meeting, or sit in a grieving person's home with a pot of Lapsang souchong tea going cold on the table between us. Amid the demands of a personal life, engagement with the world, and ministerial responsibility, I hope those theological foundations sustain me. I trust my continued study keeps the reflections fresh.

Perhaps this story—Catherine's story—sounds familiar. Maybe it is true for you, too. Or maybe you are in the midst of studying now. For many ministers, the pleasure we once had in leisurely conversations has accelerated into an urgent calling. Pastoral care, church budgets, social action, congregational change, and the weekly rhythm of Sunday worship preparation require immediate attention. When is there time for long theological conversations? How do we recall the joy we had in those conversations? How do we make time to read?

We sign up expectantly for conferences, workshops, and webinars; invitations from across the continent arrive in our inboxes. Sometimes there may be a long conversation about the authority of scripture or the sovereignty of God, atonement theories or human depravity. Every now and then we taste again the pleasures of those debates. Then we return home, where relentless demands call on our energy and thought.

In this activity we find the reality and the expression of our faith; we are busy with meaningful work. We are aware, too, that the external world judges us by how we live and how we give, by where we show up and what we do. More weight is given these days to action than to speech. Yet the meaning behind all this activity is *why* we do it. The meaning is the reason; it generates the energy.

The experience of weekly worship opens us to the presence of God. A regular worshipping practice can focus our awareness of the Holy and of God's touch in our lives. Our congregations hope ministers do many things. But they invite us into their midst primarily to help them with basic religious questions. Who am I? Why am I here? What is the meaning of life? Who is God? What wisdom will sustain me through trouble?

It is in hard times that people lean into what they believe. So ministers aim to provide worshippers with sufficient resources to strengthen the faith that will inform the decisions they make at work, in the community, and at home—in other words, to guide their thinking about how they lead their lives. We assist as they make sense of their lives. That is a remarkable task, and pastoral care is a privilege as well as a calling. In that calling, the practice of theology sustains us.

What we believe energizes what we do. Preaching for the long run, we need sustenance. Words are powerful; ask anyone who has felt bullied. Confident, strong, vulnerable, open-minded, deeply rooted, and loving words crafted into sermons have transforming power. What we say—Sunday after Sunday, year after year—in some sense becomes who we are. The word informs our expression. What we proclaim becomes who people know us to be.

I return to the Sunday sermon. Sitting at my desk, I am aware of the commotion in the front office, of the appointments on my agenda, and of the shelves of books along the wall. Twisting my attention away from pressing tasks, I turn to the wisdom of the church to guide me so that I can offer leadership. Others have walked these paths, prayed these petitions, thought through the challenges, and written theology that speaks to the issues of our lives.

This is "faith seeking understanding." The phrase *fides quaerens intellectum* comes from Anselm of Canterbury (1033–1109), who posited that after faith comes the call to reason the faith. When we incorporate reasoning the faith into Sunday preparation, it is apologetic preaching. Beyond what we do, this is the *why* of what we do.

The Origins of This Book

Worship Matters was a series of national events on preaching, music, the arts, and worship leadership in The United Church of Canada. At the symposium held in London, Ontario, in 2007, the co-authors presented a keynote address called "Shortening the Distance between Podium and Pulpit." We discussed how to sustain our preaching, season after season, through pastoral care and congregational change. We acknowledged that ministers are outrageously busy. There is no such thing as a "low Sunday" anymore; preachers are "on" constantly.

We recognized that in the midst of these constant demands, it is difficult to integrate the lectures we heard in the classroom. How could we bring that material to our pulpits? Pastoral need, our social justice commitments, and the study groups we lead drive the bulk of our theological study. The common lectionary guides us through three years of biblical material. Many of us preach on grace regularly, but beyond that, we lack the breathing space to pick up a theological text for personal pleasure or supplementary study.

At Worship Matters we argued that it was important to preach about doctrine, and illustrated how one might do that for four topics: Sovereignty of God, Human Depravity, Grace, and Vocation. We wondered how our colleagues would receive our work. We also wondered what they would think of bringing inflammatory and controversial topics like the Sovereignty of God and Human Depravity to a national event. At the end, we were given prolonged applause.

Three years later we presented again, at the Queen's Annual Theology Conference. We brought resources on Sin and Regeneration, Scripture, Last Things, and Ecclesiology (the church). We wondered particularly if Sin and Last Things would be welcome. Again, the idea was well received. Attendees asked us to put our approach to preaching doctrine into a published form so they could try it out themselves.

Now we've taken those lectures, reworked them for a broader audience, and added five other topics. The result: *Preaching the Big Questions: Doctrine Isn't Dusty.*

Our Interest in Preaching Doctrine

When *doctrine isn't dusty,* how are we using the word *doctrine?* The term can refer to a denomination's formal statement(s) of faith, as in the Doctrine section of the Basis of Union. It can also be used as a synonym for *theology,* or comments about or reflection upon some aspect of the Christian faith tradition. It is in this latter sense that we use the term *doctrine* in this book. So, for example, when we speak about a doctrine of ministry, we are talking about a theological understanding of ministry. Christian denominations hold doctrinal understandings of the Christian faith and sometimes in particular ways that vary from one denomination to another. So do individual Christians.

Doctrine addresses the big questions of our lives, our relationships, and our understandings of God. Faithful and questioning people have brought their best energies to these questions over the centuries. Tradition, inspiration, and fresh possibilities informed their responses to the dilemmas they faced—and that we often face. We are a living part of doctrine, as we sift inherited wisdom and bring fresh ideas.

Attention to doctrine in preaching, as we understand it, is less about attempting to be correct and more about exploring possibility. Striving to be correct gets dry fast. Having said that, preaching ought to have a solid starting point. There is wisdom in our traditions that speaks—in fact, declares—relevant truths. Sermons about doctrine should mean something useful, uplifting, and worshipful. Doctrine can be a solid path to fresh thought, relevant commentary, and faithful proclamation. Doctrine won't be dry if we preach it with joy, and with both feet on the ground.

Preaching doctrine is a crucial issue for the contemporary United Church, and our comments may well be true for other mainline denominations in Canada and the United States. That issue is the need to emphasize theology in the life of the church, particularly in its preaching and teaching ministries in the local congregation. We do not mean heavy-handed pronouncements of perceived right thinking. We mean the skill of talking theologically. The skill calls on the heritage of faith and the wisdom of forebears who faced human dilemmas, while also taking into account contemporary thinking that is considered and fresh. Our sense of its importance has become ever clearer to us during our years of ministry.

We met three decades ago while John was in his settlement charge, and Catherine was a divinity student and candidate for ministry. Christianity was significantly more culturally dominant then than now; changes were happening but we were slow to recognize them. In such an environment, being a Christian was rather akin to being a good Canadian—you paid your taxes and supported the government, you treated your spouse and children well, you didn't break the law (except, perhaps, with regard to the speed limit), and you acted toward your neighbours as you hoped they would act toward you. You really did not need to think about theology or what you believed; belonging to the church was the thing to do.

Also at that time, Christianity was about what we did: social justice, keeping a lid on misdemeanours, being kind. It was a common, popular morality rather than doctrine. There was still a culture of Christendom, in which, if you belonged to a so-called mainline denomination, government and religion were intertwined. It is fair to say that being a Christian was often understood as being a nice person who went to church each week.

That time is not our time. We are not sure that the overlap between culture and religion in which we grew up was a healthy one for Christianity. But whether it was healthy or not is immaterial; that world is not our world. Now, the values the Christian tradition espouses are usually at variance with the values of the culture. Sometimes they are diametrically opposed.

Our values can be articulated when we examine our doctrine. In an increasingly secular Canada where other values are dominant, we need to teach the traditions of our faith—which is to say, teach doctrine—for three related reasons: formation, ethical living, and pastoral care.

Formation

First, those who would be part of the Christian community need to understand what the Christian tradition is about; they need to be schooled in it. *Formation* is a term for that. People who are drawn to check out Christianity and who desire to become part of the church want to learn about the Christian tradition and be formed in it. They are new to a life of faith, or new to our denomination, or new to a specific congregation's expression of faith. Many long-time members of the church are also interested in learning about our heritage of faith and fresh perspectives on it. When church membership classes are opened to anyone who is interested in attending, long-time members often outnumber the recently arrived.

Our Christian point of view is different from the view of our culture. Our faith tradition leads us to value ourselves, and our place in this world that God has made, in a way that is not the way of the world. People in the congregation can only come to value themselves and the world as

Christians if they are offered formation in the traditions of our faith. Yes, we learn by doing, but we fine-tune the learning through conversation, teaching, and listening. We are going to form opinions about personal self-worth, the value of relationships, the rights of others, and the wider world. Preaching doctrine gives words to the *why* of the opinions, and allows those opinions to be considered and faithful. Listening to well-taught doctrine helps us explain our countercultural behaviour, both to ourselves and to others.

Catherine ran our ideas about doctrine past some colleagues at lunch. "They've all got doctrine," one said. He's a Presbyterian, and he wasn't referring to a presbytery meeting; he was referring to churchgoers. "They've all got doctrine. It's not orthodox, or rigid, or catalogued. It's not unfriendly or defensive. It's simply ways of living, expectations, a story."

How deep does it go? we wondered. In this postmodern world of questions and subjective truth, how much of life is sustained simply by ways of living, expectations, a story? When the hard times hit, is it enough?

Ethical Living

For those who would be Christian, the faith tradition represents a spiritual home. It roots the ethics according to which we lead our lives, the position from which we approach the world. And that perspective is different from the mindset of secular North American culture.

We need to teach the doctrine of the church because our faith tradition represents a particular spiritual home. Christian teachings and Christian values speak to our finitude, to the reality that we are stewards and not owners of the things of this world, to the need to love our neighbours as ourselves. Our culture teaches us that we human beings are self-made and that we are to put our own well-being first. Christianity presents an alternative way of viewing the world and therefore of living. Members of our congregations, and those who are curious about Christianity because of something they have read, heard, or experienced, are only going to be able to live according to such a perspective if church leaders present it to them. Teaching the tenets of the Christian faith is the way we do that.

Here's an example. One of the kindergarten children in the K to 12 school stood in the hallway as the teenagers milled past. He was lost; his classroom was at the opposite end of the building. Quiet sniffles and tears began. One of the teens, dressed fully in goth style, stopped and turned toward him. He removed a black glove and stretched out a hand. The child looked at the hand and reached for it. Five minutes later at the kindergarten room door, the teacher asked the teen how he came to respond to the child. "I was taught to see people in need," he replied. "I go with my mum to church."

Pastoral Care

Finally, the Christian faith offers us the means through which to make sense of our own lives, of our personal high points and our times of crisis. In other words, it makes available to ministers the pastoral care we offer to others and need for ourselves, a theologically based pastoral care.

There are pastoral reasons to help members of our congregations deepen their understanding of the Christian faith. We have not talked much for most of the past century about the concept of original sin, let alone the overlapping concept of human depravity. But recovering solid notions of the meaning of sin, depravity, atonement, and the sacraments would be useful for us. "I don't ever take communion," a woman said to an elder. "I don't deserve it. I know you talk about forgiveness, but what I've done won't go away. You decent people go ahead." Clarity in our doctrines of sin and communion would serve her well.

In summary, we are proposing that a conscious, specific, open, and thorough wrestling with Christian doctrine is crucial for formation, for ethical living, and for effective pastoral care.

Preaching about doctrine and our faith tradition has influenced how we view ministry. At some point in John's pastoral ministry, he concluded that his role for his congregants was a modified form of "rabbi." They had called him into their midst to do what rabbis in the Jewish tradition have historically done. The rabbi is the one called to be the teacher in the congregation, to be the resident theologian who helps members of the congregation with their religious, theological, and ethical questions. Our congregations may hope we also do other things, particularly in the area of pastoral care. But they invite ministers primarily to help with their basic religious questions.

A minister's calling is to help provide those who gather for worship with resources to enable their faith to inform how they lead their lives. It is to enable them to make meaning. It is about equipping the saints. It is about the cure of souls.

You may have some other individuals in your congregations who also do such equipping. If so, you are very lucky. But it is the responsibility of ministers to do so. No other professionals in society play that role, and it is a crucial one. Ministers function in the congregations we serve, and in the wider church, as the "stewards of God's mysteries," to borrow a phrase from Paul (1 Corinthians 4:1).

It has always been an important role for a minister to play. It is particularly so in the times in which we now live. And our hope is that as we accept the challenge, this theological thinking will become even more deeply a part of us.

Our Invitation to You

We have had the good fortune and privilege of listening to many of our colleagues preach. Each preacher brings faith, imagination, study, and a unique understanding of their particular context. Each has a singular voice, an individual practice of preparation, and a personal prayer life that makes every sermon a work of Spirit. There are many styles of writing and presenting sermons. The work is embodied, even incarnational. We benefit from listening to one another. It is in the spirit of that sharing that we offer this book, as an invitation into our theological and homiletical endeavour.

In conversations with colleagues across our church, we hear a yearning for theological conversations. When we bring up atonement, communion, or Christology, we hear opinions. When we ask about eschatology (last things), vocation, or sin, the room rarely goes quiet. We want to bring that passion into an exercise in preaching.

It is not our intention to cover every doctrine with all its nuances in this book. Even if we wished to, we could not include every angel that ever danced on a pin! What we offer is a solid grounding for preaching in what we understand to be foundational points of doctrine with which people in our pews wrestle in a variety of ways. We hope that our offerings will inspire preachers to continue to read theology, with an eye to pastoral application and also to the pleasure of thinking theologically.

We examine 13 doctrinal issues. We'll show how we have preached on each of them, using a passage of scripture for each doctrine. Some of the doctrines we cover are not issues the preacher has to deal with every week or very often at all. We are convinced, though, that we do face each of them at least occasionally, and they form a subtext in surprising ways. Issues of sin and guilt lurk, especially if we do not address them. Existential angst—last things—drives insatiable shopping, inconsolable anxiety, and a desperate desire for security. Entitlement sneaks in and poses as grace.

Each chapter has five parts. First we introduce a doctrinal concept. Then we suggest a biblical passage that is a source for reflecting on the doctrine: of many possibilities, we have made a choice. We outline pastoral concerns that make this doctrine an important living concept, and we present how it can preach. Finally, we attach a sermon that has been created with these thoughts in mind. Some of the sermons are edited versions of sermons presented in a congregation; some were written specifically for this collection.

Here is an overview of the doctrines we address:

Sovereignty of God

When we are up against the hard things of life, our self-reliance begins to fade. We, who are so capable, are responsible for climate change and environmental degradation. How do we address the limits to our power? How do we speak about the all-encompassing love of God? This chapter will address our dependence on God, including our assumption that we are in control of our bodies—which we Westerners think of as a right, not a privilege. In the illusion of total control, the sovereignty of God comes into play. This chapter addresses our dependence on God, focuses pastorally on Alzheimer's, and leans on Job 38:4–7: "when I laid the foundation of the earth."

Christology

A Christian affirmation about the person and work of Jesus stands at the centre of our faith tradition. Yet a wide variety of Christological positions exists. Who is Jesus for each of us? How do we answer such a question in light of contemporary and popular scholarship? How, in a pluralist age, do we understand Christianity's claims about Jesus? Contemporary Christians need to claim unapologetically the particularity of this affirmation of our faith tradition, without denying the possibility of God working also through other faith traditions. This chapter offers John 14:1–7 as a passage for preaching on Christology.

Atonement

Do we really have to believe that God sent Jesus to die? The medieval theologians Anselm and Peter Abelard bring us the arguments that we loved in seminary; some of us also encountered Gregory of Nyssa's classic view there. Substitutionary sacrifice may be the most common understanding, but it is not the only Christian understanding of Jesus' death. Ransom is a cosmic conflict, and satisfaction is a legal framework for understanding our relationship with God. Christ as witness to God's love kindles love in our human hearts and becomes the moral influence in our lives. Members of the congregation may have their own questions or want to be able to discuss atonement with neighbours who belong to other churches. In either case, it is essential to develop articulate understandings. This chapter presents more than one orthodox view of atonement and suggests how to preach a non-sacrificial answer for followers of Jesus from Mark 1:16–20.

The Authority of Scripture

Many Christian denominations, including The United Church of Canada, have a high view of the authority of scripture in their formal doctrinal statements. But many contemporary Christians struggle with this authority; they equate the authority of scripture with the stories of scripture being "true" in the literal or empirical sense. Recovering the understanding that God's Living Word comes to us through the words of scripture, as we hear the biblical stories read and explicated, would enable us to experience more fully the power of scripture, and its authority, in our daily lives. This chapter approaches preaching on the doctrine using 2 Timothy 3:14–16.

Sin and Regeneration

It seems that *sin* is a four-letter word. In the United Church there is deep interest in original blessing, and the corrective away from moralistic, judgmental preaching and teaching is a good thing. Yet around us we observe the infliction of suffering from one human person to another. Within us we observe a sense that all is not well, that we harbour temptation, selfishness, and the desire for self over other. What do we do with this reality? If we are not sophisticated enough to simply overcome our mistakes intellectually, how do we account for it? If sin is no more than our bad choices, and redemption merely therapy, where is Christ's work? We find ourselves back at the concept of sin and the cure for it. In non-traditional language we will outline how sin is real—as is, significantly, being made new and free. We refer to Mark 2:13–17 and call on Joseph and his brothers in Genesis 37.

Human Depravity

The term *human depravity* fell out of fashion some time ago. Contemporary United Church members tend to reflect the societal view of ourselves as basically good people who sometimes make mistakes. But our ancestors, who used the term without hesitation, had a more profound sense of the human condition. They recognized that each of us has a "shadow side," that both our humanity and our societal structures are fundamentally flawed. Recovering this doctrinal concept is pastorally important, for it enables us to address more adequately both systemic evil and the penetrating and controlling quality of addictions. The chapter suggests an approach to preaching about this doctrine using Romans 7:14–25 as a text.

Grace and Salvation

Grace is the reassurance of God's constant presence and care. It is the fallback doctrine for much United Church preaching. Without it, we could not sally forth into the social justice and personal transformation we see in ministry around us every day. Yet our culture sees grace rooted in one another rather than in God. The first factor is to see grace without entitlement. For those of us who live in privilege, the distinction can be tricky. The second factor is to see grace as more than mere kindness. It is transformative. How do we communicate the awe of grace? The third factor is to wonder if grace is available to us all. Is salvation universal? We wrestle with Jesus' parable of the vineyard, Matthew 19:27—20:16, as a way into grace and salvation.

The Church

Concepts of the church, such as "God's gift to the world," seem meaningless to many contemporary Christians. Distinctive denominational points, ministerial rivalries, and congregational competition are at best confusing and at worse antithetical to what the church "should be."

Further, church scandals and the strong individualism of the last few decades make belonging to the institutional church uninviting for many. (Think: "I'm spiritual, not religious.") But the church remains important as one place where injustice is challenged, where alternative perspectives to a secularized and consumer-driven society are presented, and where empowerment for mission happens. Further, the church becomes a critical counter to the individualism of our era. Those who participate in this countercultural institution need affirmation for their involvement. The chapter outlines one way to preach on this area of doctrine using 1 Peter 2:9–10.

Vocation

We rarely discuss vocation, except when we are thinking about the call to some formally ordered ministry. Yet Protestantism in particular has a rich history of valuing God's call to each person, regardless of their "station in life." In a post-Christendom world, where the practice of Christianity is increasingly met with ambivalence or even hostility, members of the congregation need to be willing to talk about their faith and to stand out by virtue of their efforts to live lives that are consistent with the faith they profess. This chapter illustrates preaching about vocation, using 1 Peter 3:13–17.

Ministry

"The priesthood of all believers" is a popular and effective concept. But how does it function in a church culture of lay and ordered ministers, and a variety of streams of ministry? What did Martin Luther really mean by this phrase? The call to witness, *vocare*, is a privilege and a burden. This chapter speaks to an integration of ministers' pastoral lives, the question of ministry in a variety of expressions, and the pressures of the changing church. We lift up the pastoral life of religious vocation working with Ephesians 4:11–16, Jeremiah 20:9, and the conviction that these gifts are God-given.

Baptism

Baptism, along with communion, is one of the two sacraments recognized in the United Church. Yet when we try to think through our understanding of baptism, there are challenges. The New Testament does not present a clear and consistent picture of either the meaning or the practice of baptism. Particularly since the 16th century, Christians have debated the appropriate age at which baptism should take place. Although the United Church understands baptism as that which, in a formal way, makes a person a part of the church community, current societal trends tend to separate baptism from its close church connection. This chapter emphasizes the dominant place grace has in the doctrine and the kind of community Christians understand themselves to be creating by virtue of baptism. Galatians 3:23–29 is the text for the sermon.

Holy Communion

Doctrinal discussions about communion frequently focus on how Christ is understood to be present to us in this sacrament. Most congregations exhibit a wide spectrum of perspectives. One also still meets individuals who feel unworthy to receive communion, even as liturgical scholars for the past two generations have encouraged a more frequent celebration of communion in mainline Protestant denominations. The reflections on doctrine and the accompanying sermon on 1 Corinthians 11:23–26 include examining the concept of "remembering," what it is we are remembering, and the implications of the celebration of the sacrament for the type of community we are.

Last Things

Calves really are sometimes born with two heads. One-hundred-foot waves are increasingly common on our oceans. Nations rise up against each other with appalling violence. The shocks and surprises of our sophisticated contemporary lives involve disasters of biblical proportions, and our future gazing is shadowed with fear of personal, economic, and ecological ruin. How can we ignore these concerns on Sunday mornings? When preaching is focused on personal agency and the call to social justice, it can be difficult to address the last things, the end times, eschatology, and rapture. But what lies beyond the grave is critical. A basic message of scripture is that death does not end our relationship with God. How do we make relevant the recurring affirmation that in death we continue to be in God's care and keeping? In our lives and beyond, there will be an end, a resolution, a bringing of all things, sanctified, forgiven, and renewed, back to God. We are released from the cycle of life or the circle of eternity. The doctrine of last things also concerns the purpose of time. This chapter outlines how to bring a message that we can rest assured that death is not the final word, referring to the frightening images in Revelation 6:12–17, and the words from the burial service in Revelation 21:1–7.

Preaching as a Transformational Practice

"He always comes up with something that probes your mind," a woman said to Catherine of her minister when she visited a neighbouring congregation. Catherine was glad to hear it. The spiritual nurture we offer in sermons shows concern for the deep experiences of congregants' lives, for our impact on this earth, and for our relationships with God. Week by week preachers create trust as we speak truth, faith, and hope and acknowledge the hardship within and around us. In comments after worship, we listen for indications that we have touched a nerve. In messages through the week, we agree to pastoral care appointments to further the conversations. In the determinations of congregational boards, we see the connection between faith and action. In all of this, we trust that the creation of sermons is worth it, that it is transformative, that it matters.

Taking the time to know the members of our congregations, ministers hear truths about their lives. We have the opportunity to reflect on their stories. Pastoral care is a great privilege. We cannot underestimate the importance of pastoral visitation: in emergencies, yes, when people are vulnerable. But also in the day-to-day routine of ordinary time, learning about where they live and how they work and play. To their lives we bring our interest in the traditions of the faith and our imagination as we create sermons. Steeped in prayerful writing, we are making meaning. More importantly, we are providing them with the tools to make Christian meaning themselves.

Some church libraries make a brisk business of lending books on contemporary theology. Members of our congregations also experience contemporary theology through the Internet and other media. As preachers we bring faithful, trained imaginations to make that learning lively. We offer an experience with God in the sermon.

As we engage the practice of preaching week by week, our personal worship experience transforms us, too. The rich experience of a preacher's growing faith deepens the congregation's faith. Our curiosity and our changing ideas benefit the listeners.

Studying theological texts enriches faith. Bringing those theological texts to our weekly practice infuses the realities of our times with the wisdom of the church. We can contemplate the possibilities in a particular doctrine as we read in our study, drive to the hospital, pray at the nursing home, pull on our boots for a political meeting, read news updates on our phones, or sit on the veranda at sunset. The connections are profound.

A Gift of Fresh Air

Doctrine is a gift. It is a breath of fresh air when everything seems routine. It is finding a new path of adventure when every other way looks predictable. Doctrine is meant to open our minds, to present possibilities, to engage us in transformation. It is not a constriction. Our hope in this book is that readers will enjoy doctrine and continue to explore it.

The way we present the 13 chosen doctrines is not exhaustive. There are many ways into each of them; doctrines are living concepts. Each doctrine guides us in the *why* of what we do. There are more ways of writing and presenting sermons than we can begin to imagine. Sermons are always written and delivered in the context of a specific time and place.

We can preach doctrine in a way that people will sit up, take notice, and say, "That's my life!" With attentiveness and care, we can preach Christian hope and the sovereignty of God at the time of a suicide, and predestination to God's realm by God's grace at a time when people feel entitled to greatness by their own achievements. We can strip the veneer off comfort theology, and look sin and depravity straight in the eye. We can get beyond default preaching and find the energies bubbling up out of the ground of our being. Life decisions are made in the deep-down places. We can preach solid doctrine with which listeners can go down deep, with confidence that they'll come back up.

A colleague at one of our presbytery meetings said to Catherine, "Oh yes, you're the one studying doctrine. Don't you get bored?" She responded, "Mostly not." We tell you that story not because we are judging her colleague—we're not—but because we wondered why he would find this work boring. Catherine asked him to say more, and he said it was about the vocabulary. "Doctrine, dogma, theology: they're old," he elaborated. "I'm interested in what we do, in how we show ourselves in the community."

The church brings the gift of theological reflection to social action. Partly it sustains us. Partly it calls us. Partly it brings us solid company, the reflections and assertions of others who have walked the path of justice and recorded their experience.

To those who say that doctrine is at best irrelevant and at worst a negative for the church and for contemporary Christian life, we say, *Try it.* Try it not as something that holds you back, but as something that offers you an adventure.

Here We Are

I gave the bicycle back to the professor. I have my own library now, shelves of accumulated texts. I prepare meals, drive to evening presbytery meetings, and listen to grief in coffee shops near congregants' workplaces. I trust my continued study keeps my pastoral care fresh. Perhaps this story is your story, too.

John and I remembered the leisurely conversations about meaning in theology classes. We wondered what would happen if we drew upon the vigour of our seminary experience and found a tool to bring it to the pulpit. From the joy of faith seeking understanding, we developed a formula for faith speaking understanding.

We hope this book will be helpful. We hope it will be a pleasure. We hope it will reconnect you with the theology you love to study, through the preaching you are called to proclaim. We hope that we inspire your imagination to do your own thing. Love your people. Stand with grace. Bring the Word.

Chapter 1
Sovereignty of God

Between a Rock and a Hard Place

The Doctrinal Concept

Wondering who is in charge puts us between a rock and a hard place. Part of us yearns for the solid comfort of a God who knows every breath that we take, guards every move we make, and comforts us at every moment. That is the rock. The hard place is squaring this 16th-century understanding of God with events in our lives that seem ours for the making, or governed by circumstance, or sometimes even random.

Wondering who is in charge is an important spiritual reflection, and one with a lot of history. Most potent perhaps is the heritage of the Reformers, and of John Calvin in particular. In the 16th century, they spoke of a God who is so thoroughly engaged with the world that nothing happens by chance. Were we to trust in that model of the God of Providence, the anxieties of our lives would slip into God's care. God, we would reason, must know what we cannot. Tragic loss, for instance, must be part of God's plan. Our finite and limited lives would be lived in an understanding that God is God and we are not.

The sovereignty of God is a way of acknowledging that God is present in ways that we cannot be. It is a mystery that requires a willingness to depend on God. It is not an easy way to live, although it can be a naïve way to live. It is difficult to prove, yet it can be fulfilling and a tremendous comfort. The language is awkward, and the concept can take your breath away. This doctrine is a mix.

Sovereignty by definition is monarchical. Elizabeth is queen and sovereign of Canada. In historical terms, a person who has supreme authority or power is sovereign. This language of sovereignty comes to us from scripture, from the ancient world where those scriptures were cultivated, and from the traditions of the church. But language changes and with it, our concepts change. The words and phrases we choose define the ideas we put forward, and the ideas we put forward determine the words and phrases we speak. It goes both ways. If I say the word *Lord*, for instance, you may think of medieval manor life. You may feel the heavy hand of one who "lords it over" you. You may do an etymological search and discover that it means "loaf ward," the one who was responsible for seeing that everyone had enough bread. If I ask you to bake the bread for communion, though, you will not likely think yourself lord for the week. All of which is to say that the words we choose are powerful. So it's difficult to untwist sovereignty from monarchy.

Another model of sovereignty is something, or someone, complete unto itself. It is intact. From the outside, events on the inside are untouchable, distant, and unfathomable. One thinks of massive creatures of the sea—called Leviathan in scripture—or perhaps the separation the Iron Curtain made between the West and the USSR.

A further model of sovereignty is something or someone outside our control, not governed by us. A sovereign state, for instance, is governed without interference from outside populations.

But to speak of the sovereignty of God requires yet another understanding: that God encompasses power we do not have. God is more than we can comprehend. The thing that might alarm us about government or incite us to political change is, when we speak of God, the very thing that draws us to this word.

There are dangers in this concept of God. There is the danger of anthropomorphism, that people claim for themselves a power arising from sovereignty. We know how easily dominant cultures appropriate an image of God. This can result in triumphalism, masculinism, racism, heterosexism, Eurocentrism—any of the ways we "lord over" others.

Another danger is a loss of self-respect. Lamps are hidden under bushels all over the place. If God is all-powerful and I am not, perhaps my powers are of no value. Connected to that is the danger that we give up: it can be a short road from "let it be" or "let go and let God" to despair. Then we lose our human agency and abdicate our energy to create and make positive change; we enter into despair and become impotent.

But let us not belabour these dangers. The point of this discussion is why the doctrine of the sovereignty of God is life-affirming and beneficial, and how it can be true. Many would say it is no longer worth the risk of the dangers to assert the doctrine: in human hands, it has brought dismay.

This is the rock and the hard place. Yet, if indeed doctrine is a tool for wondering and guidance more than a series of correct answers, let's look for the merit in the doctrine of the sovereignty of God. Doctrine is meant to open our minds, to present possibilities, to engage us in transformation.

So let us look for the blessing in the sovereignty of God. We find blessing as we consider the limits to our human experience. We have boundaries all around us: boundaries of time, place, energy, experience, physical ability, wisdom, and language; boundaries of patience, forgiveness, generosity, hospitality, hope, and love. To encounter God who goes beyond our limits and our restraints is to meet holy possibility. To encounter the sovereign God is to meet love that is all-encompassing.

This doctrine also addresses the regret we experience for our existential finitude. Our lifetime is limited and that saddens us to some extent, yet the concept of God's unlimited nature stirs our imagination. It speaks to there being life beyond life as we know it, and possibility of a better world than we ourselves make.

Among the four faith standards that the United Church recognizes as doctrine (subordinate to the primacy of scripture),[1] the 1940 Statement of Faith addresses the sovereignty of God most clearly. Here is Article I:

> **God**
> We believe in God, the eternal personal Spirit, Creator and Upholder of all things.
>
> We believe that God, as sovereign Lord exalted above the world, orders and overrules all things in it to the accomplishment of His holy, wise, and good purposes.
>
> We believe that God made man to love and serve Him; that He cares for him as a righteous and compassionate Father; and that nothing can either quench His love or finally defeat His gracious purpose for man.
>
> So we acknowledge God as Creator, Upholder, and Sovereign Lord of all things, and the righteous and loving Father of men.

The 1940 statement was prepared by a generation who experienced the First World War, the repercussions of the Russian Revolution, the 1918 influenza pandemic, the Great Depression, and the rise of fascism. The shock of violence, devastation, distress, and the breakdown of trust across borders reverberated in spirituality and also in theological articulation. The statement reads in tones of humility and grave hope: God is in charge; God is caring and compassionate; God stands against domination, violence, and greed.

Karl Barth, the towering Swiss Reformed theologian of the early and mid 20th century, wrote with unequivocal certainty about the radical otherness of God, and at the same time made a strong assertion of God's love for creation. He was clear that we have no capacity to set limits on God.

The kind of grief and regret that generation experienced is not wholly unfamiliar to us. We worry about climate change, extreme fossil fuel development, and islands of plastic floating in the Pacific. Perhaps our self-reliant determination that we know what is best begins to fade as we see ourselves resisting constructive change and wilfully damaging the planet. As we relinquish the illusion of being totally in control, the sovereignty of God comes into play.

We may not reiterate the language of the 1940 Statement of Faith, but we *can* speak about the all-encompassing love of God. We may not believe that God "orders and overrules all things"—or we may—but we can at least say that we place our hope in a God who is more comprehensive than we are, and more loving. Awe in God can transform our experience of domination, violence, and greed. Awe does this by setting our lives in a context that is greater than our own. When we acknowledge our finitude, some of our anxiety is released. Hopelessness, poured into a crucible of awe, loses its steam. We arise prepared for action, with an honest accounting of our own limited powers.

What we seek in the sovereignty of God is an object of our trust, a reliable One in whom to hold faith when the rest of the world lets us down. When we choose to claim the doctrine of the sovereignty of God, we relinquish our tight hold on our lives and allow the mystery of God to unfold. We claim an authority for God that supersedes the other authorities in our lives. It brings a reordering of our priorities. And we live with awe.

Scripture for Preaching

Job 38:1, 4–7
Then the Lord answered Job out of the whirlwind:...
"Where were you when I laid the foundation of the earth?
   Tell me, if you have understanding.
Who determined its measurements—surely you know!
   Or who stretched the line upon it?
On what were its bases sunk,
   or who laid its cornerstone
when the morning stars sang together
   and all the heavenly beings shouted for joy?"

Why Is This Doctrine Important?

"I love to pray," a woman said to me. For many years her mother had been living—housed, one might say—in an extended care unit for people with Alzheimer's disease. She spoke of her experience of prayer, less as comfort or a meditative practice, but rather as a connection to magnificence. "When Mum was so lost," she went on to say, "praying was a way of reaching beyond the fog to God. I knew that no matter how lost she got, God would find her."

The point of preaching doctrine is not so much to arrive at correct definitions of God and the spiritual life as it is to encounter God and experience spirituality. From there, ethical action, personal coherence, and right relations may issue. With this in mind, let's explore the sovereignty of God as a pastoral concern.

The daughter was unable to keep her mother from the outcomes of a disease that affects memory and other mental capacities. She believed firmly that beyond the ability of the rest of us to keep her, God had kept her mother. Any regret for her existential limitations was channelled into a trust that beyond her understanding, there God could be.

The doctrine of the sovereignty of God is helpful when our commitments to social action are waning. It reminds us that the cause is much larger than we are, much more long-lived. It reminds us that it's not all about us. When we experience despair at our ineffectiveness against systems of inequality, the long road behind and ahead of us comes into view. We see God's purpose stretching beyond our sight.

Also, it *is* about us, about situations we experience. When our care for another person simply isn't enough, when our hold on life or possibility is loosening, we are reassured that this is not all there is. One understanding of a sovereign God is found in the popular saying "God won't give you more than you can handle." Many of us find this approach distinctly unsatisfying, or even offensive. If we were weaker, would this experience not be happening? A corrective can be offered: that a sovereign God can be present through all the difficulties, in a more personal manner than any human or created effort. When finitude is all we have, a sovereign and transcendent God is great comfort. Pastorally when we offer comfort, support, or prayer to someone in need, it is not our personal energy that is responsive but rather a holy and other power.

On a personal level, exploring the sovereignty of God can open us to new freedom. In a culture where dominant values are found in a race for first place, in accumulation, in privilege, and in extreme living, deep relief can come with an understanding that we don't need to—in fact, cannot—have it all. The confidence that there is so much beyond our grasp that we cannot attain it can reduce our anxiety about striving. We can relax. We can admit that not everything goes according to our plans or wishes. In the end, if not in this circumstance, God's love will be visible. God is God and we are not.

The sovereignty of God can help us recover from tragic loss. There are many things we simply cannot fix, many endeavours for which we do not have enough resources. Our capacity for creativity or resourcefulness is limited, whereas we believe God's is not. We cannot eliminate poverty, for instance, but we can alleviate some poverty. The sovereignty of God allows us to come to the point where we can say, "I have done all I can." It can be a truly liberating thing to acknowledge.

This concept may be very helpful as we navigate the issue of assisted dying. It is, of course, a theological as well as an ethical matter. It is about existential meaning; it is about our nature and God's nature as well as about the moral values that hold our society together. As we create increasingly sophisticated technologies, particularly medical technologies, we must ask: Who holds our spiritual questions, our emotional needs? In the face of the sovereignty of God, we can with humility acknowledge the limits to our power.

To sum up, God is God and we are not. We are finite; we are creatures. God's nature is more than we can comprehend. And we are not alone.

The sovereignty of God is freshly relevant. This doctrine may have been more in character with the theological sensibilities of the 16th century, but it does not follow that God's sovereignty has no meaning for us. On the contrary, finding ourselves between the rock and the hard place gives us motivation to explore transcendence with congregations who share our common creed—A New Creed, another of the subordinate standards:

> We are not alone,
>   we live in God's world....
>
> In life, in death, in life beyond death,
>   God is with us.
> We are not alone.
>
>   Thanks be to God.

How Does It Preach?

The sovereignty of God will preach well in a time of anxiety. It reassures us that we are not alone: our current situation is part of the long reach of time and divinity. It preaches well when we desire motivation for social action. We are not alone: we are part of a cause that is longer running than we can know. It preaches well when we are grieving. We are not alone: even though we are powerless to reach the object of our grief, God can.

Ash Wednesday is an excellent time to preach this doctrine because we speak of our mortality: "Remember that you are dust, and to dust you shall return." Beyond this vivid admission of our finitude is a celebration of God's ongoing presence.

Seasons of expectation are also good times to call on it. The expectant waiting of Advent expresses both our awe and our humility before the great wonders and intentions of God.

When members of the congregation are dealing with loss, limitations, and regret, it is a good time to preach the sovereignty of God. We need to lean on God. This is the between-the-rock-and-the-hard-place element: we are so very capable, and yet we need to affirm our dependence.

One of the great fears of our generation is dementia. The loss of memory brings up the question of identity: Will I still be myself if I forget who I am? It brings up the question of relationship: How do I love this person when she can't remember me to respond? It brings up the question of limits: I can't do enough; how do I cope with that?

The doctrine of the sovereignty of God lends itself to reflection on things over which we have no control. It may seem a surprise to hear it preached with regard to degenerative diseases such as Alzheimer's. There are those who would expect such a sermon to be about disease as part of God's plan. That is definitively not the belief of this book's authors. Increasingly we lead funerals and memorial services for people who have died after long years, apparently unaware of who they are and often behaving in ways they would never have countenanced. So the sermon that follows is a funeral sermon for someone who died of Alzheimer's.

Listeners attend to funeral preaching with a different quality than the Sunday morning routine. Sometimes, of course, people are overcome with grief and recall hardly anything. At other times, though, there is an openness to the Word that comes from seeking comfort or encouragement. Guilt—for example, for not having done enough—may also be at play. Such a funeral sermon needs to address not merely the finitude of death but also the finitude of human reach and action. Then it needs to call on the ongoing presence of God, far and away beyond our sovereignty, to heal, to comfort, and to commission for further living.

A recitation of "We are not alone..." would set up the doctrinal theme of the sermon. There is room for several scripture sentences throughout a funeral. It would be appropriate to read Psalm 90:1-2, 10:

> Lord, you have been our dwelling place in all generations. Before the mountains were brought forth, or ever you had formed the earth and the world, from everlasting you are God.... The days of our lives are seventy years, or perhaps eighty, if we are strong; even then their span is only toil and trouble; they are soon gone, and we fly away.

The service might close with Philippians 4:4-7:

> Rejoice in the Lord always; again I will say, Rejoice. Let your gentleness be known to everyone. The Lord is near. Do not worry about anything, but in everything by prayer and supplication with thanksgiving let your requests be made known to God. And the peace of God, which surpasses all understanding, will guard your hearts and your minds in Christ Jesus.

Sovereignty would be an unusual word to many listeners in this circumstance. They might find it quite familiar in a political discussion, but a funeral is not the best time for defining vocabulary. I would mostly use the word *trust*. In sovereignty we are not looking for an assertion that God is authoritarian over you, but rather that God can be trusted to be in charge so listeners can let go of their anxiety and regret.

Sample Sermon

Sighs Too Deep for Words

> Likewise the Spirit helps us in our weakness; for we do not know how to pray as we ought, but that very Spirit intercedes with sighs too deep for words. (Romans 8:26)

You know a thing or two about "sighs too deep for words." You know about the way a heart can feel cold. You know about the way everything in front of you is fog.

You know what it is to love someone with the brilliance of the fullness of your life, and to walk across a threshold and realize: that is over. You know about the sighs too deep for words.

You know how deeply you hold onto the stories. The teaching career and long evenings of prep, the golf and the skiing, the political rallies and the family street parties, the mix-up in travel trailers—the quiet disapproval when you did that and the gentle forgiveness that followed. You know the love in a house, the simple pleasures of being together; you know the last time she recognized you and the sweet sorrow of that memory.

You know that this is the mix in which we live: this mix of sorrow and joy. But most of it, frankly, is ordinary time, the ordinary time when it mixes all up and we're not really paying attention. We simply do what we do, we breathe in and out, we come in and out. Perhaps through the ordinary time we're often in a hurry, or perhaps we're often feeling blue. As our usual selves, that is the most of life, the mix of life.

In all of that you gather to celebrate the life of Nancy, whom you love so deeply. You knew what it was like for her when the sighs were too deep for words. You knew what it was like for her when she showed such joy at the birth of a great-grandchild. But you didn't know what it was like for her when she lost that child's name, or yours, or hers.

I know someone told you that God won't give you more than you can handle. Oh, my. I'm here to tell you I don't believe that's true. I don't believe for a minute that God gives you what you can handle or what you cannot. I don't believe God gives suffering. I don't believe God gave you that suffering, with or without enough perseverance to get you through.

What I do believe with my whole soul is that God holds your expectant waiting. I believe God holds your sorrow, your prayers, and your memories. I believe God holds Nancy's memories. That the Nancy you knew to be intact is still intact in God's love.

I believe that God is present where we are not able to be, that God was present where you could not be present, that God was present to Nancy when you were not able.

Here's a word:

> Then the Lord answered Job out of the whirlwind:…
> "Where were you when I laid the foundation of the earth?
>   Tell me, if you have understanding.
> Who determined its measurements—surely you know!
>   Or who stretched the line upon it?
> On what were its bases sunk,
>   or who laid its cornerstone
> when the morning stars sang together
>   and all the heavenly beings shouted for joy?" (Job 38:1, 4-7)

Job knew a thing or two about sighs too deep for words. He knew about the way a heart can feel cold. He knew about the way everything looks like fog.

God told Job it wasn't up to him to comprehend everything. He couldn't know it all. When the morning stars sang together, you and I weren't paying attention. We were doing ordinary things: getting born, learning to love, beginning to grieve. When the morning stars sang together, you and I were striving to make everything perfect, hoping we were good enough, desperately trying to solve Nancy's problems. But the disease marched right on in, despite our ministrations, and took hold.

Now we can hear the morning stars because we are sitting still, straining to hear. Now we hear them singing together because we have had to stop trying to fix things for Nancy. We accept our tragic loss and understand that there are some things we simply cannot fix, no matter how hard we try, no matter how hard we love. We have come to the point where we can say we have done all we could and it wasn't enough. And oddly, we are liberated.

Our capacity for creativity and resourcefulness and love is limited. But God's capacities are not. Where were we when God laid the foundation of the earth? We were being ourselves, our wonderful, blessed, limited selves. And God was being God: unlimited, fully loving, the One in whom we can trust when there is no one else, when there is nothing else.

You will honour Nancy's friendships and her accomplishments and the way she made the community a better place than it would have been if she hadn't been around. You know what the gentleness of Nancy really means. You know how she liked to sing in harmony and how, in place of her voice, the morning stars seem now to sing.

In all of this comes the reassurance that God has been here all along. More than that, God has been where you and I could not go. We trust that these last years for Nancy have been in God's shining presence, and that now—beyond our powers—she still is.

You gave Nancy your love. She was a gentle, caring person; she was able to accomplish far more in these 85 years than many of us would hope to in 185. We celebrate her for that, and in this holy place we also remember the sighs too deep for words.

We remember that the love of God is not just a love that comes in the good times, or that comes when we're feeling satisfied, but that it's also a mystery. It's a love that comes to us when the sighs are really sobs.

It's a love that comes to us when we cross that threshold and we know it's over.

It's a love that comes to us even in the ordinary days when we are not paying attention.

In the language of the church, the reassurance, the source, of this love from beyond our vision is the sovereignty of God. We can also refer to it as *trust*. It's a nice word; it rhymes easily: trust, dust. "To dust you shall return." Trust is easy to say—but in fact it's a great mystery: the presence of God with us, despite everything and through and beyond all. The old hymn perhaps says it the best: to "trace the rainbow through the rain" ("O Love That Wilt Not Let Me Go," *Voices United* 658). And as the rain softens and the fog lifts, to let the morning stars sing.

In the days beyond this week as you remember Nancy and cherish her and sigh your own sighs, may you feel God holding you, bringing you a love that is beyond any love you might expect. A mystical love. A love that doesn't come because you've made something happen, it simply comes because God is. In your grief, missing Nancy and grieving the missing years, continue telling each other who she was. She wanted this service to be a celebration and it is—and in celebration there is room for the mix of tears with the song of the morning stars, and the sighs too deep for words. Amen.

—Catherine Faith MacLean

This sermon is edited from a funeral sermon for a person who died of Alzheimer's. Her name has been changed, although the family did give permission to publish reflections from the funeral.

Chapter 2
Christology

"Who Do You Say That I Am?"

The Doctrinal Concept

Jesus' question to his disciples, "Who do you say that I am?" (Matthew 16:15), echoes down through the centuries. The question confronts and demands an answer from us in the 21st century even as it confronted his immediate followers. Historically, Christians have understood Jesus as the Christ to stand at the centre of the religious tradition of Christianity. Expressed another way, the centrality of Jesus, for the Christian, is found in the claim that one is Christian because one sees God most fully revealed in Jesus as the Christ. However, many contemporary Christians are unsure in what way, or even whether, they can adhere to such an understanding. At least three factors contribute to that uncertainty.

First, there is the matter of interfaith relationships, or the implications of what is sometimes called religious pluralism. How can one square the Christian claim that "in Jesus we see God most fully revealed" with a positive valuing of other religious traditions? Some Christians have no difficulty seeing Jesus as the only way to God, and they view practising any religious tradition other than Christianity as a certain route to damnation. However, an increasing number of contemporary Western Christians judge that other religious traditions (or certainly at least some of them) are also viable routes to relationship with God and to salvation. But if one sees Islam, Hinduism, Judaism, or some other religion or religions as valid paths to God, how can one sustain the claim that Jesus is that "most full" revelation of God?

It can be a struggle to hold a positive valuing of other world religions in tension with historic Christian claims about Jesus as the Christ. That struggle makes attractive for some the Unitarian-Universalist position of a belief in God but a view of Jesus as, for example, a great teacher or a model human being, but certainly something less than God in human flesh. Unitarian-Universalists are also quite clear that for a number of reasons—including their understanding of the person and place of Jesus—they are not Christian, although their origins as a religious group lie in Christianity. A few Unitarians in Canada define themselves as Christian

Unitarians, precisely because they do want to accord to Jesus a higher status than he is given in the Unitarian-Universalist tradition.

Second, there are the effects of the Jesus Seminar, a group of biblical scholars meeting under the leadership of American Robert Funk in the late 1980s and the 1990s. They sought to determine which of the New Testament sayings of Jesus were likely "authentic" and which were probably the creation of the early church. While offering much valuable background about the times and the context in which Jesus lived, the effort to determine what Jesus "really said" has led a number of Christians to place an increased emphasis on the "historic" Jesus. To some degree, this has meant focusing their faith on "the human Jesus." This development, if potentially challenging to Christianity's emphasis on Jesus as a revelation of God, also brings its own set of problems. It makes faith contingent upon what we are able to know historically about a figure for whom extra-scriptural sources are few and fragmentary. The main biblical sources consist either of testimonies to why he was significant to his followers (that is, the gospels) or references in letters written to encourage early Christian congregations (the epistles). These biblical sources are neither biography nor history as we would understand these genres today.

There is another related problem. Albert Schweitzer, the famous physician who spent his life working in Africa, was also a very fine theological scholar. Early in the 20th century, Schweitzer studied the 19th century's "quest" for the historical Jesus.[2] This scholarly quest bears, at points, some striking resemblances to the work and motivations of the Jesus Seminar. Among other things, Schweitzer concluded that each scholar's own particular context and perspective heavily influenced what that scholar saw as the characteristics of the historical Jesus. Schweitzer commented that what each scholar saw looking "down the well" was his own face reflected back to him. The danger to which Schweitzer pointed, and the danger to which a misuse of the work of the Jesus Seminar could lead us, is that rather than wrestling with the biblical text and what these testimonies about Jesus might tell us—or, even more, how they might challenge us—we concentrate on trying to construct a historical Jesus.

The Jesus we construct, if history is any indication, is likely to be a Jesus heavily influenced by the thinking of our time.

A third factor contributing to uncertainty about the historic Christological claim is that we wrestle with the two natures of this figure, especially the divine nature. Christianity, with its proclamation of the incarnation, asserts that in this figure God took on human flesh and dwelt among us. Almost from the beginning of Christianity, Christians have struggled to hold together the claim that Jesus, the Christ, is both human and divine. One nature is almost always emphasized, or overplayed, at the expense of the other. At some points in history, the tendency has been to deny Jesus' humanity or to so concentrate on his divinity that any sense that he shares our humanity is virtually lost. At other points the focus on his human nature has been so heavy that the divine nature all but disappears.

The concluding half of the 20th century was a period when the human Jesus was heavily emphasized in the West. This is seen not only in hymns and church writing of that era but also in popular culture. Think, for example, of the musicals *Jesus Christ Superstar* and *Godspell,* or the movies *Monty Python's Life of Brian, Jesus of Montreal,* or *The Last Temptation of Christ.*

The challenge with an overemphasis on Jesus' humanity is that we may then overlook some basic insights connected with the incarnation: that God took on human flesh and dwelt among us, that God is active to work for our salvation, and in surprising ways, and that we are not on our own. At the heart of the incarnation lie divine love and divine grace, a love and grace that come to us in human form. The sense that we receive divine grace, not because of what we have accomplished or who we are but simply as *grace,* is a challenging one for Western Christians. (See chapter 7, Grace and Salvation.)

Our culture teaches us that it is all up to us. Such an attitude, aside from being contrary to the faith tradition, leads, as Walter Brueggemann has observed, either to "inordinate pride" or "deep despair."[3] An understanding of Jesus the Christ as having both a divine and a human nature, of representing an initiative of God, can help to overcome such pride or its alternative of despair.

Scripture for Preaching

John 14:1–7

"Do not let your hearts be troubled. Believe in God, believe also in me. In my Father's house there are many dwelling places. If it were not so, would I have told you that I go to prepare a place for you? And if I go and prepare a place for you, I will come again and will take you to myself, so that where I am, there you may be also. And you know the way to the place where I am going." Thomas said to him, "Lord, we do not know where you are going. How can we know the way?" Jesus said to him, "I am the way, and the truth, and the life. No one comes to the Father except through me. If you know me, you will know my Father also. From now on you do know him and have seen him."

Why Is This Doctrine Important?

A faith statement about who Jesus, as the Christ, is for the Christian stands at the very centre of the Christian tradition. It is that confession that defines us—not other aspects of our doctrinal confessions, nor our activity in local communities or the wider world, nor the statements or stances of any one denomination or combination of denominations, important as each of these other things is.

Further, many Christians, at least in Canada, the United States, and Western Europe, are today unsure how, or whether, they can continue to subscribe to the historic Christian confession that understands Jesus the Christ to be the One in whom God has been most fully revealed. It is not a lack of desire on the part of these Christians to hold such a view, but an uncertainty about whether it is now possible. Or, if it is possible, how one would do so, especially in light of religious pluralism. Jews, Muslims, and Hindus are our neighbours; our children play together and we volunteer together at the local food bank. Members of our congregations wonder, and some ask: How can we hold a view of Jesus that seems to suggest that other world religions are objectively lesser than Christianity?

This uncertainty on the part of many Christians associated with mainline denominations results in silence or weak expressions of Christology. That leaves the paramount expression of the traditional Christian confessional statement to those who would claim for Christianity an exclusive pathway to a right relationship with God. Buttressing this claim is a particular understanding of John 14:6 ("I am the way, the truth, and the life. No one comes to the Father except through me.")

History informs us of the potential consequences of such an understanding. If one truly believes that in Jesus as the Christ one finds not only God's fullest self-revelation but also, and more significantly, God's only saving revelation, then it becomes understandable that one would perceive a need to convert members of other religious traditions, by force if necessary. If one genuinely believes that a person practising any other religious tradition, or none, is certain to experience eternal damnation, is it not loving to do whatever is necessary to prevent these "misguided" individuals from suffering such a fate? There is a compelling logic to this position, if these presuppositions are held. Such a Christological understanding needs to be challenged. There are other faithful possibilities for a robust Christology.

How Does It Preach?

The first decision regarding a sermon on Christology is which of the challenges experienced by so many contemporary Christians in the West to address. Multiple sermons are possible on most doctrinal topics, but that is especially true with Christology. And there can be a temptation to try to do too much. A given sermon needs a clear, central focus. With a sermon on Christology, one must choose among related but distinctive challenges. There will always be another chance for a sermon on Christology!

With such an approach in mind, I have opted for a sermon

addressing the interfaith or religious pluralism challenge that many Christians experience. All three challenges are important, but this one seems to me currently to create the greatest uncertainty and anxiety among Christians in Canada and the United States. This passage from John's gospel is the suggested lectionary reading for one Sunday during the season of Easter, so that would be a good occasion for such a sermon. Another opportunity would be shortly after Pentecost, for during the Sundays from after Pentecost Sunday through to the end of the church year the gospel lessons often contain sayings of Jesus. That said, a sermon on Christology could be preached at almost any time.

Given that choice to look at the potential challenge of religious pluralism, I would use John 14:6 as the key scriptural text. This passage frequently serves as a proof-text for the claim that Jesus is the only way to a saving relationship with God. Many members of the congregation will have at least some familiarity with it. They may be aware that the verse is used by some Christians to support the claim that Jesus, as the Christ, is the only route to salvation. They will also likely have heard it as part of a scripture reading used frequently at funerals. I do not usually focus a sermon on a single verse of scripture, but the use made of John 14:6 as a proof-text leads me to want to keep the sermon centred on this particular verse.

To set John 14:6 in context in John's gospel, I would read more than just that one verse. The context in which this verse sits is, in my view, crucial for understanding how we ought to think about it. When preachers think about a biblical passage in relation to a sermon, it is always important to look at a passage in its broader context. How does the content that precedes or follows the passage that we are looking at help us to understand that passage? So, for this sermon, I would read at least John 14:1–7. (One could also make a good case for John 14:1–14; beyond that, the chapter goes on to introduce other themes.)

In a congregation where it is important also to have an epistle reading, I would suggest Romans 11:25–36 as a supplementary lesson. In any case, I would make reference to this passage in addressing the challenge of religious pluralism for Christology.

Why, for many Christians, is John 14:6 a troubling verse? I want the congregation to think about the challenges of this text and why it troubles them or people they know. I would name quite explicitly the challenge that the sense that Jesus is "the only way to God" causes for some Christians. For example, what would that claim, understood literally, mean for our Jewish or Hindu neighbours? What would it mean for people who lived before Jesus or who never in their lifetimes heard about Jesus?

Many Christians through the ages have understood this text as saying that the answer to those questions is that unless one is a Christian one cannot have a saving, or redemptive, relationship with God. A number of Christians still hold such a view. Yet many Christians, including in all likelihood many in the congregation, would either have reservations about that view or disagree with it explicitly. In fact, in the past 25 years, The United Church of Canada has produced statements on ecumenism that reflect a realization that we need to value and seek closer relationships not only with other Christian denominations but also with other faith groups. The United Church has worked on statements concerning its relationship with Judaism and Islam, and most recently, with Hinduism.

The scriptural setting of this verse—namely a lengthy section of John's gospel that begins near the end of chapter 13 (or, according to some scholars, with chapter 14) and runs through to the end of chapter 17—is often called Jesus' Farewell Discourse. This large section of the gospel is set in the context of Jesus' final meal and evening with his closest followers. Most New Testament scholars assert that this passage, in the form we have it, is a compilation made by the editor or editors of John's gospel. Granting that, however, does not change the reality that the passage portrays Jesus speaking to his intimate friends in the context of his impending betrayal and arrest. Whether one takes it as a relatively literal account of what Jesus said on that last evening with his disciples, or as a compilation by the editors of John's gospel of some of Jesus' teachings to his circle of close followers,[4] the intimate nature of these sayings is undeniable. In these chapters, Jesus speaks to those closest to him. His words demonstrate his deep care and concern for them. They reflect also the mutual nature of that love and concern.

Turning to the passage, the saying, "I am the way, the truth, and the life. No one comes to the Father except through me" is, I would assert, the "language of love."[5] It is set in the midst of an intimate passage. When we speak in the language of love, we speak truth. Even if the things we say are not true for everyone else, let alone scientifically verifiable, they are true for us.

I would then use a personal example—spousal, parental, or communal—of the language of love. The fact that such a claim would not be judged universally true does not take away from its truth for me. Given the view that John 14:6 is just such love language, then we have some cues for how to interpret it.

What might that interpretation look like? The claim of this passage, I would argue, is profoundly true for those of us who are part of that circle of Jesus' followers, for those of us who are Christian. For Christians, Jesus the Christ is the way, the truth, and the life; he is the means through which we have seen God most fully revealed. That is our claim, our experience. Indeed, it is the assertion that defines us as Christians. We need not apologize for making it and we ought not to cease to assert it.

We do not also have to assert—indeed, we are not able to assert—that those who follow other paths to God are, by definition, outside God's saving love. John 14:6 is, if you like, a claim internal to the Christian community—a community in love with Jesus—rather than a universal claim. That this claim might not be universally true does not make it any less true for us as Christians. To understand this verse, and the claim it contains, as the language of love does not make it less important or less meaningful for us as Christians.

Such an understanding of John 14:6 is also more congruent with Romans chapters 9—11 than a more "exclusivist" reading of John 14:6. In Romans 9—11, Paul wrestles with the question of what God's relationship is with Jews who do not see Jesus as their Saviour. He concludes that, at the end of the day, God will continue to be faithful to promises made long before to the people of Israel. God will not reject Paul's former religious compatriots. Paul reaches this conclusion in Romans 11:25–36, at the end of a lengthy argument.

To see John 14:6 in such a way in no sense undercuts the centrality of Jesus the Christ for the Christian. Jesus the Christ is, for the Christian, our path to right relationship with God. Such a view enables us to move into interfaith dialogue, whether as a denomination with another faith community, or individually with a Muslim friend next door.

People who belong to other faith traditions are, in fact, curious to know who Jesus is for us. They are interested in knowing who we say Jesus is and how that conviction influences the way we live. They do not ask us to evacuate our faith claims in order to have dialogue with them or co-operate with them in various causes. To be clear about who Jesus, as the Christ, is for us enables us to engage in such dialogue comfortable and confident in our own sense of why we are Christian. Seeing John 14:6 in this way and being secure in our own sense of why we are Christian also opens us genuinely to hear about the faith of the other.

Sample Sermon

Who Do We Say Jesus Is?

When I was a child growing up in rural New Brunswick, it seemed that everyone went to church and you did not have to think much about why you did so. But I do remember wrestling with a couple of questions. One that occurred to me several times was some version of the following: What happened to people who lived before Jesus? Were they saved?

Even to my young mind, it seemed unfair that people who had been born and died before Jesus lived had no hope for salvation. I never posed the question to any of the adults who might have been able to answer it for me or, at least, offer me an answer. But I still remember wondering about it.

In a community where everyone was connected to one of the two village churches, it did not occur to me to ponder the fate of contemporary people who might not be Christian. While I knew, even as a child, that people belonged to other faith traditions such as Judaism or Islam, I do not remember wondering in the same way about their fate. Possibly I just assumed that they had no hope of being saved. I suspect, though, that that version of my question—about the contemporary world rather than focused on people who lived before Jesus—did not occur to me as a child because I did not personally know anyone who belonged to a faith tradition other than Christianity.

As an adult, it has been that latter version of my childhood question that I have had to wrestle with. How should I, or how should we, understand the claim found in John 14:6: "I am the way, and the truth, and the life. No one comes to the Father except through me." What does that mean for friends of mine who are Jewish or Muslim? What does it mean for several Buddhist acquaintances of mine? Do I really think that their particular religious paths—different from mine but as meaningful and as inspiring for them as Christianity is for me—mean that they have no possibility of right relationship with God? Or, if I do not think that, what then do I make of John 14:6? Is this passage one that I just ignore, or dismiss, or hope no one asks me about?

For some Christians, the answer to those questions, in light of John 14:6, is straightforward: since Jews, Muslims, or Buddhists, or the practitioners of any other religious tradition, do not accept Jesus as "the way, the truth, and the life," they have no hope of right relationship with God. To put it another way, no hope of salvation. For some other Christians, and I include myself in this group, such an answer does not seem to square with our understanding of a God of love or, for that matter, with other things we read in scripture. The increasing knowledge over the past generation or two of religious practice in other parts of the world, and the increasing number of Canadians who belong to a major world religion other than Christianity, make the question of how we think about other world religions in relation to Christianity an important issue for many of us. It has certainly become a more pressing issue for the United Church and, indeed, for many other mainline denominations.

For a large number of Christians, John 14:6 has been a stumbling block in terms of viewing other world religious traditions in a more positive way. For denominations such as ours that would see scripture as our primary authority—indeed, for any denomination that takes scripture seriously as a major authority for its theological understandings—this particular text is one we must wrestle with. How should we think about this passage in relation to the faithful members of other world religious traditions?

In trying to think through what this particular passage from John might say to us, I want to begin by setting it in its wider context in the Gospel of John. When you read through John's gospel, you discover that there is a section, beginning near the end of chapter 13 and running through to the end of chapter 17, in which Jesus delivers a very lengthy address. This section contains no stories about his life. Rather, it contains a series of comments by Jesus as he tries to prepare his followers for his imminent departure from them.

Often called Jesus' Farewell Discourse, it bears some resemblance to other passages in scripture where key figures in the biblical story, Moses or Joshua, for example, make extensive comments as they prepare for death. Among the features that set this Farewell Discourse apart from those others, though, is the intimate nature of Jesus' comments. In the other examples, Moses and Joshua both make a farewell address to the gathered people of Israel about how they ought to live. These comments by Jesus do contain instruction as to how his followers ought to treat one another. But most of the comments also demonstrate his care for his followers, a care that will continue after his death. He promises not to leave them orphaned, but rather to give them a peace different from the world's peace. He will send them an Advocate or a Comforter to be with them. Jesus calls them his "friends." Just before asserting that they are his friends, not his servants, he notes that "no one has greater love than this, to lay down one's life for one's friends" (John 15:13), an especially poignant comment in light of Jesus' own impending death. He concludes this Farewell Discourse with a prayer, a prayer to God on behalf of his followers.

Two things about this Farewell Discourse need to be highlighted. First, though it is addressed to his immediate followers in the way it is presented, the gospel writer has in mind not only the group of disciples around Jesus but also Jesus' followers down through the ages. The gospel writer has people like you and me in mind. After all, the writer of John's gospel states very clearly that this gospel does not contain everything Jesus said or did. A selection process took place, and the stories and sayings included in this gospel "are written so that you may come to believe that Jesus is the Messiah, the Son of God, and that through believing you may have life in his name" (John 20:31). In the account in John's gospel, Jesus is speaking to his followers during an evening, his final evening with them. The gospel writer, however, sees that message as universal, as addressed to all Jesus' followers in the years to come.

A second important thing about Jesus' Farewell Discourse—it is very intimate. Tenderness, caring, and love permeate these verses. On this last night with his followers, his concern and care for them is palpable. That concern and care extend to all his followers in every age, including us in the early 21st century.

I have spent a lot of time talking about Jesus' Farewell Discourse, which is the broader context of John 14:6. That's because I think that context is crucial for understanding this challenging verse. When we read this verse and, indeed, the ones around it, we are hearing the "language of love." We need to understand this verse, and its claim that Jesus is "the way, the truth, and the life" and that he is the only way we can achieve a relationship with God, as the language of love. It is language internal to this community of Jesus' followers, both those who journeyed with him in person around the Galilean countryside and those of us who would follow him now in the 21st century. It is an "insider story." When we use the language of love, what we say is unquestionably true for those of us who speak such words, though the "love claims" we make are rarely, if ever, literally true for everyone else.

Let me illustrate what I mean. If I say to my spouse, "You are the most beautiful woman in the world," what I am saying is profoundly true for me. It is probably not true for others, even for those who might acknowledge that my spouse is attractive looking, kind, caring, and generous. But those words, "You are the most beautiful woman in the world," are absolutely true for me. The fact that this claim would not be universally true does not take away its absolute truth for me. My words here are the language of love.

The language of love, like the language of poetry, is true, even if such language cannot be proven to be true in terms of being verifiable through experiment, which is the way our society sometimes wants to define what it judges to be true. The language of love would rarely, if ever, be universally true in the literal sense of that word. But it is unquestionably true for those who are part of that relationship, whether it be the relationship of two lovers, or of a parent and child, or of a community for a particular member.

When I read Jesus' Farewell Discourse, especially John chapter 14, and particularly John 14:6, I am reading the language of love. This is the language of the intimate community of Jesus and his disciples, of the community of those who follow Jesus as their way to God, whether in New Testament times or in our own day. It is language that is absolutely true for this community.

To understand John 14:6 in this way in no way reduces the significance of Jesus for us. It in no way lessens, let alone disparages, Jesus' place in Christianity. For us as Christians, he is "the way, the truth, and the life." We are Christian because he is the way we see God most fully revealed. In the same way, for a Jewish friend of mine, Torah, that is, the Law, especially as it is found in the first five books of the Bible, is the way in which she experiences God as most fully revealed. To understand John 14:6 in such a manner allows us to see other religious traditions as possible ways for people to be in right relationship with God, without in any way diminishing the significance or the place of Jesus, the Christ, for us. Those other ways are not ones we have found most fulfilling, but that does not mean that other people cannot have a right relationship with God through them.

To see at least one other world religion as a possible way to God is also not something foreign to the biblical witness. The apostle Paul was convinced that Jesus was the way to a right relationship, or a saving relationship, with God. His conversion experience on the road to Damascus had cemented that conviction, and he became an exceedingly effective first-century church planter. There can be no doubt of his commitment to Christianity or of his sense of the superiority of Christianity to any other tradition.

He was not unique among Jews of his day in seeing Christ as the fulfillment of Judaism. All Jesus' immediate followers were Jewish. But Paul, whose missionary success was primarily with Gentiles, or non-Jews, also agonized about the fate of Jews who chose not to become followers of Jesus. Chapters 9—11 of his letter to the Romans deal with this question. After much wrestling, he concludes that God would not forget the promises God made to the people of Israel from the beginning of their history and that therefore "all Israel" will be saved. Paul recognizes that salvation is a gift from God, a matter of grace, and that God can choose to offer mercy and to extend grace to whomsoever God chooses. Biblical scholars have differing views on how Paul sees God accomplishing this salvation. What is not at issue, however, is Paul's conviction that members of a religious community—in this case, Jews who are not followers of Jesus—will be saved. One can hold this view together with John 14:6 without being duplicitous.

As Christians, we can make the claim that, for us, Jesus is the One in whom we see God most fully revealed. We can also see other religious traditions as pathways to a right relationship with God. We can hold these two views together, without minimizing either of them. To hold them together is both to recognize who Jesus is for us and also to recognize God's freedom and power to be in a right or a saving relationship with whomsoever God chooses.

Let me say that again, because it is the heart of what I want you to hear: to hold those two views together is both to recognize who Jesus is for us and also to recognize God's freedom and power to be in a right relationship with whomsoever God chooses. Holding these perspectives together may also help us to realize that we who are Christian have much in common with our Jewish or Muslim or Buddhist neighbours in our efforts to live our lives according to the things we profess. We share an intentionality of trying to lead lives guided by our faith convictions.

Jesus said: "I am the way, the truth, and the life." May it be so for us. And to God who created us, Jesus in whom we have come to know that God, and the Holy Spirit, God's presence with us, now and always, be all honour, glory, and praise. Amen.

—*John H. Young*

This sermon was written for this book. However, it draws upon elements from a sermon preached in a congregation some time ago and more heavily upon comments I made at a Conference annual meeting as a panel member on the topic of Christology.

Chapter 3
Atonement

Two Wrongs Don't Make a Right

The Doctrinal Concept

The congregation was at a standstill. For years they had planned to build a church and now this: the architect had drawn a cross on the steeple. "No steeple," some members said. "We don't want to look stodgy."

"Yes, a steeple," others said, looking at the plans. "We want people to know we're a church, not simply a community hall."

"Then no to the cross," some said. "We're fed up with the executing God."

The conversation got theological at that point. People offered many understandings of what the cross symbolizes. With or without a cross, the congregation would make a theological statement to the neighbourhood through the architecture of their new building. Night and day, the church would speak louder than words, broadcasting what they chose to say about God, themselves, and the life of faith.

The cross is the universal symbol for Christianity. On steeples, traffic signs, greeting cards, even tattoos and earrings, the cross calls us to pause, consider, and wonder. The intersection of a vertical and a horizontal line suggests the encounter of God and humankind. Getting it right with God has concerned Christians from time immemorial.

Atonement is the only doctrine that carries its definition in the English etymology: *at-one*-ment, making us one with God. The human yearning for something more, something right and true and complete, something that absolves the *ick* of human living, is met in the doctrine of atonement. The existential estrangement we experience is solved. Through Jesus, God gathers us back from our selfish inclinations, restores the biblical vision of the promise for the earth, overcomes evil, and lifts away our guilt. We are free to live in love.

The cross symbolizes the rather abstract question of the purpose of Jesus' work. Jesus brings us back to God. Beyond all the failings, all the hurt, all the sin, Jesus reunites us with God. Christ's life, work, death, and resurrection acknowledge human reality and reconnect us with the

Holy. This mystery goes to the heart of who we think we are, and how we connect with God.

"The cross itself has always held the hearts of faithful Christians, though no one theory about the cross has ever held the mind of the church."[6] So writes Donald Mathers in *The Word and The Way*, a theological textbook published for lay people in the 1960s. That willingness to hear more than one perspective on the cross is still true today. No single theology of atonement can be considered exclusively correct, and to some extent we must be content with mystery. As theologians, however, we do push the question. We are not content to treat it with indifference or naïveté. As theologians preaching to faithful people who have a heritage of learning *how* to think theologically, reflecting deeply on atonement is essential. My purpose in this discussion is to offer three ways into atonement, and to choose one for preaching. There are more; three suffice here.

Atonement arises from an acknowledgement that we human beings have slipped away from the intentions of God and require forgiveness. That is a huge starting place. Atonement also recognizes that something must be done, something that is beyond our ability to do ourselves.

There are three major theories of atonement, commonly referred to as ransom, satisfaction, and moral influence.

Ransom sees Christ on a rescue mission. Wrong has been done and someone must pay. The novels of C.S. Lewis are a familiar setting of ransom theology. Think about this: in Lewis's adult Space Trilogy, he named the protagonist Ransom. In *Out of the Silent Planet,* the opening novel, Ransom is abducted and taken to another world. There he is to be offered as a sacrifice to the inhabitants, part of the kidnappers' plan to plunder that planet's natural resources. As it turns out, their plan is thwarted. Ransom is sent home and will be part of rescuing this world in subsequent novels.

This theme continues through much adventure fiction: *Harry Potter, Lord of the Rings, The Hunger Games*. In each of these stories, good and evil are set in opposition. Someone must lead the battle: Harry, Frodo, Katniss. Atonement is a drama.

This theory of atonement was prevalent through the first millennium of the church's history, and brought back into common parlance by the Swedish theologian Gustaf Aulén when he published *Christus Victor* in 1931. Since 1931, one need only look to modern history to see the struggle between good and evil brought from a cosmic plane to fields in France or Afghanistan, or perhaps to our complicity in cultural genocide in the Indian Residential Schools.

The cosmic battle, then, is between God and Satan. Evil is strong. Jesus Christ is apparently defeated, but rises triumphant. We, aligned with Christ, are called to name and combat sin and evil. All the way along, we know that God will prevail. In Lewis's Narnia stories, it is a "deeper magic." Gregory of Nyssa gave an inventive explanation in the fourth century: Christ is the hidden weapon, like bait on a fishhook. Evil, unsuspecting, takes it. God wins.

Significantly, God does not save the world by responding with further brutality or coercion; the foolish wisdom, as St. Paul writes, the non-violent response to cruelty, changes the game. You can read more in Irenaeus, Origen, Augustine, or Luther. Note that we, the humans at fault, have no role but to watch the drama unfold.

What changed in atonement theology between the early Middle Ages and early modernism? In 1097 Anselm of Canterbury published *Cur Deus Homo* (Why God Became Human). He draws our attention to vicarious suffering: Christ suffers, generously, on our behalf. This *satisfaction* theory of atonement is based in the medieval reality of feudal relationships.

The feudal world of kings, lords, and serfs thrived on the premise of honour. Disobedience dishonours the lord, and punishment or satisfaction must ensue. If this sounds legalistic, you're onto the rules of the game. Humankind's disobedience and distance from God must be punished or paid: divine justice will be satisfied. Given the elevated status of God, payment could only come from a pure source. The perfect lambs of the

Hebrew scriptures were insufficient. A substitute is sought. Humankind must do it, but only God could provide the perfect sacrifice; hence, Jesus' death. Christ, the true and pure human, bears our punishments. The divine innocent suffers for the guilty.

One wonders why God, Creator and Provider of all, might be caught in the web of medieval legal systems. God's power, mercy, forgiveness, and grace seem stuck in an old-fashioned structure of justice. Yet we note there is more of a role for humankind in satisfaction atonement than in ransom atonement; the playing field is human, not a cosmic battle.

Calvin and Barth will tell you more. Righteous anger appropriately seeks restitution in a legal system of satisfaction: certainly there is a lot of righteous anger in both scripture and our lives. It is energizing. Freely given love is another energizing element: love, too, can be the source of atonement by satisfaction. "No one has greater love than this, to lay down one's life for one's friends" (John 15:13).

Disagreement with Anselm was swift. Only a few decades later, Peter Abelard wrote about Christ's perfect love, a love that transforms us through awe and gratitude. This atonement by *moral influence* changes us deeply. We are made at one with God not by a remote cosmic battle or a representative death, but by our participation in holy possibility. We are changed, and we change our ways. Abelard describes Jesus as a divine gift of love that generates love in us. He did not mean that Jesus is only a teacher or merely an example, but rather that the holy mystery of Jesus' life, work, death, and resurrection includes our willingness to change and our participation.

Christ as witness to God's love kindles love in our human hearts. We cannot do it alone, but we do participate. It doesn't happen on some divine stage or behind our backs. Again, this understanding of atonement is based in a conviction that we need to be changed—not just taught or encouraged or guided, but changed. We demonstrate our witness to Jesus' emptying love in our action, in service, in how we live out love. This theory of atonement steps away from the concept of a vengeful God, a

God who comes to make us pay. Jesus is not appeasing the wrath of an angry God. Moral influence atonement rinses the violence of the cross with meaning rising out of love.

We need to acknowledge our need for transcendent power, and yet, a particular merit of the moral influence theory is the motivation to become activists. We strive to alleviate the world's pain and speak of the example of Christ that leads us to create justice, fairness, and freedom from strife.

This moral influence understanding of atonement is where many of us in The United Church of Canada have pitched a tent. Here it is in A Song of Faith, the church's most recent statement of faith and another of the subordinate standards (italics added):

> The Risen Christ lives today,
> >   present to us and the source of our hope.
> In response to who Jesus was
> >   and to all he did and taught,
> >   to his life, death, and resurrection,
> >   and to his continuing presence with us through the Spirit,
> we celebrate him as
> >   the Word made flesh,
> >   the one in whom God and humanity are perfectly joined,
> >   *the transformation of our lives,*
> the Christ.

Admittedly, satisfaction shows up in our other statements of faith. Here it is in the Twenty Articles of Doctrine, the original Doctrine section of The United Church of Canada's Basis of Union (italics added):

> **Article VII. Of the Lord Jesus Christ.**
> We believe in and confess the Lord Jesus Christ, the only Mediator between God and man, who, being the Eternal Son of God, for us men and for our salvation became truly man, being conceived of the Holy Spirit and born of the Virgin Mary, yet without sin. Unto us He has revealed the Father, by His word and Spirit, making known the perfect will of God. For our redemption, He fulfilled all righteousness, offered Himself a perfect sacrifice on the Cross, *satisfied Divine justice,* and

made propitiation for the sins of the whole world. He rose from the dead and ascended into Heaven, where He ever intercedes for us. In the hearts of believers He abides forever as the indwelling Christ; above us and over us all He rules; wherefore, unto Him we render love, obedience, and adoration as our Prophet, Priest, and King.

The moral influence understanding of Christ's atonement infused the liberal theology that was dominant in the latter part of the 19th century through the early part of the 20th. It was motivating in the mainline churches in the last century partly because it resonated with the modern sensibility of progress. Change for the better would happen.

It resonates today in a different manner. We as religious people are challenged to prove what difference our faith makes. We can point to our discipleship following the example of Jesus. The social justice to which we are called comes from our faith, from the moral influence of Jesus. This version of atonement opens us to imaginative, lively, non-retributive social justice.

You may be wondering about the congregation arguing with the architect. In the end, there was no cross. Neither was there a steeple. Years later the congregation would ask the presbytery to erect a sign so people would know they were a church. Words alone would spell the name of the building and the times to gather. Perhaps this absence of symbol—cross or steeple—reflects our hesitation about atonement. No executing God, nor empty cross, nor steeple lifting the eye skyward would be a symbol for the faith expressed inside.

Scripture for Preaching

Mark 1:16–20
As Jesus passed along the Sea of Galilee, he saw Simon and his brother Andrew casting a net into the lake—for they were fishermen. And Jesus said to them, "Follow me and I will make you fish for people." And immediately they left their nets and followed him. As he went a little farther, he saw James son of

Zebedee and his brother John, who were in their boat mending the nets. Immediately he called them; and they left their father Zebedee in the boat with the hired men, and followed him.

Psalm 82
God has taken [God's] place in the divine council;
    in the midst of the gods [God] holds judgment:
"How long will you judge unjustly
    and show partiality to the wicked?
Give justice to the weak and the orphan;
    maintain the right of the lowly and the destitute.
Rescue the weak and the needy;
    deliver them from the hand of the wicked."

They have neither knowledge nor understanding,
    they walk around in darkness;
    all the foundations of the earth are shaken.

I say, "You are gods,
    children of the Most High, all of you;
    nevertheless, you shall die like mortals,
    and fall like any prince."

Rise up, O God, judge the earth;
    for all the nations belong to you!

John 3:16
For God so loved the world that [God] gave [God's] only Son, so that everyone who believes in him may not perish but may have eternal life.

Why Is This Doctrine Important?

In the poignant depths of our lives, we come to faith for experiences that we cannot find elsewhere. In the depths of sorrow, we reach for holy comfort. When depleted of hope, we seek inspiration. Through the guilt of our everyday living, we look for forgiveness. Where do we find release from the weight of our lives, but in God?

The traditions of the church have taken this longing seriously, and the doctrine of the atonement of Christ is where we find it. We witness to *at-one*-ment, the reassurance of God's loving presence and Christ's saving actions. Here are ways the doctrine of atonement shines in our contemporary lives.

Pastoral visitation is an enormous privilege. Pastoral ministers have the unique opportunity to show up at any time, to phone anyone, to send a text and inquire about any topic. Small wonder *pastoral care* was once called the "cure of souls." When we ask quiet questions, we are often given private answers that reflect agony. Doubts about personal value run common as fog on a Bay of Fundy morning. We frequently hear: "I did something bad." "I never got to say sorry." "I don't deserve to be loved." To this despair we bring the good news of the atonement.

Atonement is not a punishment imposed by God but rather reunion with God, a healing of spiritual wounds. It is not so much washing away our faults as absolving the underlying issues of why we act this way. Through Christ's atonement we are released from the selfishness, fear, or bitterness that leads to our actions. We are embraced in the timeless love of God, in which there is no further isolation, abandonment, or separation. As preachers, we assure our listeners of their sacred status as children of God, sisters and brothers of Christ.

Guilt is a short word with large ramifications in Christian circles. I remember studying for exams at seminary in the communal kitchen. In response to the moans from several students about not having prepared week by week, the Buddhist priest also studying at the table smiled and teased, "You Christians and your guilt." Funny as it was at the time, he had hit a nerve. He noticed that we were often motivated by guilt.

We preachers can bring the welcome message that although human wickedness is widespread, the cross is more than a symbol of guilt. It is an act of the love of God. Guilt is a reasonable response to an innocent suffering for others' faults. But Jesus is not a scapegoat; he is the compassionate presence of God. God's love is wider and deeper than our guilt.

Because Christ suffered, we do not suffer alone. Suffering can extinguish hope, humanity, and dignity. God has been there; God knows our anguish. God is with us in our distress, and has overcome it. The atonement of Jesus is more real than infusing tragedy with meaning. It is more personal than making a sacrifice worth it. It is God's presence in the most dreadful of times. My phone rang today with a notification from a news service: a man was being burned alive in Syria. In the ordinary passage of my day, on the privileged device that is my phone, this dreadful news arrived and brought me to prayer on his behalf. This death will never be made right, but I trust God was with him.

Atonement is key to the Christian life because we cope with violence. What is violence doing in our religion? The violence of the cross is no surprise in human history, but what is it doing in Christianity? The authenticity of this question is borne out in Good Friday service attendance. Choir directors, worship committees, and ministers prepare poignant liturgies for this holy day, and few people attend. The violence is horrifying. People stay away: the terms for reconciliation and salvation seem too fierce.

Atonement brings the all-encompassing love of God into the worst of our human constructions, the use of violence. Jesus faces violence with boundless love and apparently succumbs, but he rises from the dead. He responds not with more violence but rather with compassion. The deadly circle is broken. The answer to our question is that God calls a halt to the cycles of domination, violence, and retaliation in which we are ensnared. Whether it is mean-spirited cheating or physical harm, we know the violent ways of the world. Christ breaks the ways of the world and carries the day, and we see that this is God's world.

Two wrongs don't make a right. Atonement is not revenge. In the teaching, ministry, and crucifixion of Christ, God engages violence, but does not confront evil with evil. God breaks the deadly circle.

As the deadly circle is broken, the whole of creation is atoned and becomes at one with God. God's love atones all who suffer, and those who practise violence as well. Even the perpetrators are loved. This love is God's nature. It is not perhaps an easy nature for us, but it is the nature of God.

Our call is to follow, to be brave, and to love. This calling can be difficult. Forgiveness is another crucial part of the Christian life, but it is not what I am speaking of here. Human forgiveness is a process that heals the wronged and may help the wrongdoer. In preaching about atonement, we need to acknowledge that God gathers us all, the whole inhabited world, into love. When people live with righteous anger for wrongs done to them, the pastoral response can be found in atonement. It gives us a way to cope with anger, resentment, bitterness, or hurt by handing them over to God.

How comfortable are we talking about atonement? The key to understanding atonement is acknowledging that we need to be saved. This concept can be difficult in our culture of autonomy. We are powerful. We have been taught that we are capable, and we must step up. It is worthwhile considering whether we, the preacher or the people to whom we speak, believe we need to be saved.

How good are we at looking after our sisters and brothers? Do we behave as though we love our neighbours? What kind of ecological footprint do we leave? These questions are worth thinking through in preparing to preach a sermon. And there is nothing wrong with taking our questions into the pulpit, providing we consider how this particular listening congregation will feel about our uncertainty. We can acknowledge that we are not completely helpless, but we do need help. We cannot save ourselves.

Atonement can also be difficult because we may be confused about what we are being saved *from:* the world? temptation? evil? the penalties of sin? Foundational to it all is sin itself, which is to say separation from God. Pastorally we can clarify this differentiation and help people reunite with God, leaning into God's love to extricate themselves from debilitating guilt.

For some of us, popular understandings of atonement may get in the way. Ideas about a vengeful God, ransom, or a scapegoat may present challenging problems. For others, trust in a transcendent divinity may be a stumbling block. For still others, the stark realities of our world may be too big to overcome. These things we need first to address in our own minds, and then in our pastoral care and preaching.

Atonement promises a better future. Congregations need to hear that. A future where justice will "roll down like waters, and righteousness like an ever-flowing stream" (Amos 5:24), a future where God "will wipe every tear from their eyes. Death will be no more; mourning and crying and pain will be no more, for the first things [will] have passed away" (Revelation 21:4). This future of peace and reconciliation is already appearing among us. We can identify that. The empty cross, standing in most of our churches, is the strong symbol of the end of violence, guilt, death, and domination. This promise can be the genesis of social justice. Seen through the morning dawn of resurrection, atonement can be the motivating energy as we transform the world.

The empty cross hangs in most of our churches. It is the singular symbol of the love of God, through the whole of Christ's life, transforming our world. In pastoral care, through issues of guilt, suffering, violence, perpetrators, and our own theological or academic questions, the cross points toward atonement. An image of pain and death is imagined afresh as a sign of holy, healing life. There are other images: dove, cloud, rainbow, sun, manger. But the cross speaks louder than words and most incisively to our *at-one*-ment with God.

God's transforming love is what pastors and preachers are called to proclaim to our congregations.

How Does It Preach?

The doctrine of atonement scares many of us. It is a large chunk of Christian heritage to interpret. It carries power as mystery but also as horror, a bloody reconciliation between God and us. Looking at atonement as the whole gospel story somewhat ameliorates this fear. The ministry, teaching, death, and resurrection of Jesus put us "at one" with God.

All the theories of the atonement have merit. There is no need to attempt to put them together as though they could be synthesized. Part of the mystery of theology is diversity. Part of the truth of doctrine is multiplicity. So I made a choice. I read up on our old friends Anselm and Peter Abelard, and Gregory of Nyssa, knowing I would take Abelard's part.

I began planning the sermon where we are: we in the United Church are people of action. We are proud, rightly so, of showing our faith, living love, and demonstrating what we believe through how we act. Let's begin, then, from a desire for action. Let's consider how the doctrine of atonement brings holy energy to our social justice.

The *ransom* interpretation brings us the determination on the part of God that things will be made right. *Satisfaction* brings us the holier-than-we-are Jesus, who can carry our debt. *Moral influence*, however, can strengthen us more immediately and directly to be followers of Jesus.

God's saving work in Jesus is presented in some manner in every gospel story, much of the writing of Paul, and most of the other New Testament writings. On this occasion I chose to preach chiefly from Mark 1:16–20. Simon and Andrew are fishing; James and John are mending nets. They encounter Jesus. As followers, we, too, find ourselves in this encounter. The sermon expands upon the disciples' response to the call of Jesus and puts it in the context of a non-sacrificial understanding of atonement. Our own discipleship is energized through this *moral influence* interpretation. We demonstrate that in our commitments to social action, daily honest living, and inclination toward forgiveness and reconciliation. I created a "follow me" sermon out of atonement.

In the course of the sermon, I drew on Psalm 82. This psalm calls for God to judge the earth. It is a court scene or a council; God is holding a conference with a pantheon, a divine assembly. It comes from Canaanite roots, and demonstrates the universality of human yearning for God's justice, intervention, judgment, and salvation. Psalm 82 speaks of the conspicuous and demoralizing power of wickedness, with an aching call for deliverance. I also referred to John 3:16, a beloved passage often displayed at football games, to define atonement.

This sermon would be well set in a season when a congregation is considering discipleship. November is often a month of stewardship campaigns: discipleship in giving. Epiphany is the season when God is made manifest and we "see" God in the person of Jesus: discipleship in our holy brother. Lent is a time to prepare for the outrageous mystery of the cross and resurrection: discipleship in preparation. Any of these seasons would work well. Good Friday is a pertinent time to preach atonement, focused on the cross. Yet Good Friday services are famously ill attended. The services are beautiful, sorrowful, and poignant, but attendance in United Churches is often sparse. I chose a Sunday in Epiphany. The passage from Mark situates the disciples learning to follow Christ. We are all learning to follow Christ. The doctrine of atonement tells us whom we are following.

I prefaced the sermon with a gentle hymn, "Dear God, Who Loves All Humankind" (*Voices United* 608). It speaks tenderly about our wrongs and asserts God's relentless care. Sung to the alternate tune, Repton, the final line repeats, and the words "rise up, and follow thee" from verse 2 segue into the sermon. Then I read Mark 1:16–20. The passage is sparse; the disciples rise immediately and follow. Immediately before the sermon I reprised verse two of the hymn; it could be sung by a soloist, the choir, or the congregation.

John Greenleaf Whittier's hymn poetry sets the theme of following Jesus. The sermon tension is the question, Why follow Jesus? The focus is the scripture passage. The doctrine is atonement. The title needs to indicate a motivation to action—"Two Wrongs Don't Make a Right" or "Follow Me."

In this sermon I began with an outline of what to expect. I don't usually do that, but this is a teaching sermon, and I wanted people to have a framework for what was coming. Next I introduced the gospel, indicating that Mark's primary purpose is to tell who Jesus is, and his second objective is to clarify the role of the disciples. We are disciples, too, people who encounter a call to follow Jesus, and to follow him not alone but together. There are other faithful paths, and I would want to be sure to speak of them respectfully. There is often someone in worship who is wondering about our view of the veracity of other religions.

But why do we choose to be followers of Jesus? The doctrine of atonement can answer that question. The world needs saving, and we follow that One who transforms the world. I offered a few situations that need to change. And Psalm 82 is eloquent on our yearning for justice. Then I moved into the doctrine. A succinct biblical passage is John 3:16.

Movie references, and a little storytelling, help. Each of the theories of atonement is part of our heritage. Each carries truth that is valuable to the followers of Jesus. Briefly, I outlined the three theories, to acknowledge the power they each carry. Assuming that this sermon arises out of a question of discipleship, I outlined how they lead us into, or do not lead us into, service. I was seeking motivation for action, sustenance for discipleship. Atonement in Abelard's understanding is at God's initiative and involves human response.

Then I returned to the call to discipleship as a motivating element of the commitment to service of which the United Church is so rightly proud, and drew upon the third theory as our source of inspirational doctrine.

This sermon is unapologetically didactic. The theories of atonement are serious business, and the mythological battle in heaven is frequently presented in popular culture. To balance the didactic tone, I used casual phrases such as "lean in" and "fascinating." I stopped midway to ask, "Are you finding this fascinating?" That is in no way a reprimand; it is an attempt at humour. When I preached this sermon, people laughed; it must have worked. This is a sermon, not an academic lecture; it is intended to mean something that will shape our Christian living.

I chose to reference five current issues in our Christian living: a local RCMP officer had been killed; the Boko Haram group in Nigeria had kidnapped almost 300 girls (note that I did not name this group—a way of respecting the girls, not the perpetrators); the Target corporation had announced it was about to withdraw from Canada; communities in the United States were protesting the deaths of African-Americans when police were involved; our congregation had just voted to host LGBTQ refugees.

As a bulletin cover I used a drawing of the fishermen leaving their nets. That or a simple empty cross could be created for a PowerPoint slide. I suggest spending time with Francisco de Zurbarán's painting *The Crucifixion* as part of the sermon preparation. The image, readily available online, is of Christ on the cross, suspended out of time and place, not touching earth or heaven. It is tremendously lonely.

Another hymn about calling the fishermen could follow the sermon. I chose "Jesus, You Have Come to the Lakeshore" (*Voices United* 563). The words are poignant and the tune is a contemporary contrast to the more traditional Repton. Augustine said, "Those who sing pray twice." The words we sing, as the words we speak, become what we believe.

Sample Sermon

Follow Me

> In simple trust like theirs who heard,
> beside the Syrian sea,
> the gracious calling of the Lord,
> let us, like them, without a word,
> rise up and follow thee,
> rise up and follow thee.
> ("Dear God, Who Loves All Humankind," *Voices United* 608, v. 2)

"Let us, like them, without a word, rise up, and follow thee." I do have a word, though. The word is *why*. Why follow Jesus?

The scripture passage is at the very beginning of the story of Jesus, in the oldest gospel we have. "As Jesus passed along the Sea of Galilee, he saw Simon and his brother Andrew casting a net into the lake—for they were fishermen. And Jesus said to them, 'Follow me and I will make you fish for people'" (Mark 1:16–17).

This sermon has three parts. The first part is didactic, it's a bit of a teaching. The middle part is fascinating. The end part is about wonder and awe and the journey that we share.

So first the didactic bit, the teaching. When Jesus comes along and meets the fishermen and says "Follow me," he says it to all of them. Two of them here, two of them there, and as the chapters go on he is going to find more and he is going to call them, in the plural. He calls the disciples together. And in the oldest gospel that we have about Jesus Christ, the first thing that is important is, who is Jesus Christ? Sounds kind of primary, don't you think? But the second thing that is almost as important is always the disciples. When the early church read the book that Mark wrote, they understood that there were 12 disciples who did what they did, and failed and succeeded, failed and succeeded, and kept showing up. And they said, "That's who we are. We're the disciples. They may be called Simon and Andrew, they may be called James and John, but it's really us."

That's how we read this book. It's about Jesus, who he is, and why he matters. Secondarily and almost as important is who we are, why we are important, and why it matters that we show up.

So here's the question: Why follow Jesus? This is a good world, and life can be fine. There are lots of paths that we could follow that, quite frankly, are fabulous paths. There are many ways of faith that are full of mystical holiness, and they are true and right. All you need to do is sit with a friend who is Muslim and listen to her tell you that her religion is about peace, and how most Muslims are changing the world for peace. All it takes is to sit with someone who is finding again his Aboriginal roots in faith, listening while he tells you about Creator and the splendour of the world and how we are all interconnected. You are moved and you think, "This way, too, is a very good path." He may even choose to integrate both ways of faith. So what is it about following Jesus?

We follow because it's a possibility, because it's an adventure, because we can, because we're invited. For some of us it's our heritage and tradition, our habit. For others of us it's because we have heard the voice of Jesus saying, "Come to me…and I will give you rest" (Matthew 11:28).

Some of us follow Jesus because someone has looked us in the eye and said, "What you are doing is very good. I see in that the hand of the Christ." And then you say, "Really? You see in me and what I'm doing the hand of the Christ?" You reflect on the work of your life and you think yes, I am in fact following Jesus.

So the didactic point is that Jesus will say "Follow me," and that he doesn't mean just me or just you or just another person. It's always a communal call. We don't have to do it alone.

Now: Why follow Jesus?

Perhaps we crave a more organic connection with the wonder of the world, the beauty of possibility, the intentions that God has. Perhaps it's about awe and inspiration and response.

Perhaps it's because we want to change the world. We want to change the world where the world needs changing because we see so much distress. We know that we have some skills, some personality, some companionship to bring to that distress. We want to change the world. We cannot do it alone; we hear the voice of Jesus saying, "Follow me." And we say okay. We want to change the world. We want to make a positive difference. None of us is going to do the whole thing alone. We want to be part of a community of love that saves the world with love, not coercion or violence.

Now this is where we go into the fascinating part. This stuff is old, it is important, and it has changed lives. It still changes lives. I believe it saves the world. As Christians we believe that we are with God. We are in a pattern where we are one with God, we slip away, God calls "Follow me," and we come back again. We yearn to be at one with God, to feel that we are rested, contented, energized, on the right path, open to mystery and awe, changing the world, making a positive difference. In scripture the most succinct passage is John 3:16: "For God so loved the world that [God] gave [God's] only Son, so that everyone who believes in him may not perish but may have eternal life."

In academic Christian terms it's called atonement. *At-one*-ment. It's the only Christian doctrine that is in English first.

It's a dangerous word because it is about God saving the world.

Primarily we need to have an understanding that the world needs saving. Quite frankly this week, looking at anything in the news, I'd say: "Absolutely, pick me, I'll follow you because this world needs saving." Whether it's the friends around you who are sick and in despair, whether it's family members who are having a struggle, whether it's mourning RCMP officers in St. Albert, whether it's a group in Nigeria who are hurting people, whether it's a large department store abruptly leaving Canada and its 17,000 employees, whether it's the plummeting price of oil, this world needs saving. The voice of Jesus says, "Follow me." How can we be at one with that?

God is unfailingly committed to justice for the most vulnerable of earth's inhabitants. Here's a biblical way of saying it. There's no improving on the Psalms:

> "How long will you judge unjustly
>> and show partiality to the wicked?
> Give justice to the weak and the orphan;
>> maintain the right of the lowly and the destitute.
> Rescue the weak and the needy;
>> deliver them from the hand of the wicked." (Psalm 82:2-4)

Okay, here's the thing. Here's where you get to lean in. There are three words—bright, shining words. They are words you may have heard before, but not so often from me. I find two of them difficult. The first word is *ransom*: a disturbing word. The second word is *satisfaction*: a legal concept that makes atonement a commodity. The third word is *example*. Ransom, satisfaction, example.

This is where you lean in. It's fascinating but it's not easy. How does Jesus save the world? How do people line up to follow Jesus and make a positive difference? What are we looking at in terms of what the Christian faith *does*?

For years and years and years, the Christian church believed God had sent Jesus as a ransom. The overwhelming story of the Christian drama for many generations was a struggle between God and the devil. Who was going to win?

Well, we know who was going to win. Or do we? But in the story, God sends Jesus as a ransom. Jesus was payment for the salvation of the earth. We run across this understanding of Jesus as ransom in Christmas carols, in some of the big Easter hymns, and in tons of scripture. God sent Jesus as a ransom to save us; we, God bless us, get to be loved by God so much that we get picked up and saved. The merit of this is that when people find themselves in a really rough place, there's a doctrine that says God is going to save you in the end. You may not be able to get out of this by yourself, but you are not alone.

Hear that? You are not alone. We are not alone.

But the challenge of the drama is twofold. One is that we really don't have a role. Jesus shows up, brings God's love, and we are free. It doesn't leave me with any kind of response, except an enormous gratitude.

Perhaps that is enough.

The second problem is that in the drama there's a little trick. God was always going to win. The battle had a forgone conclusion, but it took a while to get there. Gregory of Nyssa, one of the early fathers of the church, said that the trick is like a fishhook. God dangled a fishing line in front of Satan, not a net like the disciples were using to gather in the fish, but a fishing hook that went under the teeth of Satan and reeled him in. The trick makes it a predictable drama. This drama is the theme of adventure literature: *Lord of the Rings,* the Narnia stories, *The Hunger Games*—it's all about somebody who goes in on behalf of somebody else, and pays the price. In the Narnia stories the lion dies and upon his return, Aslan lays claim to an older magic. The White Witch, the queen of winter, finds her world shaken and then loses it all.

Ransom is one atonement understanding of how we can line up and follow Jesus. We can accept the relief of being ransomed. Quite frankly with the power and volume of evil in the world, *ransom* is a welcome concept.

What's missing is human agency. What's missing is a role for you and me. How do we follow Jesus?

I hope you are still leaning into these thoughts. Here's *satisfaction*:

I encountered substitutionary atonement for the first time when I sang "How Great Thou Art" (*Voices United* 238, "O Lord My God"). I didn't sing it as a child—it was not in United Church hymnaries until this latest one. I went to a nursing home to lead a service. Working with a talented musician, we sang a couple of hymns and then I said, "Is there a favourite?" Somebody said "How Great Thou Art." The pianist rolled up his sleeves and started to play.

We began to sing this hymn—I was appalled. God, not sparing God's Son, sent him to die—and "I scarce can take it in." I could scarcely take it in. I thought, *God sent him to die? I don't think I believe that.* I had never been taught that God sent Jesus to die. *God sent Jesus to bleed and die "to take away my sin"? Die for me? Did I ask for crucifixion? Would I want somebody going through that horrible death for me? No.* Well, I was appalled.

The idea of...just a minute—are you finding this fascinating? Or are you finding this snooze time? Okay, all right, it's not the end of the world if you are nodding off. I simply want to clarify that I am taking you through some concepts that have shaped the life of the church. They have saved lives. These ideas probably shaped some of your friends and brothers and sisters in Christ, and you may have wondered why. That's why I'm here.

Back to it: the idea of satisfaction came about in medieval times, the feudal world of lords and serfs. Bless his heart, St. Anselm—whom we thank for many things that are precious—lived in that system. He said that this ransom theory of God coming to rescue us seems a little thin. He suggested a system that works well in a medieval system of lords who are in charge and serfs who are servants. When a serf does something wrong, he has to make it up. The lord accepts payment in a legal, courtroom, commodified, marketplace fashion. Anselm suggested we think of God as a lord and ourselves as serfs. We serfs have committed heinous crimes. We have to pay up.

Indeed, heinous crimes are real. Paying for those crimes is a legal concept. How, though, do you pay it back if you don't have the means? Poor serfs have no means. God, then, supplies the payment price, which happens to be the person of Jesus.

Then we will be at one. *At-one*-ment. God gives Jesus as the payment price. Jesus is substituted for all the wrongs of humankind. He is sufficient because he is pure, good, and unlike the rest us, perfect. He can make the sacrifice. That's what Anselm taught: none of the rest of us is good enough to make the sacrifice for humankind, so God sent Jesus as the satisfaction for divine justice. The whole concept of Jesus being the really pure and good human being who really gets it, who lives *at one* with God and then pays the price on the cross: that's what it's about. We are unable to make it right; we don't have the resources to pay to make it right. God supplies the payment to make it right. God gives the price of our salvation. God saves us all by giving us Jesus. This concept, that God required satisfaction, involves a strong sense of what is right and due to the lord and to the lord's honour, even if the wronged party—God in this case—did not want or wish it.

This theory works because there is so much wrong with our world that we really do need someone to come and make it right. It works because it acknowledges the damage we do to ourselves, to one another, to the earth.

But we don't live in a medieval world anymore. We choose not to look at faith as a kind of legal justice, a courtroom scenario. In a courtroom scenario, when costs are paid, they cover the wrong that's been done. Sin, however, is less about the particular wrong and more about a proclivity to wrong, the grounding of the actions. It is not clear whether God pays the price of the sinful action, or the price of the underlying sin.

With ransom, it's all about high drama. With satisfaction, it's all about the courtroom.

Again, do you feel a little like you are just watching this? Not the sermon, but watching God do things on our behalf? If that's the case you may ask, "How come God set up a world where God would have to intervene and save it, without us even taking part?"

I got lost in the Art Institute of Chicago once. Art galleries are great places to get lost. Eventually someone will guide you to an exit, but meantime there are awe-inspiring surprises. I found myself in the Counter-Reformation room.

Much Counter-Reformation art is terrifying. If it was meant to send the faithful wailing away from the new Protestantism, and back to the traditional church, I'm sure it worked. Suffice it to say there is lots of gnashing of teeth. I spun on my heel away from one set of demons working on a near corpse, and stopped in my tracks. In front of me was the loneliest painting I have ever seen.

Francisco de Zurbarán's *The Crucifixion* is oil on canvas, painted in 1627. Against a black backdrop, Christ is on the cross. He is beautiful, clean, shining, and very dead. The loneliness is what stopped me. The cross is completely isolated, abandoned, as though floating in the blackness. There is no connection, no rootedness in earth or heaven, nothing around him but darkness.

It's the loneliness I'd like you to consider. Christ in isolation, even saving the world in isolation, is a lonely action. How does one follow an isolated Christ?

Frankly, what is the point of all our social justice if God is simply going to come in and make it right? Does that sound familiar? Perhaps you know people who say, "Let the end times come. Let God take care of it." I know people who say that.

If God simply came in and made it right, we wouldn't be in tears at the bedside in the hospital. We wouldn't be worrying about what's happened to some of the girls around the world. We wouldn't be anxious about what's going to happen when we've lost our employment at Target. God would make it right.

I don't think that is how it works. We have lots of friends around us, however, who think that it does. My, oh my, there's great appeal in expecting God to simply come in and make it right.

Ransom is about a cosmic drama. Satisfaction is about God sending Jesus to put payment for all the things we've done wrong, for all the sins of the world.

It wasn't very long after Anselm's work that Peter Abelard responded. He didn't offer Jesus as an isolated Saviour, nor suggest that God acts to save us as bystanders. Peter Abelard said Jesus is the shining example, he is the moral influence, he's the one who does it because we can't do it alone, and he calls us to join him in the ensuing work. Jesus lives his life in love, not with violence. He lives his love by calling and drawing and loving people, not by coercing them.

He faces violence with love. Atonement by Jesus' example deeply changes us. We are made at one with God by our participation in holy possibility. We are changed, and we change our ways. Abelard describes Jesus as a divine gift of love that generates love in us.

Jesus is a divine gift of love that generates love in us. We are changed. *At-one*-ment happens.

The disciples—Peter and Andrew and James and John and the others—were there with Jesus to see his life, work, death, and resurrection. They became part of it. And he calls us: "Follow me!" We follow that shining example of working for peace and justice and dignity and health and well-being for all the people, all the creatures, all the earth, and to make that part of who we are.

When we stand with people in Ferguson, Missouri, and say "Black Lives Matter," we face violence with love. When we apply to host a Rainbow Refugee family, we challenge systems of heteronormativity. When we refuse to accept a scapegoat mentality, but rather extend friendship, we offer it from an example that calls us into relationship with one another and into relationship with God. *At-one*-ment.

When Jesus says "Follow me," the invitation is to come and get involved! Come, many of you, not just one at a time, come and bring your brothers and mother, bring your sisters and the other people who are fishing in your boats because we are going to find out what we are called to do, and we are going to do it together.

So the fascinating part is over: ransom, satisfaction, example. What we come to at the close of the sermon is this: we are on a journey and we are on it together. When Jesus calls "Follow me" to us through the evangelist Mark, he is calling us to the adventure of our lives. He is calling us into wonder and mystery and awe. He is calling us to acknowledge that there will be suffering and hurt and trouble. We will walk through all of that in good company.

The great symbol of our atonement by Christ hangs right in front of us. The empty cross in the chancel painting is not only a reminder of death, but also a reminder of the life, teaching, healing, and resurrection of Jesus. It is a reminder of the salvation Jesus brings. It is a reminder of the risen Christ, and his call to us: "Follow me." We go in good company.

What does it mean to follow Jesus? The gospel writer Mark, I think, would say that it means one takes up a cross and bravely points out evil and injustice, and even one's own self-destructive powers, so that God's desire for love and peace can come on this earth.

When Jesus says "Follow me," he is calling us into a journey that will be the adventure of our lives. We will bring the best of who we are, the possibilities, the brilliance, the strength, the courage, the companionship, and he will put that together with the shining example of living in love. In a world that operates by coercion, we will follow in love. On this changing way, Jesus calls us into a journey of adventure, and he says, "Follow me." Amen.

—Catherine Faith MacLean

This sermon is edited from one given at St. Paul's United Church, Edmonton, during a series on following Jesus. The series was called "Is It about the Journey or the Destination? The Changing Way."

Chapter 4
The Authority of Scripture

The Word of God?

The Doctrinal Concept

I recall late one hot summer morning getting a telephone call from a very active member of the congregation. Sarah said, "Bill and I wonder if you could come and see us. There is something we really need to talk with you about. Would you be free to come to our home sometime today?" She was clearly anxious, and I agreed that I would come and see them after lunch.

When I arrived, Sarah and Bill (not their real names) took me outside to the shaded picnic table already set with large plastic glasses and a jug of lemonade. A well-used copy of the Bible, the Good News version, also sat on the table. After I had drunk some of my glass of lemonade, Bill said, "We need you to look at this passage and tell us what it means." Both of them were deeply committed Christians who read the Bible with regularity. He opened the Bible to a bookmarked place and pointed to Luke 12:49–53, a passage that runs as follows:

> "I came to set the earth on fire, and how I wish it were already kindled! I have a baptism to receive, and how distressed I am until it is over! Do you suppose that I came to bring peace to the world? No, not peace, but division. From now on a family of five will be divided, three against two and two against three. Fathers will be set against their sons, and sons against their fathers; mothers will be against their daughters, and daughters against their mothers; mothers-in-law will be against their daughters-in-law, and daughters-in-law against their mothers-in-law." (*Good News Bible*)

Bill said, "What is this passage saying about the kind of relationship we are to have with our family?" And the conversation went on. I spent much of the afternoon there. I should also say I was glad to be there, glad that these members of the congregation who read the Bible and who had been puzzled, indeed troubled, by what they had read had felt free to call me to come and talk to them about it. Such calls and the subsequent visits and substantive discussions are a rich part of pastoral ministry. I should also note that I have Bill and Sarah's permission to share the account of this pastoral visit.

Now one could argue that Bill and Sarah's issue was an understanding of Jesus as nice, the "Gentle Jesus, meek and mild" version of the children's hymn of that title among other sources. But it seemed clear to me that day that, while they may possibly have had such an image of Jesus, their concern was different. The passage itself had set off questions for them about the authority of scripture. They simply could not accept that a Christian would have to be divided against family members in the way a straightforward reading of the passage suggested. In addition, these words were not just "in the Bible"; they were on the lips of Jesus himself.

It is one thing to be troubled by a passage such as Psalm 88, an unrelenting account of the psalmist suffering via God's hand. Or by Psalm 137:8-9 (in which the psalmist, in exile in Babylon, hopes for the destruction of that empire and declares, "Happy shall they be who take your little ones and dash them against the rock!"). Or by the story of Jephthah's daughter (Judges 11), where Jephthah, who promised to make a "burnt offering" to God of whoever initially met him on his return home if God would grant him victory over the Ammonites, is greeted first by his only child when he returns home victorious, and he feels obliged to carry out his vow. While these passages are certainly challenging, and may even be deeply troubling, many Christians resolve the challenge by dismissing them as "just being in the Old Testament." Such a dismissal is not something I would do, but it is an approach many Christians, both in the past and in the present, have taken. Some of the more troubling sections of Paul's letters can also be rather quickly dismissed, even by those who tend to a quite literal reading of scripture. But, at least in my experience in ministry, it has been the more troubling words of Jesus—sayings of Jesus like this one from Luke—that can provoke a crisis of faith about the authority of scripture.

The United Church of Canada and other denominations in the Reformed tradition, as well as a number of denominations outside the Reformed tradition, have traditionally spoken of scripture as their primary authority. In looking at the United Church's faith statements, I would note that this understanding of the role and place of scripture is found not only in earlier faith statements of the denomination but also in its most recent one, A Song of Faith. Scripture is described there as "the living word passed on from generation to generation to guide and inspire" and as having "a unique and normative place in the life of the community."

That said, two groups of contemporary Christians seem particularly to struggle with this understanding. One is the group that believes scripture can have authority only if all of it is accepted as literally true, if scripture is a certain and infallible guide in a perilous age. Now while I know of no Christian who, in reality, views each and every passage as not only literally true but also of equal importance, there are those, including in the United Church, who hold to the view that scripture must be seen as literally true and therefore a certain guide to how to live. I'll call this group, in a term coined by one of my ministerial colleagues, "the literalists of the right."

While relatively few people in the United Church may hold a strict form of this perspective, a much more substantial number hold subtle variations of it. Passages such as the one from Luke's gospel that proved troubling to my former congregants can lead these individuals to conclude that the Bible is wrong. When they have reached this conclusion, Christianity can no longer function for them as a religious option. That is a pastoral concern.

The other is the group my ministerial friend calls "the literalists of the left." These people conclude that if the story is not historically and/or scientifically true (if it didn't *really* happen in that way), then there is no truth in it and therefore no reason to bother with the story. While the literalists of the left may begin with a story such as Noah and the great flood, the list quickly expands to include many of the stories of Jesus where discrepancies are found between one gospel and another. For this group most, and eventually all, of scripture ceases to have any kind of authority whatsoever for their faith life.

The crisis in the authority of scripture is not a new one. But much current wrestling with this question is the result either of an uncritical rejection of the Enlightenment's emphasis on our capacity for human reason and the concomitant rise of the scientific method, or an uncritical adoption of the Enlightenment's equation of truth with that which can be empirically proven.

Another factor, as Daniel Migliore points out in his book *Faith Seeking Understanding*, is our tendency to view scripture as coercive rather than as liberating. We know, as Migliore observes, that scripture has been used oppressively—to justify slavery, patriarchal attitudes, and so on. However, such a misuse of scripture ought not to lead us to reject a healthy—Migliore would argue "a liberating"—view of the authority of scripture. We have lost the Reformers' sense of scripture's authority as "rooted in its liberating message, in the good news of God's gracious acceptance of sinners offered in Jesus Christ. The Bible was experienced not as an arbitrary or despotic authority but as a source of new life, freedom, and joy."[7] We need to develop again the sense of scripture's authority as grounded in the "good news" of God's saving action as revealed both in the stories of the people of Israel and in the stories about Jesus.

Scripture for Preaching

> **2 Timothy 3:14–16**
> But as for you, continue in what you have learned and firmly believed, knowing from whom you learned it, and how from childhood you have known the sacred writings that are able to instruct you for salvation through faith in Christ Jesus. All scripture is inspired by God and is useful for teaching, for reproof, for correction, and for training in righteousness.

Why Is This Doctrine Important?

First, scripture is not, for Christians, an end in and of itself. The debates that began in the late 16th century about verbal inspiration and a notion of "scripture alone" from that era have led some Christians to forget that we read scripture, and it has authority for us, as the primary means of hearing God's Living Word. Scripture is not an end in and of itself, and it should not be read as such. To do so is to engage in bibliolatry, something that Martin Luther in particular condemned; it is to make the Word dead, not living. Scripture is what enables us to be in touch with Jesus the Christ, the One who stands at the centre of our tradition. In other words, it is as we read and reflect upon scripture, in both testaments, that we are able to hear God's Word for us. Historically, Christians have believed that the Word of God—revealed for Christians supremely in Jesus the Christ—continues, through the inspiration of the Holy Spirit, to come to us primarily (though not exclusively) through scripture.

Second, our theology will have authorities. The question is which authorities we will have and how we will rank them. We use other authorities, including our capacity to reason. But it is scripture—and hearing a multiplicity of voices interpreting scripture—that can best keep us from the cultural captivity of making our particular context, experience, or history the dominant authority.

We cannot, and should not, deny that scripture has been misused to sanction authoritarian structures and oppressive regimes. That said, one of the remarkable things about scripture is its capacity to speak a grace-filled and a freeing Word generation after generation and to challenge those abuses, even those that have existed for generations. It also has the capacity to call us to account for our tendency to make our own culturally conditioned and incomplete reading of the Christian story the only legitimate way to hear and to understand the story. Scripture can never be our only authority. To claim that would be to deny the long-recognized reality that God speaks to us in other ways in addition to scripture. But scripture is our primary authority, for it is these stories that link us to the One who stands at the centre of our tradition.

How Does It Preach?

When we see a reference to "the scriptures" in the New Testament, we need to remember that this term refers to the sacred writings of the Jewish tradition, which Christians have historically called the Old Testament. Jesus, his immediate followers, and those initially drawn to the religious movement we now know as Christianity were all practising Jews. Jesus' followers differed from other Jews by virtue of their understanding that Jesus was the long-promised Messiah of the Jewish tradition, but they still saw themselves as Jews and still practised the various rituals of that religious tradition. If you are looking for a New Testament passage to preach upon, keep that meaning of "the scriptures" in mind.

Passages in the gospels that reflect what the gospel writers understood themselves to be doing as they wrote—passages such as Luke 1:1–4, John 20:30–31, or John 21:24–25—would be possibilities for a sermon on this doctrine. I have chosen 2 Timothy 3:14–16, however, because this passage has often been used as a proof-text for a literal understanding of scripture. Members of the congregation may have heard this passage in this context, perhaps from other Christians.

When might one preach a sermon on the authority of scripture? The passage from 2 Timothy appears in the Revised Common Lectionary as a suggested reading on a Sunday around the middle of October. Quite apart from that suggestion from the lectionary, sometime in October shortly after Thanksgiving seems to be good. Another option would be the Sunday just after Easter, a time when the passage from John 20 is always a suggested reading; the lesson from 2 Timothy could always be used that day. Catherine and I would also encourage preachers to consider doing a series of sermons on key doctrinal subjects such as those found in this book. Both of us have known colleagues to do such a series during the summer, though one could do so at any point during the year.

In choosing the passage from 2 Timothy, I am assuming that the congregation has the range of views about scripture typical of most

United Church congregations (or, indeed, of other mainline Protestant congregations in Canada and the United States). A small proportion of the congregation would view scripture in a quite literal way, and a few others would be "literalists of the left." Most would hold a view somewhere in between, according scripture authority but not sure why it has authority for them. They are not literalists, and yet they take the Bible stories seriously. They feel a little unsure of their ground, because they do not think the details of at least some of the biblical stories reflect the way things "really happened." But they also feel reluctant to dismiss the Bible the way they know some do.

Because this doctrine is so central for the United Church and other Reformed denominations, I would want to know as well as I could just what members of the congregation thought. What range of view exists? Who will experience a challenge to their faith in what I say? How do I address the questions congregants have in a way that helps strengthen their conviction that scripture can and will have authority for them?

If I was preaching to a group primarily made up of literalists of either the left or the right, then I would need to construct the sermon differently. In such a scenario, while the doctrinal points I would want to make would be the same, I would probably be more inclined to choose a passage such as John 20:30–31, where, after noting Jesus did many things not included "in this book," the gospel writer observed: "But these are written so that you may come to believe that Jesus is the Messiah, the Son of God, and that through believing you may have life in his name." That comment illustrates quite well that the gospels are testimonies, not biographies or histories. I would use that insight as a way of coming at the nature of scripture and its authority.

One other point needs to be taken into consideration. Over the years, I have had several congregational members tell me they were reluctant to think too much about what they believed about scripture and its authority. One put it into an insightful metaphor: "I am a little scared to get into a long discussion about what I think about scripture. If I conclude about one story, well, I don't think that really happened, then I am afraid it is like starting to unravel a sweater. Once that first thread gets loose and you pull on it, the whole thing just comes undone." This person feared a discussion about scripture and its authority; she feared losing her belief that the Bible did have authority for her.

In a sermon to a typical congregation, using the 2 Timothy passage, I would begin by raising some of the questions the related concepts of biblical inspiration and the authority of scripture raise for many contemporary Christians. How do we understand, or do we even understand, those words from 2 Timothy that "all scripture is inspired by God and is useful for teaching, for reproof, for correction, and for training in righteousness" (3:16)?

Then I would refer to a painting that deals with biblical inspiration. I would choose any one of a number drawn from the late 16th to early 18th century, paintings that reflect the "dictation theory" about the origins (and therefore the authority) of scripture. My personal choice would be *Saint Matthew and the Angel*, by the 17th-century Dutch artist Barent Fabritius (which can be found at the Musée des beaux-arts de Montréal). It pictures the evangelist sitting at a writing table over a bound book, pen and inkwell in hand. (Forget for the moment the anachronistic details of a pen, an inkwell, and a bound book in the first century CE!) Behind him, an angel leans in, apparently whispering in his ear. The artist depicts an understanding of biblical inspiration and authority: God has given the angel the words Matthew is to write in his gospel. Matthew simply takes dictation.

If possible, this image could be projected for the congregation or, with appropriate permissions, reproduced as a bulletin cover. Otherwise, describe the image in some detail. I would ask the congregation to think about the message the image conveys about how the Gospel of Matthew came to be written. You might allow 45 to 60 seconds of silence for the congregation to study the painting. (If the congregation is not accustomed to any silence in a service, even 45 seconds will seem like a long time.) If the congregation is small (25 or fewer), end the silence by asking those present to share aloud what struck them about the painting and what they think it conveys. (In a larger congregation, this exercise could take considerable time, so I would be less likely to ask.)

We cannot, of course, simply accept the artist's understanding, an understanding that developed in the late 16th century. We also cannot accept the corollary notion that if the Bible's authority and inspiration comes from divine dictation, then each and every word in scripture has equal value. None of us live that way. I would likely note a few examples here—perhaps asking whether the prohibition against sowing two different kinds of seeds in a field is of equal importance with the admonition to love God with heart, soul, mind, and strength, and our neighbours as ourselves.

I would also speak about the nature of authority in general—how we use and understand that term. How do we think about, and experience, authority in everyday life? Then I would move on to the authority of scripture. It is not the words on the page but the Word of God, the Spirit of God, the presence of the God who meets us when we wrestle with the stories that makes scripture our primary authority.

Depending on the context and the desired scope of the sermon, I would also address the dismissal of the authority of scripture by those who conclude that the only things that are true are those that are scientifically or empirically verifiable. Some examples can be given of "truth" statements that cannot be empirically proven—sincere words spoken by a lover, or the truth conveyed by poetry.

I might also try to address the nature of so much of the biblical literature. We are not reading historical accounts when we read scripture. We are usually reading testimony or a witness to faith. Most certainly that is what we are doing when we read the gospels, according to their own internal claims.

In his book *The Word and the Way,* Donald Mathers, former Systematic Theology professor and Principal of Queen's Theological College, described the Bible as being like "a telescope," something that we look through, not at. Scripture, then, does not have authority in and of itself. It has authority because it points us to God, because it mediates God's power to us. Therein lies its authority.

In conclusion, scripture puts us in touch with the founding moments of our tradition, with its origins. The stories of our origins also remind us of other divided families, so I would point out that there are challenging, gnarly passages of scripture. We need to try not to be put off by ones such as the passage from Luke that troubled Sarah and Bill. In the church's experience the Bible has been an empowering document to each generation down through the centuries, a document that has inspired, freed, and liberated.

Sample Sermon

The Word of God? The Authority of Scripture

What do we mean when we speak about the Bible as "the Word of God?" What authority does scripture have for us? How do we, and how should we, understand that authority?

The passage I read from 2 Timothy stated that "all scripture is inspired by God and is useful for teaching, for reproof, for correction, and for training in righteousness" (3:26). But simply quoting that verse does not answer those questions for at least three reasons. First, when the passage in 2 Timothy refers to "scripture," it refers only to what we Christians call the Old Testament. At the time 2 Timothy was written, the New Testament, as a collected body of writings, did not exist. Many of the books had been written, but they circulated individually; the sense that they were scripture had not yet developed. Second, what does it mean to say "all scripture is inspired?" Does it mean that every verse in the Bible is to be accorded equal weight? If so, that is problematic. No person I have ever met accords every verse of scripture equal weight. Third, if "inspired" means something else, what is that something else?

At one time, the answer seemed quite simple. The Musée des beaux-arts de Montréal has in its collection a painting by the 17th-century Dutch artist Barent Fabritius. Called *Saint Matthew and the Angel*, it pictures St. Matthew sitting at a writing table, lips slightly pursed, pen poised in one hand, inkwell in the other, leaning slightly over a bound book in which he is writing. At his ear, an angel hovers. Eyes shut, the angel seems to be whispering in his ear, even as a child whispers a secret into the ear of her friend. Matthew looks serious, almost a bit sad. Fabritius's understanding of biblical inspiration and the authority of scripture is quite obvious. God has given the angel the words that Matthew should write in his gospel. Matthew takes dictation. He merely writes down what he has been told.

Fabritius's painting reflects the 17th century's understanding of inspiration. But we cannot accept that picture. That understanding cannot account for the factual differences that become apparent as you move from one gospel to another, let alone when you move to other books of the Bible. It cannot explain the occasional discrepancies within a particular gospel itself, let alone the serious discrepancies that arise as you compare the data in one book with those found in another. A careful reading of the books of the Bible reveals that they are the products of very human hands. Such a reading also reveals that these books come from particular periods of time and particular cultures, periods and cultures different from our own.

That 17th-century understanding of the Bible's inspiration resulting from divine dictation, with each and every word in scripture having equal authority and value, breaks down at another point, too. None of us gives equal weight to each verse of scripture. None of us, for example, sees the Old Testament prohibition against boiling a goat in its mother's milk as being of equal importance with the admonition that we should love our neighbours as ourselves. Likewise, few of us would argue that the prohibition in the Book of Leviticus against wearing clothing made of two different kinds of material should carry weight at all, and I suspect that none of us would argue that that prohibition should be seen as having equal value with the Beatitudes.

I have indicated why that particular classical view of inspiration cannot hold, because one view of the Bible's authority for the Christian has depended upon just such a view of inspiration. This view asserted that the Bible has authority because God, either directly or indirectly, has dictated each and every word, and therefore each and every word has authority for us. But if that view of inspiration and, therefore, of authority, cannot hold, does that mean that scripture has no authority for us?

Some people have answered that question with a "yes." Generally speaking, these are individuals who have concluded that because some stories have details that are not historically accurate or scientifically provable, the Bible cannot have any authority for them. These individuals would assert that the only things that are "true" are things that can be scientifically proven or verified. Since many biblical stories fail according to such criteria, then the Bible and its stories are dismissed in terms of having authority.

But there are also problems with this view. Such a narrow definition of truth fails to take into account that there are many things we believe to be "true," even if they cannot be scientifically proven. Poetry, for example, uses imagery and cadence in conveying things we think are true, even though the images that evoke such feelings may not be historically accurate or verifiable in scientific terms. The lover who says, "You are the most wonderful person in the world" unquestionably speaks truth regarding her beloved. You and I, though, might well not make the same judgment that her beloved is the most wonderful person we know.

Most significantly, to approach the stories of the Bible as histories or scientific accounts is to misunderstand the kind of literature the Bible is. The gospels and many of the historical accounts we find in stories in the Old Testament were not written as biographies or as histories. They were written as testimonies of why Jesus was significant or of how God had acted to save the people of Israel. That is not to say that these stories do not include historical details that are accurate. But we need to remember that they are testimonies, witnesses of faith, and theological reflections, not historical or biographical accounts as we would understand those terms.

Let me illustrate this point with an example. If you ask me to give you a brief biography of my father, I would offer details such as where he was born, what he did for a living, and the various places he lived. If, however, you ask me how and why he was significant for me, I would give you a very different answer. It might include some of those factual details, but my response would reflect much more my sense and my memories of how he interacted with me, influenced me, cared for me, and loved me. Much of the Bible reflects the second kind of inquiry and the resultant type of response.

So, how might the Bible have authority for us, and how might we see it as inspired?

I need to start by defining the word *authority*. For some of us the notion of authority might be a comfortable one; for others, the term has negative connotations of control or even of oppression. I want to suggest what may to some of you be a different definition of authority. It's one that I believe works well both for thinking about the authority of scripture and for other aspects of authority. The Latin word from which our word *authority* comes meant that which authors, empowers, invents, brings into being, or makes possible. Authority, both in biblical terms and, I think, in secular terms, means that which "authors" or "empowers."

By way of illustration, let me use two quick secular examples. When I drive on the highway, the province "empowers" me to drive on the right hand side of the road. It empowers me to do so by assuring me, at least in theory, that all the drivers I meet will also be driving on the right hand side of the road. The authority of the province, far from being a negative force, authorizes or empowers me to drive in that way. Likewise, when the province "authorizes" me, as a minister, to perform marriages in this province, it gives me a licence to do so. That licence, and the authorization it symbolizes, empowers me to perform such services.

When I speak about the authority of the Bible or of scripture, I am saying that the Bible, through its stories and teachings, "authorizes" or "empowers" the Christian to live a Christian life, to live in a way pleasing to God. Far from being a straitjacket or a thumbs-down type of authority, the authority of the Bible comes from its ability to empower Christians. That authority arises from the Bible's ability to draw forth from within Christians power they did not know they had, power to live in a particular way.

I have asserted that the Bible empowers or authorizes us in some way. I need to explain just how the Bible or scripture has authority for us. When the founders of our denomination asserted that the Bible was the primary authority for Christians, I think they wanted to say two things. The first is that God's Word comes to us as we read and enter into dialogue with those biblical witnesses. The authority of scripture is not found in the words of the text itself. The authority of scripture comes from the God who meets us *through* the text.

By way of illustration, let me quote at some length from a book written in the early 1960s by Donald Mathers, then a professor at Queen's Theological College. On this point, Mathers wrote:

> The word of God means a lot more than words about God, it means God...come face to face with... [human beings]. This is true for the Old Testament prophet when the word of God comes to him. It is true about Jesus Christ, the Word of God incarnate. It is even true about preaching, which we call the ministry of the word because in preaching it is expected that we will be brought face to face with the majesty of God and with [God's] power.[8]

What is Mathers saying? He wants to make clear that when we talk about the Bible as the "Word of God," we are talking not about the words on the page but about the Word of God, that is, the Spirit of God, the presence of God that meets us when we wrestle with the stories we find in the Bible. The stories tell about human encounters with the Divine, and they become the occasion for our encounters with the Divine. They become the primary means, though not the only means, through which Christians come to know God and to meet God. Inspiration is found not in the text itself but in the Word of God that comes to us through the text. When we read in 2 Timothy 3:16, "All scripture is inspired by God and is useful for teaching, for reproof, for correction, and for training in righteousness," it is in this sense that all scripture is "inspired." In all scripture, there is the possibility that, as we read and reflect, or as we hear scripture read and then explicated through a sermon, the Word of God may come to us.

In a later place in that same chapter, Mathers uses a wonderful analogy to express this point about what the Word of God is, and is not. He writes:

> The Bible is like a telescope: it is for looking through, not looking at. It is not itself revealed, it is the witness to revelation, the record of revelation, it is the testimony of the

church that God has [been] revealed...to [God's] people, to the prophets, to the apostles but most of all *in* Jesus Christ.[9]

Scripture, then, does not have authority in and of itself. It has authority because it points to God, because it mediates God's power to us. Therein lies its authority.

In speaking of scripture as the primary authority for Christians, I think our denomination's founders also wanted to remind us of a second, related point. They wanted to remind us that the Bible has authority for us because it alone puts us in touch with the founding moments of our tradition, with its origins. It has also been the church's experience that the Bible has been an empowering document to each generation of Christians down through the centuries. Hence the Bible has authority for the Christian community. It is, in that sense, the church's book. It puts us in touch with our roots. It empowers us for our time. In this sense, the Bible differs from every other book for the Christian. Other books may be inspiring. Many of them are much more inspiring than ploughing through the dietary laws of Leviticus! But for me as a Christian, the Bible is always a necessary source for Christian living, something I must take seriously in my effort to lead a Christian life.

But if it is a necessary source, even the primary source, for doing Christian theology, for weighing out Christian moral questions, it is neither all-sufficient nor the only source. If we believe in a living God, a God who speaks to us in the present, rather than a dead God whose only possibility for revelation is found in the literal words of texts that date back 2,000 years or more, then we also believe in a God who is able to reveal God's very self to us in this day. The biblical writers themselves borrowed concepts and wisdom from other cultures and writers in their own day. We need to be open to the other ways God speaks to us, namely through nature, through tradition, through others, through our experience of the Spirit of God in our own lives.

Whence comes the authority of scripture? It comes from God who meets us there, whose Word and Spirit empower us for our living as

Christians in our time and our place. May we be open to this God who meets us in scripture and in other ways, and to that God be praise and thanksgiving, this day and always. Amen.

—*John H. Young*

This sermon is a significant revision of one preached some time ago, the revision incorporating new elements from a sermon on the authority of scripture preached in 2015.

Chapter 5
Sin and Regeneration

There's an Elephant in the Room

The Doctrinal Concept

"Behold, I make all things new!" Twenty-four times this message comes through scripture. All things new, a new creation, new humanity, clothed in a new self, new birth, new heart, new mercies, new covenant, new way: "Behold, I make all things new!" Beyond those 24 passages are witnesses to miracles, release from domination, second chances, deep transformations, increasingly vigorous spiritual communities, resurrected life, reconciled relationships, sinners who are cured: regeneration as far as the eye can see. Life is rich and full. Our cup runs over.

Such are the promises of God, and such are our Christian expectations. Drawing on our trust in God, we celebrate that we are made in the image of God.

Yet we acknowledge that this exciting newness is not the full story. We carry a core human question: Why are we not good all the time? From this dilemma about our existential identity, our failure, and our hope for regeneration comes the doctrine of sin.

A Song of Faith expresses sin in this manner:

> Made in the image of God,
> we yearn for the fulfillment that is life in God.
> Yet we choose to turn away from God.
> We surrender ourselves to sin,
> > a disposition revealed in selfishness, cowardice, or apathy.
> Becoming bound and complacent
> > within a web of false desires and wrong choices,
> > we bring harm to ourselves and others.
> This brokenness in human life and community
> > is an outcome of sin.
> Sin is not only personal
> > but accumulates
> > to become habitual and systemic forms
> > of injustice, violence, and hatred.

Most of us are humble enough to feel all right not being perfect. We absorb failure and mistakes, and we keep going. We may think of sin as bad choices. This doctrine opens up to us the ambiguity of the human condition, the flawed nature of humankind, and the pernicious systems or contexts in which we live, move, and have our being. This further understanding of sin conflicts with our cultural expectation that we can and do make our own way with enough salary, enough education, enough determined hard work. Into this understanding comes the question of our interest in hurting other people. If we can work to be whatever we wish, and we still find ourselves hurting one another, we run into a wall: we must be responsible for our unkind desire; there must be something wicked within us.

For anyone who has spent time reading Milton's epic poem *Paradise Lost,* or watching horror movies, "something wicked within us" may ring a bell. Let's look at that, turning to the two accounts of creation in the Book of Genesis.

The second creation narrative, in Genesis 2, is the earlier of the two. It comes from the 10th century before the Common Era, at the beginning of the Israelite monarchy. The first parents experience temptation and estrangement from God. The myth of Adam and Eve brings us colourful, memorable ways to address trust and faithfulness, and to cope when we fail. Often the concept of original sin is read into this narrative; we may also call it first sin, universal sin, inherited sin, and the Fall.

Original sin is a helpful concept when we are beyond our own capabilities and yearn to lean on God's grace; it is dangerous when we read it to mean we are rogues at heart. Furthermore, interpretations about the Fall have less to do with the ancient biblical writers, and more to do with Paul's concept of the first Adam in Romans 5 and 6, and further with the bishop and theologian Augustine of Hippo (354–430), the reformer John Calvin (1509–1564), and the poet John Milton (1608–1674).

The story in the Garden brings us many issues such as domination of nature, religious exclusivism, heteronormativity, and ambivalence about sex. But the question of alienation, of estrangement, is the foundational question.

The first Genesis creation narrative, starting with "In the beginning" (Genesis 1:1) is the more recent story. It comes from the time of the Exile in Babylon, in the sixth century BCE. The creation story of the Babylonian Empire was violent. Apsu and Tiamat, the gods of fresh and salt water, are killed by their children. Marduk is victorious and creates heaven and earth from their dead bodies. He enslaves and abuses humankind. Continued tyranny follows. Against the backdrop of this hope-defying, brutal myth, our ancestors in faith told a contrasting one of goodness. "And God saw that it was good," rings the refrain, and then at 1:26, "Then God said, 'Let us make humankind in our image.'" At verse 31, further good news: "God saw everything that [God] had made, and indeed, it was very good." The cosmic creation story asserts that we are made in God's image; we are creatures; we are not God; and creation is very good.

At the outset of Genesis, then, we find two conflicting issues: we are made in the image of God, and we are estranged from God. What we need is assurance that God wants us back. We call that *regeneration*.

Here are the pertinent definitions that were drafted in the Statement of Faith written in 1908, which became part of the Twenty Articles of Doctrine accepted at church union in 1925:

> **Article V. Of the Sin of Man.**
> We believe that our first parents, being tempted, chose evil, and so fell away from God and came under the power of sin, the penalty of which is eternal death; and that, by reason of this disobedience, all men are born with a sinful nature, that we have broken God's law, and that no man can be saved but by His grace.
>
> **Article IX. Of Regeneration.**
> We believe in the necessity of regeneration, whereby we are made new creatures in Christ Jesus by the Spirit of God, who imparts spiritual life by the gracious and mysterious operation of His power, using as the ordinary means the truths of His word and the ordinances of divine appointment in ways agreeable to the nature of man.

Living with an assurance that God wants us back, that the nature of God is to love us, not to shun us, we have a constructive way into reflection on sin.

The freedom to make choices is part of the first parents' story. Apples may never recover from iconic scenes with the fruit of the tree of the knowledge of good and evil! Are our first parents prototypes of bad choices, and is sin then disobedience? Paul writes, "the wages of sin is death, but the free gift of God is eternal life in Christ Jesus our Lord" (Romans 6:23).

Let's look a little more deeply at disobedience. Disobedience can, of course, be understood as a series of bad behaviours. It can also be understood as a denial of our heritage as children of God. Seen in this perspective, the sins we commit become symptoms of our pulling away from God, something deeper than bad choices. I am thinking here of *why* people do what we do, more than *what* it is that we do. I am thinking about why we hurt other people, our ecological balance, and the systems we live in. Often we are bewildered, confused, and dismayed by our proclivity to do the hurtful thing.

In this perspective, an understanding of sin is less moral and more spiritual. It is less behavioural and more existential. It is less about what we do and more about who we are. We are made in the image of God. We are creatures; we are not God—and creation is very good.

It goes on. Cain and Abel, the first siblings, come to us in Genesis 4. Verse 8 is larger than life: "Cain rose up against his brother Abel, and killed him." We continue to rise up against one another. Violence and selfishness run rampant in our world. There is a universality to sin, and to yearning for regeneration.

The narratives about first parents and first siblings bring the question of sin home. The stories are anthropocentric: centring on humankind, they are dramatic, vivid, powerful, and memorable, and we can identify with the protagonists. Metaphoric engagement with the narratives allows us to extrapolate the meaning into other forums for sin. We understand the drama to be corporate, ecological, political, and economic as well as personal. Secrecy, theft, jealousy, deceit, murder: all these parts of the stories issue forth in systemic sin as well as interpersonal relations. Sin becomes more than mistakes or bad choices; sin becomes a corruption of the sacred meaning in everything around us. Sin becomes contempt for the good creation we live in. Sin becomes a disparagement of the very blessing we were created to be.

The stories beyond Genesis 4 allow us to move our biblical connection to sin out of the Garden and into a wider-ranging culture. In a similar way, our connection to sin begins with a personal understanding and involves everything we touch. Politics, economics, sex, stewardship of the earth: sin is everywhere. The point, however, is not brimstone and shame, but rather awareness that God is yearning for us. God is waiting for us to turn around and return to the way of love. Politics, economics, sex, stewardship of the earth: restored to beauty, pleasure, and mutuality. "Behold, I make all things new!" As our denominational founding theologians put it in Article IX, God will make us "new creatures in Christ Jesus by the Spirit of God, who imparts spiritual life by the gracious and mysterious operation of His power."

Acknowledging that we are not perfect, and that sin is not the end of the world, we may celebrate the image of God in which our human nature is based. The merit of the doctrines of sin and regeneration may truly be that they allow us to live with ourselves. The mystery may be that we can lean into God and celebrate that.

If it seems that I am sounding cheerful about sin, that's not quite it. I thoroughly acknowledge the anguish of people hurting people. I also acknowledge that there is a cure, a hope, a confession, a renewal, a regeneration that comes through Jesus Christ—and about that I am excessively cheerful. That is what the church is for, to be a community that proclaims human value, hope, love, forgiveness, and a God who yearns for us. That is the intent of preaching doctrine.

Scripture for Preaching

Mark 2:13–17

Jesus went out again beside the lake; the whole crowd gathered around him, and he taught them. As he was walking along, he saw Levi son of Alphaeus sitting at the tax booth, and he said to him, "Follow me." And he got up and followed him. And as he sat at dinner in Levi's house, many tax collectors and sinners were also sitting with Jesus and his disciples—for there were many who followed him. When the scribes of the Pharisees saw that he was eating with sinners and tax collectors, they said to his disciples, "Why does he eat with tax collectors and sinners?" When Jesus heard this, he said to them, "Those who are well have no need of a physician, but those who are sick; I have come to call not the righteous but sinners."

Why Is This Doctrine Important?

Sin is important because many of us ignore it. We draw a curtain over it, and hope decency will prevail. I speak for myself: it is much easier to keep the peace in a pastoral charge by focusing on governance, baptism policies, Sunday music and liturgy, or basement repairs than to unveil a nasty term such as *sin* and set things on fire. Governance and these other issues require our attention. They are not incidental. Yet under the surface runs a current of unease, a sense that not all is well. Echoes of the old Babylonian creation myth reverberate; for instance, in pastoral care we hear people lamenting that they don't deserve to be loved, that they felt diminished as a child, or that they don't know how to love unconditionally.

"Is it not enough to be decent?" a member of a church board said to me once. I expect she meant that behaving nicely toward one another was sufficient, that we don't need to unearth the old theologies, that we ought to move on. Do we believe, though, that the doctrine of sin is indeed archaic, spent, or irrelevant? If this doctrine is an outmoded belief, we need to explain why. If not, let's engage it.

Our call is not to preach old doctrines simply because they are written down, because they are ours, or because they are interesting, but to preach doctrine because it matters. Doctrine is relevant; it saves lives. Preachers do not bring spiritual truths about sin to make intellectual or academic points. Rather, we offer an encounter with the Author of Life, the Holy One, the Reality that goes deeper than our imagination, the God who loves us and our lives and calls us to honesty, forgiveness, grace, and regeneration. Sin is more than an old concept, a tired tool of chastisement. It is a deep and transformative acknowledgement that all is not well, much is wrong, and much is unhealthy.

People who seek us out for counselling often recognize sin in their spirits. When we fail to address it in preaching, it is as though we keep it behind closed doors. It is as though we define it as one person's particular issue, not an issue common to us all. Preaching about sin normalizes it, takes the stigma away, and gives us opportunity to speak about confession and the new freedom in Christ. When preachers acknowledge sexual abuse in a sermon or in a prayer, for instance, we give permission to people who have been abused to talk with us. The same is true generally for sin.

Attentive pastoral care brings crucial issues into the light. We know that a thoughtful visit from a minister can uncover uncomfortable realities. "Help me pray," a member of the congregation asks. "Teach me to pray about what I've done wrong." In preaching we can acknowledge deep pastoral issues—not in a way that calls out that person, of course, those visits are confidential—by speaking about the wisdom of the faith. In this case, of the doctrine of sin. Teaching this doctrine faithfully can bring the listener hope and comfort through a new perspective.

Preaching on sin and regeneration gets at the central pastoral question: Where does our interest in hurting other people come from? We cannot ignore our hurtful behaviours, the gratuitous violence of our world, and the harm we do to our planet home. Many of us write prayers of confession every week because of the sins of the world. Some of us lean away from that heavy language, yet still include confession and forgiveness. After one particularly volatile conversation about the prayer of confession, I tried a change in the vocabulary with "Prayers from the Bottom of Our Hearts." The conflict disappeared. I tell you that story because preaching about sin can touch fire.

What is more, there is a cure for it. Our listeners may not know about that cure. Confession is the cure, and it is rooted not in subservience but in God's yearning for us, in regeneration through Christ.

A pastoral sermon can call for honesty in our lives and our living. A sermon written out of love for one's listeners can relieve the burden of sin. It can awaken fresh possibilities. It is, of course, our privilege and pleasure to be called to do just that.

Sin is a word that has been appropriated by those who have chosen to use it. Because others use it forcefully, it has become awkward for many of us to retrieve it. In much popular memory sin is a large stick, used with guilt to press people down, to submerge creative abilities, and to dominate others' theologies. Shame follows quickly where sin is invoked, and bad things happen. Bringing sin into the conversation in our congregations gives members the opportunity to address those concerns.

Our tolerance for sin is on a spectrum. From personal white lies through cultures of brutality to insidious anti-ecological practices, we learn to tolerate sin, to the detriment of all, of course. We acquiesce to pressures around us, and find ourselves estranged from God and from our own existential identity, made in God's image. Systemic sin looms. Here is a description from A Song of Faith:

> We are all touched by this brokenness:
>   the rise of selfish individualism
>   that erodes human solidarity;
>   the concentration of wealth and power
>   without regard for the needs of all;
>   the toxins of religious and ethnic bigotry;
>   the degradation of the blessedness of human bodies
>   and human passions through sexual exploitation;
>   the delusion of unchecked progress and limitless growth
>   that threatens our home, the earth;

> the covert despair that lulls many into numb complicity
> with empires and systems of domination.
>
> We sing lament and repentance.

There are times when we are simply at wit's end with relationships, ecological issues, politics, or personal issues. A sermon that speaks to this incapacity to do enough, or apparent inability to do the right things, will give a spiritual perspective on an exasperating situation. Attention to this aspect of our reality as human beings will be helpful to all our congregants. Rather than being at our wit's end and incapacitated, we find ourselves at the beginning of a process of confession, forgiveness, and restitution that may solve a problem.

The sins of our living are often identified as bad choices. A decision to drive while drinking, to purchase a product made by child labour, to leave unspoken a word of forgiveness: these decisions are the symptoms of sin. They do need to be addressed. The spiritual work is reaching underneath them to find the motivator. A sermon can offer Christ's objective work and get to the bottom of things, changing us, redeeming us, regenerating us into who we are created to be: made in the image of God.

As much as sermons about sin get us thinking in very personal terms, their purpose is not therapy. Regeneration and redemption are not therapy. Therapy can change lives, but it is the tool of another discipline. What the church is about is existential, the curing of souls. People need to hear that God yearns for them, and that regeneration is that gift.

A sermon on the doctrine of sin will generate thought and conversation. Rather than leaving issues to the optimistic means of decency, situations are identified and reparations can be made. Lives can be lived fully, without guilt or shame. How we speak about the doctrine can change how our listeners understand it; how we tell the doctrine can determine whether we fight it or find relief in understanding it. Questions about trusting God arise when sin is discussed. People ask, "Does God hold people accountable with punishment? Are we squashed because we make mistakes?"

Many in our congregations resist the concept of original sin. Members resist the idea that a baby brought forward for baptism could be tainted with sin, having no maturity to be disobedient. They resist an assumption that we are basically immoral or evil at root. And of course! We are made in the image of God; this is a fundamental part of who we are. It is important to address this apparent dichotomy, to speak about the church traditions of original sin and blessing. The fundamentally flawed nature of our humanity and of our societal structures brings us close to the concept of "original sin."

What if our congregations do not want to hear about sin? Perhaps they think it is old-fashioned and irrelevant. "You catch more flies with honey," a member of the congregation told me in a conversation about Sunday worship. We were standing in the church parking lot. "You'll keep them coming if they feel better when they leave than they did coming in." This warning, I think, reveals an expectation about sermons on sin.

Our calling is not to put people down, as people may expect in a reflection on sin. That is why preaching sin and regeneration together is essential. The good news is that God yearns to have us back. In fact, I have found people deeply attentive when I preach on sin; preaching the hard theologies can satisfy the mind and spirit of listeners. It gives them something to chew on when they get home. The parking lot fills up when something hopeful, relevant, and meaningful is going on inside.

In this age of disillusionment with authority, it can be challenging to speak of sin. The threat of punishment echoes from other places or distant times. Although The United Church of Canada has a heritage of open-mindedness, forward-thinking, and acceptance, there are listeners who fear what they might expect in sermons about sin, and more specifically that we harbour judgments about sinful behaviour. Frankly, the six-word phrase "preaching about the doctrine of sin" delivers three heavy-handed words: *preaching, doctrine,* and *sin.*

What happens to our Christian living if we ignore the doctrine of sin? We may be made just a little lower than the angels, but we are lower—

we are so remarkably capable, and yet we are so merely human. We are capable of so much destruction and creative nastiness. We assume that with enough willpower and money, we can accomplish what is needed. If we ignore the doctrine of sin we can easily fall into entitlement, and that is a problem of another sort, requiring humility and grace.

Sin shows up in the backyard, along the streets, in the neighbour's life, on the front page of the morning paper, in my congregation, and in pastoral care. People need to hear that God yearns for them, that Christ makes everything new, and that we live in hope that things can and will change.

How Does It Preach?

The sermon that follows is an introduction to talking about sin in Sunday worship. A preacher or a worship committee might well plan to deal with sin in a reflective season such as Lent. A circumstance of apparent sinful behaviour may hit the headlines (when does it not?) and provoke a sermonic response. There is also something normalizing about offering a reflection on sin in ordinary times such as October or May, as an acknowledgement that sin is an ordinary thing. A sermon on sin deals with bringing the topic out of the confines of personal or private conversations and into the community. If individuals are wondering about the church's opinions on sin, this sermon begins a public discourse. People may feel that their questions about sin are too personal to ask; by acknowledging the elephant in the room, issues about sin become a conversation for us all to share.

It's important to say that sin and guilt are a formidable, crushing combination. This sermon recognizes that sin is a fact of human nature, a fact that in no way overcomes the blessing in which we are created, the central and holy nature of being human. It serves to normalize sin, or at least to reduce the anxiety about sin. It is a pastoral kindness to address the heavy-handed treatment of sin, which many of our congregants have encountered.

Jesus or Adam? I needed to make a choice. The sermon would be too long for one morning with both the second creation story and Jesus. I preached a separate sermon on Apsu, Tiamat, and Marduk. The material is fascinating. What I wanted to get at in this one, though, was Jesus' recognition of sinners. The passage from Mark is clear on that point. Then I could move into a conversation about who we are, existentially, and why we hurt one another.

In Mark 2:13–17 Jesus speaks of sinners. It is not an act of sin of which he speaks, but the people. It is an issue of identity, spiritual identity. Jesus says he calls not the righteous but sinners. This passage gets to the heart of the issue straightaway. We might wish to be part of the righteous, but perhaps we wonder if we are truly among the sinners. It is a goal of this sermon to accept sin as part of who we are. It is a spiritual issue, and it is spiritual language that I use to distinguish it from behaviours. With that in mind, I speak of a monarchical model and a spiritual model of sin. These two models help distinguish between sin as bad choices and sin as part of our nature.

We are astonished at our tendency to cause harm. Small wonder we need a commandment to love one another! To bring a familiar moment to the sermon, I drew on a comment from an older member of the congregation. In her wisdom she spoke of "not being good all the time" as simply part of the human condition.

I chose not to use the word *regeneration* in this sermon. This word would sound archaic or unfamiliar to many ears: it was enough to deal with vocabulary about sin. I chose instead to use descriptions of God yearning for us. For the purpose of this sermon, it is more pastoral and more poetic to make the point that the God who loves us and who made us in God's own image is more powerful than sin. There would be opportunity in subsequent sermons to define and use *regeneration*.

In the sermon we also hear the beginning of the story of the family of Jacob. The narrative of Joseph and his brothers is a wealth of sin: jealousy, attempted murder, despair, depravity, lying, cheating. I referred to this story because the congregation had spent nine weeks on it recently;

it was familiar. Reading these narratives, we recognize that biblical authors have long addressed sin.

The sermon takes the doctrines of sin and regeneration and focuses them through these questions: Where does our interest in hurting other people come from? Why are we not good all the time? The doctrine of sin has more to do with our interest in hurting other people than with the acts themselves.

Sin is insidious. Sin is a mystery that compels us. Yet as people made in the image of God, we are offended by the power of sin.

I chose to explore the power of sin in two contrasting ways. I outlined pride and inflation of self, through which we become dominating and self-aggrandizing, not acknowledging our finitude or our dependence on God. And I outlined servility, unworthiness, and despising oneself, feeling undeserving of God's love and subsequently of our own or anyone else's love. These two powers of sin, self-aggrandizement and diminishing ourselves, are where we find answers for our questions.

Near the close of the sermon, I brought us back to Levi's house, where Jesus was eating dinner with sinners. We have nothing to fear if that is the company we keep. If Jesus is there, God's love is there. Any healing we need will happen; any estrangement from God will be overcome.

We need assurance that God wants us back, that we have not made too many domineering mistakes, nor shrunk too far from God's eye. This sermon reminds us of the purpose of the church: to be a community that proclaims human value, hope, love, and forgiveness, and to deepen a relationship with the God who yearns for us.

I ended the sermon as it began, with words and phrases that lift us up and bring us down. If the word *sin* has pushed us down, if concepts of sin have alarmed us, these thoughts may change that. I finished by addressing sin as the elephant in the room, driven away by the God who does love us beyond sin. God will never let us go, for we are created in God's very image.

Sample Sermon

The Elephant in the Room

There are words in our common speech that energize us. Words such as *laughter, beauty, welcome, thanks*. There are phrases that relax us: *free parking, breakfast all day, students and seniors' half-price admittance*. One of the most energizing phrases in our common life is the phrase *I forgive you*.

There are words in our common speech that bring us down. Words such as *vigilante, brutal, morgue, poison*. There are phrases that cause us anxiety: *road closed, sold out, proof of membership required*. One of the words that bring us down as faithful people is a word you don't hear very often from me. It's one of those words that I find to be so very true and powerful that it's almost better to find a synonym. It's ubiquitous. We don't really need to acknowledge it. It's like an elephant in the room.

It's the word *sin*.

If you were to collect all the Sunday DVDs that Luc and Daniel and Luke and Jack and John and Irl and Serena have produced for us over the years, you would find very few times that I have used the word *sin*. It's a short word that's large, like a mouse in front of a flashlight, making a shadow big as an elephant. It takes all the air out of the room.

Frankly, preaching about sin keeps me awake. I hesitate to preach about sin when we have friends and guests present because we in The United Church of Canada are proud of recognizing that we are made in the image of God, that everyone is made in the image of God, and that human nature is a blessing.

Human nature is a blessing, not a curse, because we are made in the image of God—that is our primary identification. From our identification comes our primary purpose. Who we are leads to what we do, and we are proud to do much for justice, much for equality, much to shine the light on the image of God in the world. But there is never a Sunday without friends and guests present—and so they are welcome to hear our dilemma, my dilemma, that is called sin.

The word *sin* has been appropriated by other people. And because we let it go, because we let others seize it, the short word *sin* has become a very large word. We have let others define it, and today we will correct that. Another short word follows quickly on sin, and it is the word *guilt*. Although there are times that we may think guilt is motivating, it's truly debilitating. It brings us down. Guilt calls on our anxiety, and shrouds sin with a thin, bitter chill.

"I have come to call not the righteous but sinners," Jesus says. "Those who are well have no need of a physician, but those who are sick; I have come to call not the righteous but sinners" (Mark 2:17).

Let's figure out who the sinners are and why they make excellent company. Jesus sat with them; in my book, that is excellent company. Let's figure out why we might want to be at that table, too.

In a monarchy, sin would be disloyalty to a king. Sin would be disobedience to laws. In a monarchical model, sin would be a commodity with market-priced costs.

But in a spiritual model, God is love, not a king. In a spiritual model, sin is separation, our wilful and deliberate separation from God.

Our fundamental problem is not sin in a monarchical model, but sin as we relate to the God who loves us, the God who created us in God's own image. Sin is estrangement in a spiritual model. Sin is being separated from that to which we belong. Sin is a disposition revealed in selfishness, cowardice, or apathy.

Sin is an elephant in the room. Sin is real. It is crucial to know that we have an antidote for it. We call it *confession*. It is bringing the prayers from the bottom of our hearts into the open, into words or song or sighs. It is trusting that God will hear those words or song or sighs that come from the bottom of our hearts, and loving us still, will forgive us and bless us on our way.

You see, sin is not simply about making bad choices. It's about acknowledging that we are not perfect. Olive Elofson used to sit in this sanctuary every Sunday. She said to us in Bible study, "We're so human, we're not good all the time." Why are we not good all the time?

The sinners at dinner were seen to have broken the laws of God. Some sins were easily identifiable. The sinners were shunned—that's why the religious authorities were perhaps surprised that Jesus was eating with them. Yet it's not about bad character. Our existential character is a blessing; it is in the image of God.

So we are created in the image of God, and all the faithful people in this story are aware of that. The word *sin* is often thought of as identifiable crimes against the law of God. That is the monarchical model. But really just doing something wrong is part of human nature. We all do things wrong. In many instances we can ask for forgiveness and do what we can to alleviate the pain, to reconcile with the person we've hurt. That can't always happen but it often can.

Here's a story: Once there was a family, the children of immigrants, who were ranchers. The sons looked after the sheep, keeping them from wolves and poachers. The youngest of the children was the apple of his father's eye. As a teenager he had the run of the ranch and told tales on his brothers to their father. They resented him as a favourite and a tattletale. The father had a fancy coat made for him. It was a long coat with sleeves that made it impractical for wrangling sheep.

You know this story, don't you? The youngest brother had dreams, too, about the sun, moon, and stars bowing to him. He told his brothers the dreams and their jealousy increased. The brothers started a plot to kill him. When circumstances came together, they threw him into a pit. One brother persuaded the others not to kill him, but they bound him up and sold him into slavery. Years later the family of Jacob would be reunited, but not before the kidnapped boy had interpreted dreams in a faraway land, become the chief economic officer in the empire of the day, and saved the empire from famine. Eventually the father would die happy at a fine old age.

Scripture itself brings us narratives that remind us what it is to be human. Jacob's sons knew a thing or two about sin—and we can learn from them. The humanity of the characters is the crucible. The failings of every single member of the family become apparent. The jealousy, attempted fratricide, and cover-up at the beginning of the Joseph story describe the indiscriminate nature of our human proclivity to sin. As well, there is no good guy/bad guy set-up: Joseph is naïve or perhaps he flaunts his father's favouritism; the brothers keep their heads low and grind their teeth at his insolence; the father may be ignoring the rift he is causing. No one is beyond judgment. Are any of us free from the disposition to greed, cowardice, apathy? What do we do with the guilt and shame of our sins, of the hurts we have inflicted and incurred?

If we were Knights of the Round Table fighting chaos, we could see ourselves as the privileged, entitled people of the kingdom. But that is not who we are. We are not defending a set of laws or a king's honour. We are not looking for an answer about living in a monarchy. We are looking for an answer about living spiritual lives in our real world.

The spiritual questions are the deep ones. So here are the deep questions about sin: Where does our interest in hurting other people come from? Why are we not good all the time? The thing about sin is that it has more to do with where our interest in hurting other people comes from than the acts themselves. The acts can be identified. People can be made to pay, or shunned. But what is it that draws us to hurt other people? Pride comes to mind; selfishness and greed come to mind. Are pride, selfishness, and greed the answer? If so, where do they come from? These are spiritual questions.

In our daily lives we encounter sin. In the mix of wonder, pleasure, and goodness that we find in, for example, our ecosystem, our school boards, our sexual relationships, and our children's friends, we also encounter sin. This is our daily living. We would rather not admit that it was there; we might rather call it growth, addiction, or perspective. But truly, it's just plain sin.

The power of sin works in two contrasting ways. In one way, it builds us up and aggrandizes us. In the other one, it diminishes us and brings us down.

In the first way, the power of sin wants us to lift ourselves up over other people, to be seen to be the better one, to be seen to be more successful, whatever it takes. Those are the kind of things traditionally identified with sin. We puff ourselves up; we self-aggrandize.

When I was young and smaller than I am now, one of the worst things people could say to you was "You think you're so big." That is the root of that part of sin: thinking you are so big, so fine, so invincible, so unassailable, so close to perfect, so wonderful, so ideal that other people could suffer a little to acknowledge that. We are made in the image of God! So in the first power of sin we acknowledge that we are creative, exciting, dynamic, and marvellous—and we puff ourselves up. We see that on a personal scale; we see it on a community scale. We see it on a scale of whoever claims to be the dominant culture; we see that on a global scale.... But there's another side to sin.

The second power of sin is the opposite of the first. In sin we also diminish ourselves. We are made in the image of God! In the second power of sin we forget that. Maybe somebody teaches us to forget that, or perhaps we were never taught that in the beginning, taught that we are born in the image of God. So we diminish ourselves. We may become apathetic. We may say, "The world is the way it is and I can't do anything about it," and we sit down rather than stand up.

Or worse yet, we say that we don't deserve to live as an image of God. We say that other people are bright and brilliant and wonderful and follow God and follow the light and seem to make the right decisions and make a positive difference—but that we don't. That kind of insecurity, anxiety, and dishonesty about who we are as people of God creates a possibility for dissolution of the person and of relationships. It makes us feel like we could just be squashed, that maybe we should just be squashed. Doesn't it break your heart?

The power of sin works in two ways. In one it puffs us up and aggrandizes us. In the other it diminishes us and brings us down.

That is the spiritual nature of sin. It's not about a list of things we've done wrong. Frankly we've all done things wrong. It's part of human nature to be drawn to doing things wrong. That's just part of who we are. It's not good, but it's part of who we are.

The power of sin, where we puff ourselves up or we shrink ourselves down, is the part that's spiritual. It's a part that hurts deeply. It's the part that causes devastation. It's the root of violence, privilege, greed, and all the things that tear apart our relationships and our world.

That's why sin is a spiritual issue, not just an ethical issue. And that's why Jesus went out to dinner at Levi's house. At the outset of Mark's gospel, before you even turn a page, straightaway in chapter two, Jesus sat down at a table with people who were most easily identified as sinners, most easily identified with human nature.

Do you remember that at the beginning of the sermon I said our primary identification is God's image? At root we are loving, peaceful, hopeful people, drawn to be generous with one another, drawn to see beauty, and to hold this world that we are given in compassion and forgiveness. That's the primary part of who we are. But would you maybe agree with me that it could be possible that once in a while, every now and then, we are also drawn to the power of sin that wants to puff ourselves up or squash ourselves down?

We need to talk about the elephant in the room as a spiritual question. Certainly it is also an excellent ethical question, or a political question, or a relationship question, or an ecological question. The reason we need to talk about the elephant in the room as a spiritual question is because the heart that pounds within us stirs with God's image.

When we acknowledge that beyond God's image we are capable of sin, then we get honest. We can breathe deeply. We don't need to hide things. We can pray from the bottom of our hearts. Indeed, there's stuff we would rather tuck down inside. When we actually acknowledge that we walk in sin, though, it gets lifted away from us. There is something about honesty that makes a person breathe more deeply. Yes, it is hard. It is embarrassing. But honesty—a spiritual honesty—can help us breathe deeply, freely, and with great joy.

We are made in the image of God, and we are estranged from God. What we need is assurance that God wants us back. That's why we're here. That is what the church is for: to be a community that proclaims human value, hope, love, and forgiveness, and to deepen a relationship with a God who yearns for us.

We have nothing to fear. God loves us. We will sin, and we will confess. We will love. We are free.

Somebody's going to take the DVD home and count the number of times I used that word this morning. You can report that I used the word *sin* 25,000 more times than in any of my other Sunday sermons, because I preach on sin with some trepidation. The word *sin* has been snatched, used as a club, infused with guilt—and I just claimed it back. It might have been easier not to do so, but it is the elephant in the room.

There are words and phrases that lift us up: *beauty, light, I forgive you, thank you, good morning, good-bye, I love you*. There are words and phrases in our common speech that bring us down: *vigilante, brutal, morgue, poison, get out, I'm not worth it.*

The word *sin* is a short, large word that lets us be human. In a spiritual model, sin is estrangement. Sin is being separated from that to whom we belong. And the One to whom we belong yearns for us. God created us in God's own image, and God will not let us go, not even to a short, large word.

There goes the elephant out of the room. Amen.

—*Catherine Faith MacLean*

The sermon title the following week was "The Elephant's Little Buddy: Entitlement."

Chapter 6
Human Depravity

Talking about Our Shadow Side

The Doctrinal Concept

I need to begin with a confession. We noted in the introduction that the idea for this book originated with a presentation at Worship Matters, in which we talked about the importance of preaching on doctrine and illustrated how we would do so with four doctrines. In preparing for that presentation, Catherine suggested that human depravity should be one of the doctrines. "We need to talk not just about easy ones," she said to me, "but about some of the topics we avoid addressing." Well, human depravity certainly qualified on those criteria! So, with some unspoken reluctance, I agreed to address the doctrine of human depravity.

About a month before the event, I began to get cold feet. I feared being mistaken for a holder of archaic theological perspectives if I even tried to take the topic on. *Human depravity* is not a term in fashion these days, at least not in mainstream Protestant circles. It is simply not discussed. A debate in the Reformed church in the Netherlands about "total depravity" in the early 17th century, combined with slightly later creedal statements in the English Reformed tradition asserting a similar understanding of the human condition, have caused a strong distaste for—indeed, an outright horror at—this term. Those 17th-century formulations have so tainted the term *human depravity* for many moderns that it may not be possible to rehabilitate it. And many might say that that would be a good thing!

Having cold feet, I argued for using other theological terms that speak to some of the same realities, though with different nuances. I wondered about doing a presentation on "fallen humanity." Then Catherine, concerned that maybe I was right, had lunch with some ministerial colleagues who opined that we need not worry about using the term *depravity*. Debates about total depravity were long in the past, and terms like fallen humanity seemed pretty bland. They judged that there was something about human depravity that needed considering.

So, we have this chapter. Even if one might hesitate to use the term *depravity* in a sermon to a congregation, preachers need to find the language and the courage to talk unapologetically about the dimension of human sinfulness the term *total depravity* (the traditional theological term) conjured up for our forebears of several centuries ago. That dimension is still with us—and, I realized, it is a fruitful context for pastoral issues that come up. For this book, we chose *human* rather than *total depravity* to avoid the notion that there is "no good in us," and to concentrate explicitly on human nature. In colloquial conversation, the terms are often used interchangeably.

What has the church tried to get at with the doctrine of human depravity? This term has been a way to describe the fundamentally flawed nature of humanity—namely, its sinfulness—and the inevitability of that sinfulness. Traditionally, sin was primarily understood as putting ourselves in the place of God (as in the story of Genesis 3, when the serpent tempts the first humans with the forbidden fruit by telling them it will make them like God, knowing good and evil). In the latter half of the 20th century, primarily through the work of feminist theologians, discussion of human sinfulness moved to recognize that self-negation or self-loathing could be equally sinful. They can be their own form of idolatry, their own denial of God's grace.

Feminist theology has suggested that sinfulness, and therefore what the "shadow side" of humanity might look like, can be different for women—particularly for poor and marginalized women—than for societally privileged men. Women, especially marginalized women, often need encouragement to cease being totally devoted to a self-denying care for others at the expense of developing their own full humanity. Both dimensions are important.

If our creation in the image of God means that we are created for relationship with God and with others, then sin is a denial of that relatedness, whether with God, with others, or with both. Some of us are still imbued with the understanding of late-19th-century liberal theology that if only we were all a little better educated, a little more progressive, a little better at making the right social conditions, we could create the perfect world. Indeed, we really would not need God. That is the idolatry side. Others of us, in the face of the massive problems of global warming, environmental degradation, conflicts in Syria and Iraq, sexual abuse, violence, and so on, become passive, asserting we lack the power to do anything. Both views are problematic.

Our forebears tried, through their use of the term *depravity*, to get at a dimension of our humanity that we still struggle with. That dimension is the sinfulness that infects us and our actions, whether as individuals or as groups. John Calvin, who used the term in describing the human condition, believed that our God-given nature was not inherently sinful; if it were, we would have to blame God. Further, why would God have created human beings in this way? Our human nature was pure and good before Adam sought equality with God rather than accepting contentedly to be a child of God. What Adam "lost" (to use Calvin's term) was lost for us all. Our corrupted nature is something we inherit, though Calvin did not associate that inheritance with conception. Sin, something outside our human nature, so "wounded" our original God-given human nature that it has become corrupted in every part. Not only do we human beings have a sinful nature, but that sinful nature also produces sinful acts.[10] Only God's grace, known to us in Jesus Christ, can restore our human nature to its original, God-given and God-desired state. Such a grace is God's gift, Calvin asserted. We cannot earn it. It is given.

Contemporary theologian and Reformed scholar Serene Jones writes with deep insight on this topic. Feminist theory can take much of Calvin's framework for sin and total depravity and rework it in ways that are helpful for women who are making sense of their lives and their faith. Jones works effectively with Calvin's insight that sin comes from outside us and is not inherent in us, yet penetrates our being and the societal structures in which we live our lives. She shows how it shapes our embodied being, in ways both conscious and subconscious, at least until the latter are brought to the fore.[11]

Human depravity refers to that shadow side of our existence, the side we overlook, suppress, and deny. The insight of our ancestors in the faith, one that Western society since the Enlightenment has been tempted to reject, is that each of us has such a shadow side. Most of us would readily admit that we are not perfect, that we make a few mistakes. However, we often think of sin as making bad choices, rather than recognizing the ambiguity of the human condition, the fundamentally flawed nature both of our humanity and of our societal structures. Such an understanding of ourselves is particularly difficult for middle- and upper-class Western people. Our society tells us in so many ways that we can be whatever we want to be, if only we work hard enough at it and make the right choices. Our ancestors in the faith knew better.

Scripture for Preaching

Romans 7:14–25
For we know that the law is spiritual; but I am of the flesh, sold into slavery under sin. I do not understand my own actions. For I do not do what I want, but I do the very thing I hate. Now if I do what I do not want, I agree that the law is good. But in fact it is no longer I that do it, but sin that dwells within me. For I know that nothing good dwells within me, that is, in my flesh. I can will what is right, but I cannot do it. For I do not do the good I want, but the evil I do not want is what I do. Now if I do what I do not want, it is no longer I that do it, but sin that dwells within me.

So I find it to be a law that when I want to do what is good, evil lies close at hand. For I delight in the law of God in my inmost self, but I see in my members another law at war with the law of my mind, making me captive to the law of sin that dwells in my members. Wretched man that I am! Who will rescue me from this body of death? Thanks be to God through Jesus Christ our Lord!

So then, with my mind I am a slave to the law of God, but with my flesh I am a slave to the law of sin.

Why Is This Doctrine Important?

Some of my views on this doctrine, and on the importance of approaching it in preaching, were shaped by a conversation with a member of a congregation I had recently moved on from. I met him on the street of a nearby city during a time when The United Church of Canada was encouraging interested congregations to use a "hymnal sampler" as a means of testing reactions to some hymns before publishing a new hymn book.

After an exchange of pleasantries and some catching up—the garden, my dog, his family—he said, "I'm glad to have run into you today. You know we are using that new hymn sampler at church. Why did they change the words of 'Amazing Grace' in it? Why in that sampler did they change the line 'that saved a wretch like me' to 'that gave new life to me'?"

I hesitated. I knew the answer would be the wrong one. But eventually I said that I supposed the committee working on the new hymnal was uncomfortable with the "worm" theology conveyed by the term "wretch."

He looked at me rather sadly, almost pityingly, wondering, I expect, whether I shared the viewpoint I had offered as the committee's rationale. Then, in words that have stayed with me ever since, he responded, "Well, they haven't been where I was." This man had long been open in the community about an addiction he had once battled, an addiction that, like most such addictions, had threatened to destroy everything he held dear. He went on: "When I was unsure if anyone, even God, could love me, that line was what gave me hope."

I must confess that I had not been fond of the hymn "Amazing Grace" prior to that conversation. But his comments gave me a new insight into the hymn's words, and that line. By the way, when the United Church's hymnal, *Voices United,* was published, the original wording for "Amazing Grace" (266) was maintained, although there is a little asterisk beside "wretch" to point you to alternative words at the bottom of the page if you prefer to sing "that saved and strengthened me."

In the course of pastoral ministry, we inevitably deal with members of the congregation who battle addictions. When you deal with someone who has an addiction, you quickly realize that strength of will, the determination to do "the right thing," is not enough. Overcoming that addiction—to alcohol, to pornography, to gambling—becomes a lifelong battle against a force that seems stronger than your own will. It is a fight requiring resources outside oneself. Those acquainted with Alcoholics Anonymous will know the stress that organization puts on connecting both with a Higher Power and with one's neighbours who share the addiction as a means of strength for the struggle.

Many preachers were trained, with good reason, to resist the "we are worms" theology of a previous age. That approach is still dangerous. It will lead, if taken seriously, to self-negation or even self-loathing. But the more popular theology—"we are all good, though we make a few bad choices"—can prove equally problematic. A theological reset would be to see evil as something we all need to battle, with God's help, in ourselves and at all times. Talking about human depravity in a sermon may also give people who battle addictions permission to come to talk with you; they may now realize you have an understanding of what they experience.

How Does It Preach?

I need to begin with a caveat. If you preach about human depravity, be prepared the following week to preach about grace. Human depravity is an important topic to explore, but the term and the concept carry baggage. Members of the congregation might miss the point and move into self-loathing. A sermon on human depravity followed by one on grace provides critical balance. In fact, understanding human depravity can open up a deeper understanding of grace.

When might one preach on this topic? The passage from Romans I have suggested as a text is a reading in Year A for a Sunday early in the summer. Lent would be another time to address this subject, followed by a sermon on grace. Indeed, one could preach on human depravity at almost any time. Another option would be to include sermons on human depravity and on grace as part of a series of sermons on doctrinal topics.

Various aspects of human depravity are possible to address. One could examine the relationship of depravity and the way we are both victims of sin and perpetrators of sin, or the relationship of depravity to powerlessness. Serene Jones offers some especially insightful thoughts in both of these areas in her book *Feminist Theory and Christian Theology*. In the sermon that follows, however, I focus on the shadow side of our human nature, on our fundamentally flawed human nature, and then use addiction as an illustration of how we can feel divided between what we know we ought to do and what we choose to do. I thought the context of this doctrine could be helpful for listeners battling an addiction, or seeing family members or friends battle an addiction. Thinking about addiction in the context of our faith may open up a path for trying to deal with it.

I would begin with the optimistic view of human progress and possibility that was so prevalent in the West in the late 19th and early 20th century, prior to the outbreak of the First World War. Margaret MacMillan's recent book on the origins of the war, *The War That Ended Peace,* offers some examples, particularly in her account in the opening chapter of the Paris Universal Exposition held in 1900. Other possibilities for an opening illustration could be drawn from the theological writing, hymnody, or literature of that era.

Contemporary events can challenge that optimistic view of the essential goodness of humanity, though. I would discuss one of the major instances of genocide from the 20th century. Tragically, there are a number to choose from. Nazi Germany may be the example that comes most quickly to mind. Elie Wiesel's *Night,* his account of his time in a concentration camp, provides vivid material for outlining the depths of savagery and inhumanity that we human beings are capable of.

But I would choose Rwanda and the genocide that country endured in 1994. Roméo Dallaire, a now retired Canadian lieutenant-general, commanded the United Nations Assistance Mission for Rwanda during that period. One cannot read *Shake Hands with the Devil,* his account of his time of service in Rwanda, without asking mind-disturbing questions about human depravity—the same questions that we have had to ask about the Holocaust. Other accounts of the Rwandan genocide, for example, Philip Gourevitch's *We Wish to Inform You That Tomorrow We Will Be Killed with Our Families,* paint an equally horrific picture. I would choose Rwanda as an illustration for several reasons. It is more recent than the Nazi Holocaust. The rate at which Rwandans were killed, 800,000 to 1,000,000 (depending upon the estimate you use) in just over 100 days, was more rapid than in the concentration camps. And the direct involvement of some church leaders in the killings can make the example a yet more pressing one for many Christians. How do we, as people of faith, make sense of what happened there?

At this point, I would begin to analyze the lesson from Romans. Often I come to a biblical text more quickly in a sermon, but for this topic I judged it necessary to challenge conventional thinking sufficiently to allow Paul's insights to be more readily heard.

Paul vividly recounts his own wrestling with his incapacity to do the thing he most wants to do and to avoid doing the thing he genuinely does not want to do. Most of us can identify with Paul's description as a form of temptation we know well. But Paul pushes his audience. He is not talking here about a temptation to watch a Montreal Canadiens hockey game when we should be helping to put a young child to bed, or to read Louise Penny's latest mystery novel when we should be cutting the grass. He is talking first about the "sin that dwells within me," about his *incapacity* to do the good he wants to do. Even more powerfully, he names the reality that in the good he wants to do, he finds evil lying close at hand. This aspect, that the possibility of evil or sinfulness lurks even in the good things we do, is a huge challenge for our culture.

Paul's struggle, and the notion of human depravity, can be a way to think about addiction. One could choose any addiction as an illustration. Alcoholism is likely the most common one found among congregation members, but gambling may be a better choice. If one has members who are known to battle alcoholism, they may feel singled out. People with a gambling addiction often keep it very well hidden; hence, listeners are less likely to believe you are talking about them. Also, by naming the addiction of gambling, you may give permission to someone in the congregation who has such an addiction to come and talk to you about it.

In conclusion, I would assert that we need to recognize the shadow side of our humanity, what our ancestors called *human depravity*. Doing so can help us realize that it is only through God's grace that we are able to overcome such alienation from God, from others, and from our own best selves.

In the sermon, I would be trying not only to teach but perhaps even more to address the pastoral reality that we have congregants who wrestle with principalities and powers, demons, or the "sin that dwells within." An optimistic, everything-is-pretty-much-okay theology does not, among other things, address these individuals and those of us who love them.

Sample Sermon

When I'm Tempted to Do Wrong

Today's sermon title is a line from a 19th-century children's hymn, "Father, Lead Me Day by Day." [12] Its third stanza runs, in part:

> When I'm tempted to do wrong,
> Make me steadfast, wise and strong.

And its final stanza goes like this:

> May I do the good I know,
> Be Thy loving child below;
> Then at last go home to Thee,
> Evermore Thy child to be.

    Some of you of a certain age may remember that hymn from your childhood. Its author, a British Unitarian minister named John Hopps, captured well the theological sentiments of the late 19th and early 20th century in his hymn. We know what God would have us do. Following God's way is challenging. We sometimes have to stand alone, and we do face temptation. But we can, with God's help, do the good we know.

    Undergirding this theology, and hymns like "Father, Lead Me Day by Day," was a conviction that human beings were basically good and humanity, particularly in the West, was progressing. Politicians spoke optimistically. Some theologians even believed we might bring about the kingdom of God here on earth. One's environment, or a lack of education, or oppression, or something else, sometimes led people to make bad choices; however, human beings were essentially good. While much of that optimistic perspective—with its accompanying idealism and belief in human progress—succumbed to the horrors of the First World War, the popular view of humanity continued: humanity as basically good, and sinfulness as essentially making bad choices.

    But if that understanding is correct, how do we make sense of events such as those we have seen this fall and winter in Syria? How do we make sense of the shootings at the Paris office of *Charlie Hebdo* and in the surrounding streets? Even more than those events, however, whose perpetrators can rightly be judged to hold an exceedingly perverted form of Islam, how do we make sense of the events that took place in Rwanda in 1994? In that African country, in the space of a little over three months, between 800,000 and 1,000,000 people, close to one-fifth of the country's population, were killed. To put that carnage in perspective, Rwanda witnessed extermination at a much higher rate than Nazi Germany during the Holocaust. Tutsis accounted for most of the dead, though moderate Hutus were also killed.

Christians, including church leaders, played major roles in this act of genocide. Some people taking refuge in churches were burned alive there. To read Canadian Lieutenant-General Roméo Dallaire's first-person account of his time in Rwanda, *Shake Hands with the Devil: The Failure of Humanity in Rwanda,* is to come upon events that can only be called horrific. Dallaire was the commander of the UN Assistance Mission to Rwanda at the time of the massacre in 1994.

The sub-title of Dallaire's book, *The Failure of Humanity in Rwanda,* captures an important double entendre. Rwanda represented a failure of humanity by the wider world. But it also represented a failure of that basic humanity and decency many of us just assume exists inside every person. How, we wonder, can human beings decide to engage in such acts of butchery? What leads human beings collectively, as a mob or as an organized militia, to act in horrific and abusive ways that people acting individually would not? We know the power of mob thinking and acting. We see it played out on the TV news from time to time. Most of us know it in ourselves, too. For example, some of us can think of an occasion when the influence of a large group, especially the in-group, led us not to speak or act to protect the schoolmate who was a victim of that group or clique.

If I were preaching today's sermon in the 17th or 18th century, I would have had a ready answer to those questions. The answer was called *human depravity*. The concept of total depravity, which would be a good synonym for what I am calling human depravity in this sermon, was a key theological statement, one of the five affirmations adopted by a gathering of Protestant leaders in the Netherlands in the early 17th century. This theological concept also had a significant place in Presbyterian, Congregationalist, Christian Reformed, and Baptist thought well into the 19th century. Over the past century and a half we lost that sense, and the term is now rarely heard. In many ways, that has been a good thing. Most of us have an internal sense of horror when we hear it. In its 17th-century manifestation, it contained the sense that there was no good in us at all.

Now I want to stress that the lack of any sense of good within us has negative consequences. Such a feeling can readily lead to self-loathing, depression, and in some cases, self-destruction. Further, the sense that there is no good in us is not biblical. God created the world and everything in it, and called it good. That notion is found not only in the creation stories of Genesis 1—3 but also in many other places in scripture.

What is also biblical, though, is a recognition that we human beings as individuals, and the systems we create collectively, are fundamentally flawed. Each of us has a shadow side. It is this aspect of our humanity that we mainstream Protestants have generally been reluctant to explore for more than a century. I find this understanding of our human condition well captured in the following quote from Daniel Migliore, a contemporary theologian. He writes:

> We human beings are a mystery to ourselves. We are rational and irrational, civilized and savage, capable of deep friendship and murderous hostility, free and in bondage, the pinnacle of creation and its greatest danger. We are Rembrandt and Hitler, Mozart and Stalin, Antigone and Lady Macbeth, Ruth and Jezebel.[13]

We might not want to see ourselves as either of the polar opposites of these pairs. However, if we are honest we can identify both the good and the bad that lurk within each of us. Such a mixture is part of the human condition. We need to recognize it, and to acknowledge it, in order that we might then see how best to deal with it.

Migliore was not the first to make this observation about our human condition. Writing to the Romans nearly 2,000 years ago, the apostle Paul observed this conflict within himself. New Testament scholars judge that in these comments in Romans 7, Paul may well have been paraphrasing the thoughts of some ancient, non-Christian philosophers who made similar comments about their own internal struggles between good and evil.[14] Regardless, Paul certainly claimed these sentiments as a reflection of his own experience. In today's reading from Romans 7, we hear Paul's account of his own struggles. "I do not understand my own actions. For I do not do what I want, but I do the very thing I hate" (verse 15). He goes on, a few verses later, to repeat this thought: "For I do not do the good I want, but the evil I do not want is what I do" (19). He describes experiencing a war within himself, his mind telling him he should do one thing but his wants and desires leading him in another way. Paul concludes that only God, through Jesus Christ, can save him "from this body of death" (24). Paul believes that God has already done this for him, but he still recalls vividly those struggles for the benefit of the church in Rome.

The wider context of this section of Romans 7 is Paul's lengthy discussion about the Law, or the Torah, the means by which he and his Jewish contemporaries had believed that they could be in a right relationship with God. While Paul concludes that the Law is God-given and a good thing in and of itself, he concludes that the Law also opens him to greater sin. He observes that he would never have known covetousness had the Law not told him it was wrong to covet. Paul believes that the Law proved a dead end for him in terms of a right relationship with God, and he thinks that it will be a similar path for anyone else who tries it.

While acknowledging that Paul's comments here are set in the context of a larger discussion about following the Jewish Law, his comments about our general human condition ring true. Paul's frustration at his inability to do the thing he wants to do, knows he should do, but cannot bring himself to do is something probably all of us know.

Who among us cannot recall occasions when we have known full well what we ought to do, what our minds have told us is the right or appropriate thing to do, and we have chosen to do something different? The examples may seem small or indeed be small. It could be the time when we knew a child of ours wanted and needed our attentive presence at some event, and we chose instead to work on something we hoped might impress the boss, even though we did not need to do so. It could have been sitting watching the Blue Jays play when we should have been helping our spouse, partly because we really love baseball and know that every game is important.

Those examples do not qualify for what we might think of as the kind of extreme shadow side the term *human depravity* conjures up. But let me offer another example where Paul's language of struggle is a good description, and where the individual involved might confess the utter helplessness that does start to sound like human depravity. We need always to remember that when we encounter this term, *human depravity*, it does not refer to something we choose, but rather to a condition that is part of us, something endemic to our very being that we cannot shake.

I have occasion from time to time to drive past a large casino. I am always struck by the large number of vehicles in its multi-acre parking lot just off a major expressway. The parking lot even has a section for RVs, so people can spend multiple days there. Statistics suggest that a little over 3 percent of Canadians are "problem gamblers." That does not sound like a high number until you consider the fact that if there are 100 of us here in church this morning, it is likely that three among us have a gambling problem. Let me clarify that it is not 3 percent of the Canadians who gamble who have a gambling problem, but a little over 3 percent of the Canadian population.

I do not know whether you know anyone who has a gambling problem, or to put the matter more sharply, an addiction to gambling, for that is what we are really talking about. But when I read Paul's words here in Romans 7, I think that people with a gambling addiction, for that matter those battling any sort of addiction, could identify with the struggle he outlines. To use the gambling example, problem gamblers who know that once they start to gamble they cannot stop also know that they ought not to go to an online site where they can gamble, or to the casino to play the slots, or to wager on the outcome of the Super Bowl. Mentally, they know that. They are committed not to engage in such activity, strongly committed.

And they just cannot help themselves. All the willpower in the world does not seem enough. Many of them hate themselves for what they are doing—to themselves and to those closest to them. Read the account of a problem gambler who has lost his job, her home, his family, her dignity, the family's life savings. See if the agony, the regret, the sense of helplessness that permeates the pages does not come close to what Paul was describing here. It also sounds like that shadow side, that evil that lurks within us, taking over, loathe it though we might. It sounds like the kind of thing our ancestors had in mind when they spoke about human depravity, for though we may think of the term as a condemnatory one, they regarded it more descriptively.

People who have an addiction, whether it is to gambling or to something else, only begin to be able to deal with that addiction when they recognize that they need help and support to deal with the problem, that they are not able to do it on their own. Gamblers Anonymous has a good track record with those who battle an addiction to gambling. Its success lies, in significant part, in the ability of group members to support one another, to recognize the nature of the problem each has, and to hold one another accountable. Another significant element in this group's success is recognizing the need for the help of a Higher Power.

In the passage from Romans 7, Paul describes his inability ever to gain a right relationship with God through fulfilling the Law. He could and did have a right relationship with God only through God's grace, a grace known to Paul through Jesus Christ. In the 18th century, a former British slave trader named John Newton wrote a hymn in which he, too—as someone who saw himself condemned for what he had done in his life, who saw himself only as a miserable wretch—gained a sense of peace and of the possibility of a right relationship with God through grace alone. It was grace, an "Amazing Grace," he believed had been given freely to him.

Human depravity is a term Newton might have used as a self-description before his experience of grace gave him new life. I have come to appreciate, in a way I did not when I was younger, why this hymn is so powerful to people who have recognized they have an addition and either are struggling, or have struggled successfully, to overcome it.

Human depravity—it is not something we talk about much in our denomination. It is a troubling term. Yet, the insight that sin comes to us from outside and then penetrates our whole being, rather than being inherent in us, may be a helpful starting point for those among us who struggle with demons of addiction that have penetrated every part of our being. It may enable us to reach out for the grace we need, God's grace, as a foundation for rebuilding our lives. These insights can be helpful in the challenge all of us know to live as we would intend, rather than as we sometimes do.

"When I'm tempted to do wrong." In those times when we feel tempted, not to the minor things such an extra piece of chocolate cake that we know we ought not to have, but to self-destroying activities, may we both know and seek the divine aid that can strengthen us for such difficult parts of our journey. May we remember that others have been here before us and that they, too, have had these battles. May we find, as Paul did, a divine grace that saves us despite ourselves, despite our own sense of unworthiness. And to the God who made us and who loves us, to Jesus the Christ, the One in whom we have experienced God's grace and love, and to the Holy Spirit, that loving presence of God with us now, be all honour, glory, and praise. Amen.

—*John H. Young*

While I borrowed a few elements from a sermon on "Temptation" I had once preached during Lent, this sermon was written for this book.

Chapter 7
Grace and Salvation

Water to Our Thirst

The Doctrinal Concept

Amazing grace, how sweet the sound that saved a wretch like Steve.... The rest of the choir burst into laughter as the bass kept going. Steve chuckled. *He once was lost...* and then the singer lost it, too, and the whole rehearsal deteriorated into silliness.[15]

Grace, I've observed, is the fallback doctrine across our denomination on Sundays. We hear grace preached, sung, and prayed regularly. Grace is like water and air, necessary and ubiquitous. Grace is the reassurance of God's constant presence and care. It is the unmerited love God has for us; it is our unearned help and our undeserved blessing, as individuals, as a church, and as the whole earth. No wonder doxologies soar from hymnals, and worship services open with smiles. Small wonder people cross the threshold into a sanctuary expecting good news to be preached. Little surprise most clergy love their work, and many church boards have no trouble recruiting people for worship committees—even if they can't find a property chair or a treasurer. Grace, plentiful and available, shines like the aurora borealis on a warm September evening north of 60: across the whole sky.

Celebrating grace so unabashedly we might wonder, why? Why is grace such a big player? Can we even define it easily? Love, we can define. The other three Advent Sunday themes are a piece of cake: hope, peace, joy. Grace, however, is truly more like the air we breathe. It is one of those church words, and we exchange it readily, unlike heavy words such as sin or sovereignty or depravity. We are, after all, people of the good news, and grace is part of that vocabulary. Still, defining *grace* is something many of us do with similes, or with qualifying words such as unmerited, undeserving, unearned, free—and amazing.

What makes grace necessary at all? Life does. The residue of forgiveness, remembering that there was indeed something to be forgiven; the long memory of shame; the deep sorrows that form the backdrop to our commitments; the frustratingly persistent recurrences of international conflict; our failing efforts to maintain the beauty of the Garden. Divine grace saves us from carrying all these things around with us perpetually.

Grace is God's ongoing work in the world. God chooses to save us from our actions, our limitations, our sin, not because of a rule or law or necessity but as a gift. There is nothing we can do to deserve it or earn it. We don't experience an existential change and become perfectly good, but we are absolved, justified, sanctified, and saved. We are loved. God transforms what we have broken.

Humankind continues to be broken, but God remains with us and carries on loving us. God doesn't turn away. God saves us and makes us holy; in traditional language, God sanctifies us. A Song of Faith expresses it as follows:

> We are called together by Christ
> as a community of broken but hopeful believers…

Yet grace is not shallow. Grace includes judgment. I am accountable for my life, my choices, my principles, and my perspective. God chooses to address my accountability, and the judgment merited, with unmerited love. I don't have to do anything to receive that love. In fact, I can't do anything to receive that love. If I am accountable for my life, do I have a responsibility to desire and respond to grace? Is my response important? How do we explain the continued sin around us? Grace and judgment are not so much in conflict as they are part of the process.

Let's have a look at some understandings of that process over the years. In the fourth century in North Africa, after much personal spiritual anguish, Augustine came to the conclusion that sinners are trapped. Since we cannot do enough to free ourselves, our efforts must be meaningless. The true meaning, the effective power, is God's. We cannot earn grace; it is a divine gift.

Straight across Europe, in the British Isles, Augustine's contemporary Pelagius was appalled at this conclusion. What kind of ethical or moral life would that make? We must participate, he argued. We must work for grace. I think about that: what indeed is the point of a lazy spiritual life? God gives grace to those who have been making an effort.

A thousand years later Luther worked voraciously at the problem: How do you know you're doing the best you can? We are justified by grace through faith, he determined. Shortly thereafter, Calvin and other Protestant Reformers claimed that the majesty of God is so great, and we are so limited, that the things we do and the efforts we make can play no role in justification. The gift of grace is not ours because of our virtues. Grace comes without regard for merit.

The argument went on over the centuries, hotly, debating God's autonomy in determining who receives grace and thereby salvation. Perhaps not everyone receives it. Perhaps the gift of grace is determined solely by God and we have no role, nor any means of correcting our place in God's economy. We are stepping into the arena of predestination here, the doctrine that salvation and everything else has already been decided by God. That is not strictly the subject of our discussion, but you can see how it touches on an explication of grace.

Our common life is governed by a deep-seated understanding that we get what we earn. We know our borrowing power, for instance, and purchase a house that fits our budget. A neighbour brings a birthday pie, and we ask for her birthdate so we can reciprocate. We are comfortable with exchanges; we feel awkward with a free gift. How can salvation—eternal life, restoration to God, freedom from guilt—simply come to us by an unearned grace?

Back to our history: The Roman Catholic Council of Trent in the mid-1500s determined that grace is necessary for salvation, but not grace alone. Grace gets you started, and you have a responsibility to shape up and carry on better than before. Salvation is a steady progression.

Arminius, a generation after Calvin, put forward that everyone is offered grace; it's not predestined. Further, we can say no or yes to grace. That means we have a hand in the matter. Free will and response are at play. This is a question over which people were willing to face martyrdom: Is the distribution of grace the arena of God alone or do we have a role? Salvation—eternal life, restoration to God, freedom from guilt—may require something of us, or it may not. The ongoing question is whether we have the autonomy to make such a positive difference that we earn God's grace, or whether it is a free gift out of which we live in gratitude. The history of this debate can absorb your attention for a long time.

In the 17th century, Reformed churches met in the Netherlands and drew up the Canons of Dort, five points of doctrine related to election and predestination, framed in opposition to the views of Arminius. Christian Reformed churches hearken back to this church-shaping synod. Followers of Arminius presented a document called the Remonstrance of 1610, saying among other things that we can indeed resist God's grace. Remonstrance churches are scattered over northern Europe still. And these denominations, too, are our sister churches through the World Communion of Reformed Churches.

Our Methodist roots began a century later, when John Wesley took up the Arminian position. He was appalled by predestination because of the concept that some are among the elect living in God's grace, while others are not among the elect and live with the shadow of damnation. Grace, he put forward, is not irresistible; we have a choice and we can choose to act in grace. Going further he asserted that we can achieve Christian perfection. The United Church is a member of the World Methodist Council today.

All of this is to say that our understandings of grace and salvation have a lively history. Some among us agree with each of these positions. And they are represented in international ecumenical councils across the spectrum.

Another position on these questions of grace and salvation is the implication that through grace the whole inhabited earth is saved. *Oikoumene*, or ecumenical, is a term often used to mean Christian denominations, but the Greek word refers to the whole inhabited earth. If indeed grace is a gift and not earned, the whole world can be implicated. If God loves and saves me, what's to stop God from loving and saving the world? Salvation becomes understood as a gift for all: human, creatures, ecology. Universal salvation, too, would be dependent upon God's grace, not human works. It is not earned; it is not a reward, a promise. Here are words from near the opening of A Song of Faith (italics added):

> God tends the universe,
> *mending the broken and reconciling the estranged.*
> God enlivens the universe,
> guiding all things toward harmony with their Source.

This movement beyond partial salvation to universal salvation is called universalism. Sometimes it is called *apocatastasis,* which means a time will come in which everyone will be saved: given eternal life, restored to God, freed from guilt. *Apocatastasis* means, briefly, that in the fullness of love no one could be left out. There couldn't be a heaven if the residents were aware of the miseries of hell.

On this topic, there are choices! In a doctrinal consideration of grace and salvation, there is much disparity, and ideas diverge widely. God's grace is God's perpetual and caring involvement with and for the world. Not simply because we are made in the image of God, but because of God's ongoing work, grace abounds. It is better said in Ephesians 2:8: "For by grace you have been saved through faith, and this is not your own doing; it is the gift of God."

Scripture for Preaching

Matthew 19:27—20:16

Then Peter said in reply, "Look, we have left everything and followed you. What then will we have?" Jesus said to them, "Truly I tell you, at the renewal of all things, when the Son of Man is seated on the throne of his glory, you who have followed me will also sit on twelve thrones, judging the twelve tribes of Israel. And everyone who has left houses or brothers or sisters or father or mother or children or fields, for my name's sake, will receive a hundredfold, and will inherit eternal life. But many who are first will be last, and the last will be first.

"For the kingdom of heaven is like a landowner who went out early in the morning to hire laborers for his vineyard. After agreeing with the laborers for the usual daily wage, he sent them into his vineyard. When he went out about nine o'clock, he saw others standing idle in the marketplace; and he said to them, 'You also go into the vineyard, and I will pay you whatever is right.' So they went. When he went out again about noon and about three o'clock, he did the same. And about five o'clock he went out and found others standing around; and he said to them, 'Why are you standing here idle all day?' They said to him, 'Because no one has hired us.' He said to them, 'You also go into the vineyard.' When evening came, the owner of the vineyard said to his manager, 'Call the laborers and give them their pay, beginning with the last and then going to the first.' When those hired about five o'clock came, each of them received the usual daily wage. Now when the first came, they thought they would receive more; but each of them also received the usual daily wage. And when they received it, they grumbled against the landowner, saying, 'These last worked only one hour, and you have made them equal to us who have borne the burden of the day and the scorching heat.' But he replied to one of them, 'Friend, I am doing you no wrong; did you not agree with me for the usual daily wage? Take what belongs to you and go; I choose to give to this last the same as I give to you. Am I not allowed to do what I choose with what belongs to me? Or are you envious because I am generous?' So the last will be first, and the first will be last."

Why Is This Doctrine Important?

Grace is a common word in the church, and it has a wide variety of connotations outside the Christian life. It is basic to our relationship with God. It is also an indicator of self-worth, and that bubbles up into the issue of identity. Spiritually, our primary identity is in Christ.

Grace, this common denominator to our life, is more than mere kindness. It is a transformation of life. Whether you believe you are one of the elect through grace, or whether you believe you work alongside grace, it is transformative.

There is another issue related to the elect, however: not seeing oneself in grace at all. This view can arise out of experiences of abuse or addiction, or through the less traumatic experience of growing up without a faith community. Pastorally I identify two concerns, which are polar opposites: diminishment and entitlement.

I see diminishment in the woman who tells me she doesn't take communion because she doesn't deserve it. I hear it in the tones of the young man who says, "I'm no good." Pastoral care is a privilege. It is perhaps the only professional practice in which we may call on people with no particular purpose. People see other professionals for a reason: health, finances, education. Pastors may visit simply to ask after their spirits, to get acquainted, or to keep in touch; this is an expectation in many pastoral positions. So pastors hear comments such as the ones about communion and being "no good"—and we have opportunity to discern doctrines for preaching.

For these individuals, both in the visits and in subsequent sermons, there is room for grace. Some pastors could not sally forth into the social justice and personal transformation we see in ministry around us every day without our understandings of grace. We know, as A Song of Faith puts it, that God mends the broken, reconciles the estranged, and guides "all things toward harmony with their Source."

With regard to entitlement, I see it sometimes when people situate grace in themselves or others instead of in God. In the church, in preaching, we remind one another that we are not self-made, self-created beings. Rather our identity comes from God, in whose image we are made, and moreover, from Christ, in whose grace we are saved. Salvation—eternal life, restoration to God, freedom from guilt—is not something we can make happen.

Sermons can help form the character of believers. Preaching about diminishment or entitlement offers listeners possibilities, and nuances for

GIC's -

RBC -
 Invest - 83 475.00

 AIF - 53962.00

 Ins   250,000.

BNS -
 (GIC) - 67858.89
          17 719.42
         ─────────
          419053.31
                    - 50,000
                    ─────────
                    369053.31

 ÷ 2 = 184526.65

"Be brave if you lose and meek if you win."

— *Harvey Penick*

MONDAY MARCH 09	

MONTH 03 | WEEK 11 | DAY 069

living and for changing their approaches to the issues confronting them. Doctrine doesn't constrict the preacher—it gives us adventure. In the same way, sermons also can spark fresh explorations for listeners.

Working through the doctrine of grace as more than God's kindness prepares listeners with a staying power for hard times. Both when oil prices fall and unemployment looms, and when oil prices surge and ecological havoc threatens, we need God's grace. When we are not sure if we are taking steps in the right direction, we need to know that grace will sustain us. When we are recovering from mistakes, we need the assurance of grace to fortify us.

Common usage of the word *grace* appears in idioms such as "There, but for the grace of God, go I." It means that something bad has happened to someone, and it could just as easily have happened to you. It means that it is owing to God's grace that you are not in that situation. The phrase is attributed to John Bradford, an English Reformer who was martyred in 1555 at the age of 45. The English Reformation was brutal. "There but for the grace of God goes John Bradford," he was reputed to have said, as a man was being led to the gallows. Sources for this story are unreliable, and it is attributed to several other people, too. The saying, however, indicates vulnerability to a bad situation.

The reverse use of grace, indicating a positive outcome, comes to us in the current vocabulary of blessing. "I'm so blessed," the celebrity says accepting an Academy Award, celebrating a football game, or winning an election. "We're so blessed," the couple says stepping away from the car wreck, or after in vitro fertilization, or about surviving cancer. This popular use of blessing sounds like grace on the surface, but misses the universal grace. What about all those who would like to be in their shoes and are not?

Grace brings a deep understanding of God's love, and of the value of a church community that upholds people in equal value. Churches are not perfect either, and grace keeps us humble while it also keeps us celebrating. A Song of Faith tell us:

> The church has not always lived up to its vision.
> It requires the Spirit to re-orient it,
>> helping it to live an emerging faith while honouring tradition,
>> challenging it to live by grace rather than entitlement,
>>> for we are called to be a blessing to the earth.

In grace, we go with confidence and faith into the social justice and personal transformation we see in ministry around us every day. In sermons on grace and salvation, we can proclaim a hopeful vision that is universally applicable, a vision that will invigorate the listeners who go into the vineyard. Again, words from A Song of Faith:

> God transforms,
>> and calls us to protect the vulnerable,
>> to pray for deliverance from evil,
>> to work with God for the healing of the world,
>> that all might have abundant life.
> We sing of grace.

How Does It Preach?

"Paris is always a good idea," Audrey Hepburn famously said, and preaching about grace is always a good idea, too. Grace fits everywhere. It fits every liturgical season. Grace is water to our thirst. We always need to be reminded that God loves us no matter what and has unbelievably good things in store for us, salvation by another name. Certainly we need grace in the rough times. Most importantly, we need to preach grace when we have forgotten that we are a community that depends on God. We need grace when we begin to think we create our own salvation. The sermon that follows is best preached when we are coasting, or when the community is feeling smug or wantonly proud. When is that? Perhaps variously when we are overly congratulating ourselves on mission, when we are getting the church year up and running in September, when we are beginning to read the 94 recommendations the Truth and Reconciliation

Commission released (in June 2015 just as this book was being completed), or when we are pulling the drawbridge up over the moat.

I chose to preach a sermon about an understanding of grace that is all-encompassing, unconnected to merit or good deeds. That comes with some considered reflection on Calvin, and a willingness to step aside from our Methodist heritage for the day. There are other opportunities to engage the freedom of the human will. I chose the unmerited love of God partly because I believe it, of course, and partly because I am preaching in a context of privilege and affluence.

The word that follows quickly upon privilege and affluence is *entitlement*. This sermon is for people who live at the intersection of *can* and *do*. I chose to speak about living in entitlement or living in grace, and I chose a title that gets to the issue of arrogating things to ourselves. Written in a personal style, the sermon asks first-person questions. They are not dishonest questions; I do have questions about discerning grace and entitlement! But the voice is also a stylistic device. Identifying the issue as my own connects me with the listener and creates an invitational tone. Preaching about wealth, entitlement, and whether we deserve what we have can very quickly be perceived as judgmental, and people will stop listening. This strategy is part of building trust, which is essential in preaching and in pastoral care.

The context of the scripture is a conversation between Jesus and Peter immediately after the rich young ruler has stepped away. Jesus speaks about rich people and the eye of the needle, then Peter asks about their reward, and Jesus tells the story about the workers in the vineyard. These passages are rich in preaching possibilities about grace, salvation, and affluence. I chose on this occasion not to speak about the eye of the needle: it fits well, but it overpowers the vineyard story. Similarly with "the last will be first, and the first will be last"; indeed, I was tempted to leave that sentence out.

One might wonder whether Peter was prepared to bargain with Jesus about what he and the others were earning, what their reward might be: *Look, we have left everything and followed you. What then will we have?*

If the ensuing parable disturbs us and challenges our sense of fairness, so would a homiletic reflection on bargaining for reward, grace, or salvation.

Salvation is a heavy word: salvation and entitlement in one Sunday makes for a heavy Sunday. If people find in church an experience of Christianity that is only restful, comforting, and happy, though, where will they find staying power through the hardships of life? In the sermon I refer to salvation and define it each time with three phrases: eternal life, restoration to God, and freedom from guilt. I let these phrases simply be without explaining them further; again, that is material for another Sunday.

The preaching point is this: Humankind continues to be broken, but God remains with us and carries on loving us. God doesn't turn away. That is true for all of us, universally, rich and poor and in between. None of us deserve the future God has in store; there is nothing we can do to merit it. The reward given by God will far outweigh the sacrifices made by the disciples—and by us.

Here is the central question addressed in this sermon: our common life is governed by a deep-seated understanding that we get what we earn. How can salvation—eternal life, restoration to God, freedom from guilt—simply come to us by an unearned grace? Sometimes we human beings lodge grace in ourselves instead of in God. That is entitlement. I chose to preach grace as a free gift, as irresistible; grace is God's purview.

In writing this sermon I had in mind the young man who thinks he is no good, who is in church because he has small children. I had in mind the woman who doesn't take communion but comes to church because her friends are there. The grace that comes to those who feel they have plenty is also coming, in as much bounty, to those who feel they have none, or that they deserve none.

The expression "the world is your oyster" comes from Shakespeare. Pistol delivers a variation of the line in *The Merry Wives of Windsor* (Act II, scene 2). One could have a lively and enriching time developing that connection. For this sermon, it was enough to work it in as a rather lighthearted story about developing deep gratitude for God's grace. I am aware that people in congregations listen in many ways. Some will go home with vocabulary about grace and salvation; others will connect with my personal, faithful quandary. Still others will remember the oyster story and think about it during the week.

Sample Sermon

It's Not about Me, Thanks

Jesus turned it around. Their entitlements, I mean. Jesus turned it around through this story so they began to sort out entitlements from grace.

One of the department stores in our city just told people it's closing. All three outlets, right across the city—they'll all be closed by summertime. I have a friend who works there. She showed up because she was recruited and she's shown up every working day since. I have a hunch she's been well paid—I hope so—and now she's starting over. She'll be online, on the search, right away. The workers in the vineyard will be looking for work now, too. The day of labour is over and they'll begin again in the morning. They had a strange day yesterday, irritating for some and a happy surprise for others. Everyone was paid the same, regardless of the hours they worked: irritating for some and a happy surprise for others. Can God be as unfair as employers with erratic practices?

That story is set immediately after Peter asks Jesus, "Look, we have left everything and followed you. What then will we have?" (Matthew 19:27). Reward is part of our human expectation. Peter asked a very human question. "We have left everything and followed you. What then will we have?" Jesus answers with what sounds like a great reward: thrones! The compensation is good: authority, judgment—management positions. And the others, too—they'll get a hundredfold what they sacrificed, what they put into the work. Wow, a hundredfold.

Then this story. A change, a corrective to the rewards of thrones and hundredfold investments. Everyone in the story gets the same wage. Well, so much for fair pay. So much for showing up and getting in the front of the line so they could work hard all day; so much for earning a reward. Jesus turned it around.

Are there people in your life who tell you how blessed you are? Perhaps you have friends who talk about how blessed they are. I do. I choose not to use the phrase, "I'm so blessed." It's not that I am not blessed! I most certainly am. Frequently, though, when I hear the phrase "I am so blessed," it is in reference to something that has changed around for the first person that has not changed around for a second person. "I am so blessed," because the disease that was afflicting me has been cured. But the second person's disease has not been cured. "I am so blessed," because I have plenty to make my life tick. But of course, most people do not have plenty with which to make their lives tick. So it is that I struggle with this distinction between grace and entitlement. The so-called blessings that come to me but not to others seem to be more entitlement than grace. Or they may be luck, or timing, or circumstance, but I don't call them blessings. I don't call them grace.

It can be difficult to pull apart the difference between grace and entitlement. Grace is a gift from God. Entitlement is sneaky. Sometimes, though, I find it hard to tell if my gratitude is for grace, or if my gratitude is for the circumstances that bring me good things. Grace is like the water to my thirst; it is necessary to life. Grace is like the air I breathe; it is ubiquitous. Grace is like laughter when friends surround us. It is the best reassurance that I am myself, that you are yourself, and that we are loved. Entitlement is knowing that I deserve these pleasures. And maybe I do, but that's not the point. We all deserve these pleasures, of course. The point is that even when I do *not* deserve these pleasures, even when I do *not* merit these pleasures, God's love accompanies me.

God's abundant grace: oh, my. When I cannot muster enough strength, spiritual nurture, companionship, love, peace, or dignity, God is still present to me. Oh, my. Grace is the unmerited love God has for me, for us. It is our unearned help from God and our undeserved blessing from God. That goes for us as individuals, as a church, and it goes for the whole earth, too.

That's why I can say from Sunday to Sunday that in you I see the wonder of God, the movement of God, the peace of God, the grace of God. That's living fully in the Spirit of Christ. That's being who we are completely. Using all our gifts, all our talents, practising the things we are good at, working at the things we are not so good at, being able to let go of the things that we will never be able to do. Finding out who we are and being that, not being someone else or striving to be something that we cannot be. And living in God's grace because we are not afraid.

We are not afraid of carrying the burdens we carry, because we carry them in God's grace. We are not afraid of who we have been, because we live in God's grace. We are not afraid to do some serious examination, because we live in God's grace.

That's where entitlement comes in. For the most part our lives are pretty good. Most of us have more than enough so we can look after our homes, take care of the people we care for, and attend to our own needs. We can do the things that we wish to do, and accomplish the things that we have to do. In the eyes of the world, most of us have pleasant lives. We might say that is a blessing.

We might also get to the dangerous point of entitlement in which we assume that we deserve what we have: these homes, people, needs, activities, and accomplishments. We assume we've done it on our own. We assume that because many good things have come to us, many more things ought to come to us. This entitlement, of course, is a problem, because it's not happening for everybody else. If it weren't for my privilege, more people would be living happy lives. I know that to be true.

Entitlement gives me an understanding that I deserve stuff, no matter what. God's grace gives me an understanding that I don't need to deserve stuff. It is not about deserving. It is about grace.

What I learn in this difficult passage from Jesus, what stops me short in my entitlement, is that none of us deserves the future God has in store—there is nothing we can do to merit it. The issue is not merely fairness, living decently, and sharing. That's all well and good. The issue, though, is not that others can't catch up. The issue is that despite my entitlement, despite my privilege, despite my confession that I am complicit in the evils of this world, God still holds me in grace. Oh, my.

This sermon is confessional, isn't it?

Well, there's room for confession in this economy of God's. There's room to acknowledge that rewards will be subordinated by grace. Even if I got one of those 12 thrones, the others coming in behind me would get a hundredfold whatever they had invested. Those who only showed up for an hour, well, they'd get as much as all of us. No one will be left out; in the fullness of God's love no one *could* be left out. All of us who have thought about grace and love and faith and abundance and friendship and rest and justice and health for so long and prayed about it and worked for it, and those who showed up at the last minute, we all receive the same.

And the same is plenty.

This is not a particularly easy part of the Christian life. And I am quite hopeful that this sermon is going to take you home with more questions than answers—because that is part of experiencing sermons. If you go home to assess the privilege and entitlement in your life, and if you do so infused with a sense of God's grace, then you will have made me very happy. But, of course, it's not about me. That is what this passage is saying so very clearly. That it isn't about me.

A story about me, nonetheless:

"The world is your oyster," a friend told me many years ago. I do love oysters. One spring I ate an oyster burger in Maple Bay, Vancouver Island, and the oyster was as big as the bun it sat on. A few weeks later I ate oysters on the half-shell in Malpeque Bay, Prince Edward Island. But that is not what she meant, not country-wide oyster eating. She meant that I had opportunity to do whatever I wanted, and I'd likely succeed. I don't happen to think that's true. I have a lot of limitations. Many things to which I put my hand turn to dust. But many things work, too.

The point is that is doesn't matter. I am in God's grace—you are in God's grace—and we don't have to earn it. We cannot earn it. We don't earn it.

Our common life is governed by a deep-seated understanding that we get what we earn. I purchase a car because I hand over the money, you go to a beach resort in February because you can afford it, I send you a Christmas card and you feel obliged to send me one next year. Yet salvation—eternal life, restoration to God, freedom from guilt—simply comes to us by an unearned grace.

Oh, how humbled I am. Oh, my.

Is this a little difficult? This should be a little difficult, because as Jesus is calling people to follow him, he is calling us into a way of life that is not going to be easy. The way of life to which Jesus is calling us is a life with unbounded generosity. The grace of God acknowledged in our lives brings us such a sense of gratitude that we're never finished giving thanks.

Love, peace, dignity, fairness, honesty, good solid companionship: all of those things come to us by the grace of God, not by our own achievements. They are spiritual values. Judgment is real; I am accountable for the way I live my life. The challenge for me is to learn to live my life by grace, not by entitlement, knowing that I am indeed deeply blessed and that I did not do it myself. The challenge in the Christian life is to understand our lives as gifts from God—not to be denied, not to be diminished, not in a spirit of self-hatred, but in a spirit of gratitude. And when I can give my life in a spirit of gratitude, that's living in God's grace.

I expect you may be as confused by my spiritual quandary as I am. But when I get to walk through this spiritual life with you, knowing that we live in a culture of plenty, and that we are as a community looking for God's grace that will move us out of entitlement into service, then I know I am following Christ. Amen.

—*Catherine Faith MacLean*

This is a real live sermon I preached after several congregants came to me asking about grace.

Chapter 8
The Church

God's Gift to the World?

The Doctrinal Concept

What makes the doctrine of the church problematic in our time? As a starting point, what do we think when we hear The United Church of Canada's recent faith statement, A Song of Faith, describe the church as an "instrument of the loving Spirit of Christ?" Historic formulas for the church, such as "God's gift to the world" or a "divine instrument," say pretty much the same thing. What do we make of such claims?

Catherine and I have each attended a few presbytery meetings that would raise doubts about these understandings of the church! Many of us can likely think of times when the institutional manifestation of the church has been a source of pain, of bitterness, and of actions that seem substantially out of sync with contemporary or traditional expressions of the church's role. Language about the church as "the body of Christ" may not be much more helpful. While this expression is traditional, and biblical, it also does not always seem to match our reality.

Many people who come out to Sunday services have a sense that they should believe something about the church, but they are not sure quite what. The likely default is to think of it in terms of the congregation where they worship. But they also know that the church is bigger than the congregation they belong to. They know, too, that the concept of church is under attack and corroding, both from easy-to-see forces and from less visible ones.

What are some forces that work against seeing ecclesiology, or the doctrine of the church, as important, let alone central, to an informed and intentional Christian life? First, we within the church, not to mention critics outside it, are struck by some of the obvious public problems of the church. Scandals of financial misappropriation, sexual misconduct, or the abuse of power raise questions about the place and value of the church. I don't know about you, but when I hear a news headline about a cleric being charged with some form of inappropriate sexual activity, my initial thought is *please don't let this person be from the United Church.* But then I quickly realize that the person is still part of the church. In the eyes of the wider world, and even in the eyes of many who sit in our pews, the denomination really does not matter.

Second, for the church to operate, indeed to survive, it must have some institutional structure. Religious movements—whether in the shape of young people motivated to start a congregation because they cannot find one they like, or of a revolutionary remaking of an existing tradition such as the Protestant Reformation—require at least some degree of institutional structure to continue beyond the initial generation. Christianity itself began as a religious movement within Judaism. Had it not assumed an institutional form such as the church, it would not have survived much beyond the generation of Jesus' immediate followers.

However, we live in a time of deep suspicion of any institution, especially among younger people. In addition, it is easy for the church, or any institution, to become more concerned about maintaining itself than about the purpose for which it exists. There is a built-in tendency for institutions to become self-perpetuating. That said, I do chafe at the denigration of "maintenance" in the phrase "we need to be about mission not maintenance." This phrase suggests, at least to me, that the church can somehow engage in mission without expending any attention or resources on maintenance and on nurturing the membership. The dichotomy between "mission" and "maintenance" is a false one. There must be a good balance between the two.

Third, we live in a time with a strong notion of individuals following their own lights. Coming together as community, or in a community activity, is in decline. In 1986 Robert Bellah and four other authors published the well-documented study *Habits of the Heart,* which looked at this phenomenon in the United States. What they observed also applies north of the border. More recent, and perhaps more jarring, was Robert Putnam's 1995 essay "Bowling Alone" (which was later developed into a book of the same title). Assessing the decline of communal activity, Putnam called for a renewed "civics." A related trend is the sense that religion is a private and privatized affair, a concept that would have seemed most strange as recently as two generations ago.

Fourth, in addition to the disdain for the institutional church and the strong individualism of our day, there is an increased interest in spirituality that is undertaken as an intentional counter to participation in any formal religious body or enterprise. Think of the phrase "I'm spiritual, not religious." Does one really need to say more? The words suggest that "religion" and its institutional forms (the church, the synagogue, the mosque) are at least antiquated, if not bad, whereas an individual quest for some form of "spirituality" is good.

Finally, a significant number in the church have lost any sense that God could be active, in the church or in the world. Reflecting on his time in office, former United Church Moderator Peter Short observed that many within the denomination appeared to live according to a functional atheism. In other words, many people, both clergy and laity, lead their lives from the position that it is all up to us. If it is up to all of us, then it is hard to see the church as an "instrument of the loving Spirit of Christ."

Scripture for Preaching

1 Peter 2:9–10
But you are a chosen race, a royal priesthood, a holy nation, God's own people, in order that you may proclaim the mighty acts of [God] who called you out of darkness into [God's] marvelous light. Once you were not a people, but now you are God's people; once you had not received mercy, but now you have received mercy.

Why Is This Doctrine Important?

I think we need to strengthen, or in some cases recover, the sense of the church as a place where God can be, and is, active, and the related understanding of the church as an "instrument of the loving Spirit of Christ." In 1984, American Presbyterian scholar Wallace Alston wrote a thoughtful book entitled *The Church*. Alston asserted that the church is a place where the divine and the human meet. Some of us struggle with or even reject the church, he stated, because we cannot see enough of God there. Others struggle because we see too little humanity there.

To me this doctrine is important primarily because the church is, or at least should be, the place where we are nurtured and empowered for mission. The church is the body in which I find myself nurtured by the Word proclaimed and the sacraments administered. Through the prayers that are offered and the sense of community surrounding me, I have an enhanced sense that I am not alone, that I live in God's world. It is a place where, when the church is at its best, I can experience God's love. So the church is a place of nurture.

It is also a place where I am empowered for mission. The church does not exist for its own sake; it exists for God's mission. It is the place where, at its best, people are empowered to seek a more just world, a more compassionate world. It is a place where oppression can be named and challenged. I should add that the church never does this nurturing or this empowering for mission perfectly. But even with our most halting efforts, the church can still be the place that seeks justice and resists evil, that proclaims Jesus, crucified and risen, our judge and our hope.

There is another reason why this doctrine is important—in a world where we function so frequently as individuals, we need community. But we need it not to have a sense that others share our convictions, important as that can be. Rather, we need it to check our own reading of scripture, our own understanding of where and how God is active in the world. Former United Church Moderator Lois Wilson spent the fall of 2009 at the Queen's School of Religion as a scholar-in-residence. In one presentation during her time there, she offered several criticisms of the contemporary United Church. She perceived a decline of the denomination's ecumenical spirit and therefore its increasing isolation. Worse still, she said, as a denomination we have become quite contented with that, quite contented to hear only our own voice. I found her point convincing in terms of some wider denominational matters, but her comments also made me think about our reality as individuals, especially in a time when we place so much weight upon the individual. The church becomes a crucial place to check our individual understandings, a place to ensure that we are not just listening to our own voice.

How Does It Preach?

One can preach a sermon on the church, or ecclesiology, at any time in the year. A congregational anniversary is one obvious time; a Sunday shortly after Pentecost would be another. A wide variety of texts from the letters in the New Testament, especially the Pauline epistles, are suitable for a sermon on the church. Many of these texts were intended to encourage small, relatively new congregations trying to make their way in a world that was generally ambivalent, though occasionally hostile, to their presence. When we see references to a congregation or a church, we need to remember that these letters were addressed to house churches of only a few handfuls of people. In addition, for much of the first two centuries of the Common Era church members generally came from the lower echelons of society. Well-to-do members like Lydia (Acts 16:11–40) were an exception; many members were women without her means and many others were slaves.

Our congregations are usually larger than the communities addressed in these letters, and there is certainly more awareness of Christianity in our society than there would have been in the eastern Mediterranean in the first century. But the wider society's ambivalence or mild hostility to the practice of Christianity represents a growing point of similarity between the world of the New Testament and that of early-21st-century Canada.

For the sermon that follows, I have opted for a reading from 1 Peter 2. The First Letter of Peter is addressed to "the exiles of the Dispersion." The intended recipients lived in communities away from the more populous and prosperous coastline of the Mediterranean, in the back country in an area that is now part of Turkey. We do not know a lot about the widely scattered groups to whom this letter was sent, but the area where they lived was generally poor. In the passage I chose, the writer wants to encourage a small, struggling group of people who likely had little or no status in society.

As always, begin by assessing the congregation's context. While I know of some exceptions, in most congregations many of those present can readily remember a time when attendance was larger and the congregation was younger. They can remember when it seemed easier to start an initiative or undertake an outreach project. Active church members likely encounter ambivalence from at least some family and friends about their involvement. Some may experience disdain or even mild hostility from neighbours. A few may have had to wrestle with whether to take a job that requires them to work on Sunday and therefore to "miss church." Some, faced with that choice, have opted for church involvement over an employment prospect. All would be aware that, by virtue of actively involving themselves in a faith community, they are in a distinct minority in contemporary Canadian society.

So the sermon assumes that such factors form the general background of the congregation. In a different context—for example, in a congregation experiencing rapid growth and an abundance of resources—I would do something quite different.

I begin by asking, "What is the church?" Then I allow a little time for silent reflection. There are other ways of getting those present to think about the church and about what it means "to be the church," but thinking a little about what comes to mind when you hear the word *church* is a good place to start.

I move on to affirm the importance of what this gathered group is doing by being part of the church. I do this for two reasons. First, it is easy these days to see what is wrong with the church. Even if we did not want to be self-critical, there is no shortage of critics outside the church who will readily offer their views. Most media stories about the church are not going to increase the church's standing in the wider society.

Second, being active in a church community these days, especially for those in their mid-40s or younger, is decidedly countercultural. Even for people above that age, church involvement is no longer the norm.

So I want to affirm, indeed to praise, those in attendance. I am not praising their presence in worship as an end in itself. Rather, it is the willingness to be present in a community with the concomitant, and countercultural, desire to lead one's life according to this particular faith tradition. Depending on the make-up of the congregation, I might draw a comparison to the situation in the 1950s and 1960s, when the wider culture supported our practice of our faith tradition.

For that affirmation, I would repeat part of the passage from 1 Peter, a passage that concludes with comments about this chosen race, a royal priesthood, God's own people. I would then talk a bit about the likely context or situation of the early church community to whom this letter was addressed, the nature and status of those who made up these early Christian communities, and the world and worldview within which they functioned. Why does the writer of 1 Peter see them in the way the letter describes? They are a group chosen or called to proclaim God's mighty acts. The Greek word for church, *ecclesia,* means "called out." The church is called to do that proclamation through verbal witness and also through the action of mission.

Then I would speak about the particular nature of the congregation and the context in which we now live and work. Canada's version of Christendom has come to an end, and a much more secular Canada presents challenges not only to the church but also to the practice of any religious tradition. In fact, in the challenges of practising a religious tradition in our time, we have much in common with Jews, Muslims, Hindus, Buddhists—with all those who seek to lead their lives according to the tenets of a faith tradition. We have more in common with people who practise any of these "world religions" than with our secular neighbours.

Next, I would want to come explicitly to the concept of the church as God's instrument in the world and have the congregation think about what that understanding might mean for us at this time. In this regard, I would offer either of the two following illustrations.

If the needed encouragement on this occasion was a challenge to engage or continue to engage in outreach, I would tell a story about a church reaching out in mission to the wider community. I am aware of several small town or rural congregations that have done extraordinary outreach, far beyond what one would expect of a congregation of their size. Some rural church literature could provide good examples—and a gentle challenge.

Or a reminder might be needed of the importance of the congregation as an entity in and of itself, an entity that nurtures, strengthens, and encourages its members, individually and collectively, in order to be God's instrument in the world. In that case, I would introduce a story with the following reflection: Church is a place, certainly not the only place but most definitely a place, where divinity and humanity come together. In that coming together, we are nurtured as part of the body of Christ, and in that nurturing we are empowered.

The powerful imagery in that passage from 1 Peter will likely leave at least some congregants uncomfortable at first hearing. It is imagery I would have struggled with much more when the church was a hegemonic institution in Canada. I would not have preached on this passage 25 years ago; I still struggle with it somewhat. I grew up in a time when, although the church was losing its hegemony, many aspects of it still remained. That said, our situation has changed radically, and I now think of this passage as most appropriate. I want congregations to see themselves as the body of Christ, as a place where God might be present and be active, both in their nurturing of one another and of the resultant outreach.

I would then share this or another story. A former congregant of mine, in the midst of some congregational soul-searching in the late 1980s about what we in the United Church then called "the issue" (that is, the ordination of self-declared gays and lesbians), said during a congregational meeting, "For my own personal reasons, I disagree with the church's decision, but I am glad I belong to a church that could make this decision." He went on to say something I continue to find a profound and succinct description of what church, at its best, can be. He said, "I think of the church as being about the sharing of grace received."

I think that is very good theology. It speaks to what the church can be, at its best, for any one of us in our individual lives, with all the moments of triumph and of loss that each of us knows. It speaks to what the church can be, at its best, for the community and for the world in which it exists. It speaks to what I think both a contemporary expression of the doctrine of the church, as an "instrument of the loving Spirit of Christ," and historic expressions such as "God's gift to the world" or a "divine instrument" seek to convey. Let us, I would conclude, be a body that is about a "sharing of grace received."

Sample Sermon

On Being the Church

On this anniversary Sunday I want to focus my remarks around the concept of the church. It seems an appropriate thing to do on an anniversary Sunday when we want to do two things. We want to honour and remember those who founded and who have maintained this congregation down through the years. We also want to think both about the present time in which we live and about the future.

What is the church?… What do you think about when you hear that question: this congregation? the United Church? the church worldwide? the faces of people who used to attend here but have died? something else? There is not a right answer to that question. It could be any of the things I already mentioned and a number of other things besides.

For now, though, think about this congregation, the group of you who gather here each week. Most congregations I know are experiencing a challenge that still feels new to us. I was born in the early 1950s. When I was growing up in a small rural village in northeastern New Brunswick, almost everyone in that village went either to the Roman Catholic Church or to the United Church. Those were the two options.

Just as I was leaving home to go to university, the village began to grow quite rapidly; by the mid-1990s, its population was about five times larger than when I had lived there. However, despite that increased size, when I attended church there during visits to my mother in the mid-1990s, I saw about the same number of people in the pews as when I was a child. The congregation also had an older average age than I remembered.

Fast forward to 2014. I received a note during the winter from a friend telling me that the congregation had dwindled further and had made the painful decision to close. While that is obviously not the story of this congregation, does this general picture sound familiar? Certainly the story I have recounted of the village where I grew up is reflected to at least some degree in most congregations I know. Most congregations are challenged by the diminishment of the place of the church in the community and the decline in the number of people involved.

It is one of the challenges we face being the church in the early 21st century. Fifty or 60 years ago the wider society supported our practice of our faith. Whether for good or for ill (and one can argue that question either way), it was a time when there was some significant, if unspoken, pressure to be involved in a church community. In the 1950s, being involved in a church was the thing to do. But 60 years later, as I do not need to tell you, a markedly different situation exists.

Indeed, it is the opposite. Instead of being "the thing to do," to attend church now is to engage in a countercultural activity. It is to do what is not the norm. Each of you coming here today has defied the regular pattern in society, a pattern that says we have outgrown the need for church, or for that matter, the idea that any regular religious practice—whether of Christianity, Judaism, Islam, or some other faith tradition—matters at all.

So I want to commend you for your involvement with this congregation. To be involved regularly in the life of this or another congregation takes effort and requires sacrifice. For reasons I shall come to shortly, it is also to be involved in something very important. There are lots of folks outside the church who will tell us what is wrong with it. And at times within the church we rightly need to give attention to things we should try to do better. But there are also times to think about what is right with the church, and today is one of those times.

The passage from 1 Peter uses powerful titles in addressing an early Christian congregation, a group almost certainly smaller in number than our gathering here this morning. Just listen to these words, from verse 9: "But you are a chosen race, a royal priesthood, a holy nation, God's own people, in order that you may proclaim the mighty acts of [God] who called you out of darkness into [God's] marvelous light." This was not a congregation of the well-to-do, or one drawn from the upper echelons of first-century society. Most of the congregation to whom this letter was addressed came, in fact, from the lowest levels of society. Most would have been either slaves or women, two groups that in the first-century Roman Empire had no status at all.

Yet it is such a congregation that is addressed with this rich imagery. It is biblical imagery, drawn from the Old Testament, rich, powerful imagery. Their situation in their time was more challenging than what we face in ours. The Christian church has a much diminished place in Canadian society compared to its place 50 or 60 years ago. But that first-century congregation functioned on the very margins of society. In their everyday lives its members had no status and virtually no rights.

But it was such a people that God called to be the church. The Greek word for "church" means to be called out, and this group, like so many other early Christian congregations, was called out to witness to their society. They were called from a place of little or no status, to be the ones to, as the passage puts it, "proclaim the mighty acts of [God] who called you out of darkness into [God's] marvelous light."

Do we think of such titles applying to us?—"A royal priesthood, a holy nation, God's own people?" I want to argue that they do. One of our challenges these days is the much diminished view of the church in the wider society. Whether we like it or not, whether it is good or not—and both sides of those questions have been argued within the church over the past generation—we live in a society where the active practice of Christianity is generally met by ambivalence and, occasionally, mild hostility. We cannot go back to the situation where the church had status and where everyone went to church. While it was more comfortable, may have been more pleasant, may also have had challenges we no longer recognize, that is beside the point—it is not our reality.

What we are called to do is to be faithful in that proclamation of God's mighty acts on our behalf, and on behalf of our whole world. We are called, as the church, to continue to proclaim through word and through deed our conviction that, in Jesus Christ, God was seeking to reach out to us and to reconcile us, indeed our whole world, to God's very self.

What does it mean to reach out in word and in deed? I think reaching out in word requires that we become as knowledgeable as we can about our faith tradition. It means becoming as familiar as we can with scripture and thinking through what it means to be a Christian. It means thinking about how to continue, or to expand, our effort to act in ways that are in concert with the things we say we believe. It means learning to talk about our faith to others, so that we can communicate the relevant aspects in those moments when someone asks us about the things we believe or about why we make the faith-influenced decisions we do.

Reaching out in deed, in the things we do, involves the things we do as individuals, the things we do as a congregation, and the things we do as a wider church. One understanding of the church is that it is an instrument that God uses to accomplish God's loving purposes in our world. The church as an "instrument of the loving Spirit of Christ" is the language used in the United Church's recent faith statement, A Song of Faith. "God's gift to the world" is another traditional way of saying the same thing. Behind those terms is the sense that God works through and uses flawed and very human people like you, like me, to accomplish God's purposes in our world. We are not the only means God uses, but we are one means God uses. We might not be so trusting in our abilities, but God is.

There is no one magic thing that every congregation should do by way of reaching out. What I can say more generally is that we need to try to respond to the needs of the community, both the community around us and the community of the wider world. In our responding, we proclaim God's loving care in action.

I want to share a story with you. I am thinking of a conversation with an M.Div. graduate from my time at Queen's. I want also to say that I have her permission to share this story. She recounted that she had taken a call to a church in a small town, a town that was struggling as a result of the loss over the past number of years of almost every small business or industry that had provided employment. Where 20 years ago there had been 10 such enterprises, now there was only one. The congregation was, not surprisingly, struggling financially, and its membership had become composed largely of retired people.

The congregation had a long tradition of providing food vouchers to people in need. This graduate had asked the church board what the budget for this item was and had been told, we don't have a budget line. Whatever you give out is what we will cover. During her second calendar year, this graduate realized that by the end of July she had handed out almost as many food vouchers as she had during the previous year. It was also no secret that the congregation had had financial struggles for the past number of years. So she called the church treasurer to say, "Should I change this practice? Should I start to become more restrictive?" After all, she did not want to have complaints later from the board. The treasurer responded: "You know, we are having a better year financially. It is good that we are able to do this. Don't worry."

Now what I find powerful about that story is that a place that had had financial struggles and that, for reasons unknown, was starting to do a little better did not try to hoard its new-found resources. Know what? I'd like to be part of that kind of church.

I am not saying that this particular type of outreach is what this congregation ought to do. Every congregation's context is different. But the church is an instrument that God uses to accomplish God's loving purposes in the world. What does that look like for us, as a congregation, today and in the days ahead?

On this anniversary we celebrate the ways in which this congregation has been such an instrument in the past. May we be open to the strengthening, nurturing presence of God in our midst, in this place! May we be open to seeing where the Spirit of God is leading us in the days that lie ahead!

And to the God who created us and gave us life, to the God whose love has been made known to us in Jesus Christ, and to the God who continues to be present to us through the Holy Spirit be all honour, glory, and praise. Amen.

—*John H. Young*

This sermon is a slightly revised version of one I preached in the fall of 2014 at a congregation's anniversary service.

Chapter 9
Vocation

Called in Our Post-Christendom Society

The Doctrinal Concept

Vocation is not a new concept. The term comes from the Latin word for "call." Yet it is not a doctrine we talk about much. When we do, we usually discuss vocation only in relation to members of the church who are seeking to become pastoral ministers. Vocation, however, applies to every Christian. Each Christian is called to live a life that witnesses to the Christian faith through word and deed, a life of Christian service. The specifics will vary according to the context of time and place. The next chapter on Ministry focuses on people who are serving in pastoral ministry; here, we reflect on vocation primarily in relation to the laity.

The concept of vocation appears frequently in scripture. Abram and Sarai are called to leave all that is familiar by a God they do not know. Various other figures—men and women, judges and prophets—are called to be God's voice, God's instrument in the world. Indeed, the people of Israel have a vocation as God's elected, or chosen, people. In the New Testament, it is not only Jesus calling the disciples. Paul certainly thought he had been called. Early members of Christian communities understood themselves to have been called to proclaim their faith and to live lives that were consistent with the faith they professed.

The notion of vocation as Christian service, as a call to serve God in the world, has featured prominently in all four of the United Church's major doctrinal statements. In the Twenty Articles of Doctrine, Article XX reflects a key aspect of the denomination's founding vision, namely, that the United Church would be a force to bring about a Christian Canada. To that end, members of the church were reminded of a series of duties that fell to them as "disciples and servants of Christ." While the desire—let alone the possibility—for creating a Christian Canada faded long ago, the sense that God calls every member of the church to Christian service continues to speak to our understanding of vocation. The 1940 Statement of Faith's section "Christian Life and Duty," among other things, stresses the call of Christians both to support the church and to live their lives in society in a way that demonstrates love for others. A notion of service permeates the third section of A New Creed ("We are called to be the Church..."). The denomination's 2006 statement of faith, A Song of Faith, includes the following passage:

> We are each given particular gifts of the Spirit.
> For the sake of the world,
> > God calls all followers of Jesus to Christian ministry....
> To embody God's love in the world,
> > the work of the church requires the ministry and
> > > discipleship
> > of all believers.
>
> In grateful response to God's abundant love,
> > we bear in mind our integral connection
> > to the earth and to one another;
> we participate in God's work of healing and mending creation.

So, what would vocation look like now? Vocation still includes that sense of feeling called, summoned, to lead one's life in serving God a particular way. That way certainly does not need to be as a pastoral minister; indeed, as Paul made clear in his letter to the Romans (Romans 12:4–8), Christians are called to many tasks. Only some have the specific call to exercise their ministry in and for the service of the church. The denomination's formal doctrinal statements agree on that point.

Vocation, properly understood, captures Martin Luther's concept of "the priesthood of all believers." It is the sense, shared also by John Calvin, that God calls every Christian to ministry, calls every Christian to God's service. Over the past few decades that classic Protestant understanding of the priesthood of all believers has frequently been misinterpreted as saying that there is no differentiation among Christians in that to which God calls us. Now, there must be no differentiation of value. However, while we are all called, the varieties of gifts God has given us mean that we are called to different and specific ministries in the church and in the world. We are not all called to preach or to teach, but every Christian has a vocation to serve God.

For a significant portion of our denomination's history, and certainly during the period our earliest doctrinal statements—the Twenty Articles of Doctrine and the 1940 Statement of Faith—were written, the Christian church in this country enjoyed a position of privilege. It was powerfully, if informally, established. Until some point during the 1970s most Canadians had at least a tenuous connection with an institutional religious body. Operating under the assumption that almost every Canadian had a link to some religious body, the emphasis in outlining Christian vocation—heavily in Article XX of the Twenty Articles of Doctrine and exclusively in the 1940 Statement of Faith—fell on service. One served God through one's active participation in the life of the church and in activities in the wider world. Article XX did include the idea of proclamation as a part of Christian service. But one senses that the drafters of the statement had in mind other parts of the world, rather than Canada, as the place where such proclamation would occur.

The emphasis on service is not surprising. With most Canadians having a connection to a religious body, an emphasis that the laity should proclaim the good news to those around them would have looked like an encouragement to proselytize. In the world in which Catherine and I grew up in the Maritimes, most people, no matter how active they were in a local congregation, did not talk about their faith to neighbours or friends. Outside of the major cities, most people were at least nominally Christian. Serious conversations about one's faith anywhere outside of church or a church group—for example, a conversation with a Roman Catholic neighbour—would have been seen as a subtle effort to convert the person from their denomination to yours. Such "sheep stealing," to use the term of the day, was much frowned upon. Members of some smaller denominations who did engage in such activity were widely regarded with disdain.

In our present circumstances we need to rethink some aspects of our understanding of vocation. We now live in an increasingly secularized country where the practitioners of any major faith tradition, including Christianity, experience either ambivalence or mild hostility. Each new 10-year census reveals a rise in the percentage of Canadians who declare they have "no religion." More significant than that change, though, is the general disregard for religion and religious practice. Sunday morning has become the time of choice not only for children's activities, such as ballet practice or minor hockey league games, but also for charitable causes aimed primarily at adults, such as a run for the Terry Fox Foundation or breast cancer awareness. Organizers judge that Sunday morning is the one time in the week when few people are out and about doing something else. Therefore, it is a time when a run, for example, will both have the fewest traffic issues and allow for the greatest level of participation.

Increasingly the vocation to be a Christian brings members of the congregation who seek to live lives reflecting their faith into conflict in the places where they work and live. They might be faced with a choice around participating in a leisure activity versus being active in the worship life of the congregation, or with deciding whether to take a job that means not being able to attend worship. Unpopular stances on social or political questions might arise out of one's faith convictions. In our secularized society a focus on individuals caring for themselves is displacing the notion—common to Judaism, Christianity, and Islam—that we have a responsibility to care both for our neighbours throughout this world and for the planet itself. In practising their faith tradition, Christians increasingly stand out. And increasingly that prominence might attract derision rather than affirmation.

The changed context also requires of Christians in Canada a new openness to talk about their faith. Even when religious participation was high, as in the two decades after the Second World War, the assumption that people would learn something of the Christian tradition by osmosis was likely faulty. But in that period most people had at least some contact with a church or a synagogue. These days most people outside the Christian church have no idea about our faith tradition or about the nature of our worship. It has become necessary to feel comfortable discussing, and answering questions about, our faith. Neighbours or co-workers might be curious about what we believe and why we act as we do, and we may need to explain to others our rationale for a particular stance or decision.

This differentiation from our peers and need to be willing to talk about our faith makes our situation similar to that of the early Christians, such as those addressed in the New Testament epistles. Over the past generation or so, a number of writers have commented on this point. Aspects of our contemporary situation in the West resemble that faced by early Christians trying to make their way in a society that was generally indifferent, and occasionally hostile, to this "new religion."

Scripture for Preaching

1 Peter 3:13–17
Now who will harm you if you are eager to do what is good? But even if you do suffer for doing what is right, you are blessed. Do not fear what they fear, and do not be intimidated, but in your hearts sanctify Christ as Lord. Always be ready to make your defense to anyone who demands from you an accounting for the hope that is in you; yet do it with gentleness and reverence. Keep your conscience clear, so that, when you are maligned, those who abuse you for your good conduct in Christ may be put to shame. For it is better to suffer for doing good, if suffering should be God's will, than to suffer for doing evil.

Why Is This Doctrine Important?

It has always been important to remind members of the congregation that the Christian faith needs to be professed both in words and in deeds. But today they must grapple with society's increasing antipathy to the practice of any major religious tradition—think of the spate of books by so-called new atheists, such as Richard Dawkins and Christopher Hitchens, that strongly criticize any religious practice and view it as dangerous. In this context it is important to re-emphasize and help our members to think about vocation.

Members of a congregation must be prepared to face challenges that would have seemed strange a generation ago and inconceivable in the first half of the 20th century. They might need to choose between attending worship on Sunday and holding a job, as employers seek workers available on weekends, not just on the traditional work days. They can face quiet, and occasionally not so quiet, devaluing for participating in worship, taking time for prayer, making decisions informed by their faith, even saying grace.

At the same time, we must be ready to enter into conversation with others who are genuinely curious about what we believe and why we act as we do out of our beliefs. Responding to questions or providing a faith-based rationale when asked about our decisions is a form of quiet evangelism. It is likely the only effective means by which, in our time, we can spread the good news. We are called to witness to our faith, not only by what we do but also by what we say. Such a witness in our day will not be from a position of power or privilege.

It will be a challenge for many Christians in the mainline denominations to talk about what we believe and how our theological convictions make a difference to how we live. Many of us are still influenced, knowingly or unknowingly, by assumptions related to that earlier privileged position of the Christian tradition in our society. The most problematic of these assumptions, given our current context, is that we ought not to talk to others about our faith.

When the Christian church had a privileged position in this country, and when much of the population was active in some Christian denomination, such conversations about one's faith were taboo for a good reason. But today, many Canadians have no idea what goes on within the walls of a congregation. They know little, beyond what they've seen from TV evangelists and in stories in various media, about the assertions and practices of any religious tradition. They are most likely to learn more if, when they ask out of curiosity about what we believe, why we go to church, or why we make the commitments we do, we are open to talking to them about such matters.

How Does It Preach?

When might one preach a sermon about vocation? A church anniversary is one such time. Lent, with its spiritual stock-taking, is another possibility. One could preach on this topic at almost any time of the year.

In a congregation in which most people are under 45, I would begin by talking about some of the challenges of being Christian in a society that is either ambivalent or mildly hostile to the practice of the faith. If the average age was early to mid-60s, I would begin by touching on something the older members of the congregation know—that the place of Christianity in society has changed dramatically within their lifetime. There is no returning to the situation of my childhood in rural New Brunswick where almost everyone attended one of the two churches in the village and nothing was open on Sunday. I would talk about some of the challenges we now face when we seek to practise our Christian faith. Then I would describe the situation, and the trials, of being a member of a Christian community in the Roman Empire at the time the First Letter of Peter was written. Some significant parallels exist between their situation and ours.

I chose this reading from 1 Peter because of the circumstances of those to whom the epistle was addressed. A church leader in Rome[16] sent this letter to small, scattered congregations in what is now Turkey. The members of these congregations were poor and drawn primarily from the lowest ranks of society; scholars believe women and slaves, two groups with no status in the first-century world, made up the bulk of the membership. These members faced opposition to their practice of the faith. There is no evidence they risked martyrdom, but the comments in chapters 2 and 3 about suffering suggest they had to confront opposition, abuse, and some level of public disgrace or persecution. The main reason to choose this lesson is the writer's advice about how to witness to their faith in these circumstances where they experienced some societal disadvantages and suffering because they were followers of Jesus.

Part of responding to God's call to be a Christian in our changed circumstance requires us to be willing, as the writer of 1 Peter put it, "always [to] be ready to make your defence to anyone who demands from you an accounting for the hope that is in you" (3:15). I assume that almost everyone who regularly attends a Christian congregation these days does so out of conviction, out of a sense of vocation. There is no longer societal pressure to participate in a faith community; indeed, there is pressure not to do so. But practising Christians, the members of any congregation, need today to be ready to talk about what they believe and why. Several things will force that. One is the occasional questions from neighbours, co-workers, or other family members who are curious about our religious commitments. Another is the need for each of us to be an evangelist.

During the first decade of this century, The United Church of Canada had a program called Emerging Spirit. The program's purpose was to reach out to the "unchurched," particularly those between the ages of 30 and 45, and to encourage them to join a local United Church congregation. The program sought to help congregations be hospitable places where curious "seekers" who came with questions about the faith tradition would find both a warm welcome and an openness to engage with their questions. I think the willingness of people who currently attend a United Church congregation to talk about their faith with those strangers who come or, for that matter, with the neighbour across the back fence, will be a crucial form of reaching out. It is part of our vocation as Christians to share our faith tradition.

Finally, in an increasingly secularized society, practising Christians will find themselves increasingly at odds with decisions being made in the workplace or the community. It is important to be able to provide a rationale for our views not only to strengthen our own resolve but also to provide an explanation to those who ask about our decisions and practices. Our vocation as Christians will increasingly make us "resident aliens" (to use the title of a 1989 book by William Willimon and Stanley Hauerwas) or those living "in exile," as Walter Brueggemann and others describe our present reality. Being an alien or a person in exile is to be at some risk from the conventional, dominant forces in the society. It is a new phenomenon for many who attend our congregations. It is not, however, a new situation for Christians, as the world of the New Testament would attest.

Sample Sermon

It's Not Easy Being Christian

"It's not easy being Christian," a good friend said to me recently. "I need to buy a new car. What kind of car do I buy, given concerns I have, and should have, about the environment, and about how much to spend in a world where so many have so little? Do I buy one that is cheap and quite good on gas? One that is somewhat more expensive but better on gas? Or do I buy one that costs a fair bit more and will use a little more gas but will last a lot longer and so use less of this world's resources in that way?"

My friend lives with great intentionality about what she buys. Her intentionality is matched by few people of my acquaintance and surpassed by none. It arises from her Christian principles, from what she understands herself called to do and to be as a Christian. She endeavours to live out her Christian vocation.

The word *vocation*, derived from the Latin verb "to call," is not a term we use often in the church, except when we think about people who feel called to become ministers. It is a term early Christians understood and used to refer to the sense that they had felt called by God to tell others about Jesus and to live a life of service to God and their neighbours. We may not have talked much about vocation in an explicit way. However, our denomination's statements of faith, and also many sermons, without necessarily using the term *vocation*, have focused on the responsibilities of being a Christian. The emphases have been on service to others, on being God's hands and feet in our world, on acting as God would have us act. Those emphases are good ones. I very much want to encourage such attentiveness to living out our Christian faith.

With apologies to Kermit the Frog, it's not easy being Christian. The intentionality of my friend is not easy to sustain in a country, let alone a world, where so few others have such intentionality arising from their religious practice.

It's not easy being Christian in other ways, too. Many of us here can remember when the sanctuary here was much fuller than it is today. I can go to congregations, especially ones opened recently in rapidly growing suburban areas, where there are lots of children and youth and a good-sized attendance at Sunday worship. But those places are the exception. The reality most of us know is that fewer and fewer people leave their homes at any point during a weekend to attend a religious service of any type, whether we are talking about services at a Christian church like ours or a Jewish synagogue.

It's not easy being Christian. I grew up in the 1950s and 1960s. Whether or not it was really easier then to be a Christian, it certainly seemed easier. For starters, it seemed that everyone attended. In my home village in New Brunswick, with a population a little over 600, those who did not attend either the Roman Catholic Church or the United Church, the two options in the village, stood out.

Further, there was an informal establishment of Christianity. By an informal establishment, I mean that in the world in which I grew up, being a good Christian and a good citizen seemed very much alike. Worship at the local church on the Sunday closest to November 11 suggested a close relationship among citizenship, service, and Christianity. The basic rules of right and wrong—you did not steal, you did not beat people up, you paid your taxes, and so on—seemed drawn from Judeo-Christian teachings. When necessary, police officers and the legal system enforced these basic rules to ensure that a good, safe, and well-functioning Christian community resulted.

Finally, in the world in which I grew up, society supported the practice of the Christian faith in many ways, not least by what was not open on Sunday. An older cousin of mine owned and operated a garage. He lived next door. If you needed gas for some emergency or you had forgotten to get it on Saturday, you could go and knock on his door, and he would come out and pump you some gas. But his business was closed on Sunday, and you would never have thought of going to buy gas there unless you genuinely needed it. I recall that there were a total of four drugstores in two nearby towns; the four drugstores rotated which one of them would open between 2:00 p.m. and 4:00 p.m. on Sunday to enable people who needed a prescription filled that day to obtain it. You could not buy any other product in the store. No other business was open on Sunday.

I make these comments not by way of nostalgia or to wish that such a pattern could be recreated. It was a particular era, and while I think a common pause day would be a very good thing societally, I am not sure that informal support of Christianity was especially helpful to Christianity. I think that period's informal support helped to make our Christian practice more influenced by societal standards, with less attention to thoughtful wrestling with scripture. I may be wrong, but I think that was so. Having said that, it's not easy being Christian, and it did seem easier then.

It's not easy being Christian. It's not easy being Christian when you have to choose between a needed job at Walmart and attending church, because the Walmart store in the nearby city looks for folks who will work weekends. It's not easy being Christian when you have to choose whether your daughter will play soccer, with practices every Sunday morning and Wednesday night beginning in late April, or attend Sunday school, which will not finish for the summer until the second week of June. It's not easy being Christian when you could give less of your time, not to mention your money, to the church and be like your neighbours on either side of you who seem to have more leisure time than you do because they are not involved in church, or in any other community activities, for that matter. It's not easy being Christian when the general attitude of many neighbours and friends, and sometimes also family members, to your practice of Christianity is ambivalence or even mild derision. You certainly are clear that they are not supportive of your commitment. It's not easy being Christian and wondering if the church you have been a part of for so long will still be here 10 years from now, as you see fewer and fewer people in the pews each passing year.

Earlier in this service, I read a passage from 1 Peter 3. This letter was written to a group of very small and struggling congregations scattered over a part of what is now Turkey. They had been founded at some point earlier in the first century, but their existence was precarious. If you look at the material that precedes today's reading, you discover that the members of these congregations were facing abuse and suffering for their faith.

This passage has much to say to us about how we might live our vocation as a Christian at a time when our surrounding society is ambivalent or mildly hostile. While the context of these and other New Testament communities is different from ours in many respects, the ambivalence or mild hostility we experience to our practice of the Christian faith is an important point of similarity. The writer encouraged the members of these congregations to continue to witness to their faith by the way they lived, whether they were slaves of abusive masters or had unbelieving spouses. These comments spoke to what I have been calling the service side of the Christian call or vocation.

But their call or vocation to be Christian in such trying circumstances did not end there. The writer urged them: "Always be ready to make your defense to anyone who demands from you an accounting for the hope that is in you; yet do it with gentleness and reverence" (15b–16a).

Their call to be Christian, their Christian vocation, meant they needed to be ready to speak about their faith, about their beliefs. They needed to speak about how their beliefs had led them to the outlook on life they had, about how their faith led them to live their lives in a particular way.

Our Methodist ancestors would have called such speaking offering testimony. Testimony—speaking about our faith—is not something most of us do or, for that matter, feel comfortable doing. That's what we pay ministers to do, some of you may be thinking. Many of us do not feel comfortable talking about our faith and the commitments to which it leads because we grew up in, or were influenced by, that period in Canada when Christianity was informally established and when talking about your faith was something done only by those who sought to proselytize. We assumed, I think not accurately, but we assumed it nonetheless, that everyone knew a fair bit about Christianity. We tended to look down on those individuals who chose, for whatever reason, not to involve themselves in the church. Involvement in the church was then the thing to do.

That is not our reality. Our Christian vocation, our call to lead a Christian life, continues to require that we seek to serve God and others by the way we live. We continue to witness to what we really believe by the decisions we make at home, at work, at play. But we live in a time when we also need to be ready to talk about *why* we believe the things we do, to make our defence to anyone who asks of us an accounting for the hope that is in us, that Christian hope that propels us onward in this world. We need to do that when we are asked by a neighbour, a grandchild, a cousin, a co-worker, our golfing companion. We need to do so because their questions show curiosity. Whether it is only curiosity or whether it is curiosity prompted by seeing something in us they would like also to have in their lives is hard to say. But it was upon such willingness to speak to the hope early followers of Jesus found in their faith tradition that the Christian church grew. Sharing the hope that was in them led others to join them.

The Christian vocation requires different things in different times and circumstances. In our time and context it requires being open to talking about our faith with those who ask. Doing so takes courage for two reasons. First, we are not used to talking about our faith, and it makes us feel uncomfortable. Second, we are not sure what our conversation partner will think. They may even think we are foolish. But we need to respond respectfully—with "gentleness and reverence," as today's reading put it.

Let me also be clear. I am not suggesting as a model for talking about our faith setting up a little stand in front of the local Tim Hortons and passing out leaflets at the drive-through. Rather, I have in mind a much more passive approach, though a challenging one for all of that. I have in mind being open to talking about the things we believe when one of our grandchildren asks, "Why do you go to church?" Or when the person next door asks, "Why do you believe in God?" Or when the woman who cuts our hair says, "Tell me, as someone who goes to church, what you think about euthanasia?" Or our co-worker asks, "Why, when I watch an NFL game, do I usually see someone behind one of the goalposts holding up a sign that reads John 3:16? What is that all about?"

I have been stressing the need for us to become comfortable talking about our faith because we need to be open to responding to questions from those around us, genuine questions about what we believe and why. I could call it a soft form of evangelism. If we are Christians by conviction—and I assume we are, because these days there is no societal pressure to belong to a church—then we do believe that the Christian message is good news. Please be clear. I am *not* suggesting that we should foist our good news on others. But if we really do believe that practising the Christian faith is a life-giving thing, then we should be open to sharing that story with those who ask.

In our world, there is one other reason why we need to think through the relationship between the things we do and the commitments we hold and our Christian faith. The writer of 1 Peter encouraged the recipients of this letter to be ready to give an account of their faith and its implications to those who asked. They ought do so gently and with reverence. Since most of them were drawn from the lowest ranks of a society where rank and status mattered, they would often be speaking to their "betters." The writer was aware that some of the time they would need to account for the hope that was in them in defending their participation in Christian worship or in other faith-related activities to people who thought the practice of Christianity misguided, or wrong, or dangerous. In a time and society where fewer and fewer of us practise any formal religious tradition, we will sometimes be called upon to defend those actions by those who disagree with us or who think the commitments that arise from our faith convictions foolish. We need to be prepared to do so.

It's not easy being Christian. In reality it never has been, even if some of us remember a time when it seemed easier. We do need, as the writer of 1 Peter put it, to be ready to make our defence to anyone who demands of us an accounting for the hope and the joy we find in the Christian life. We also need to do so gently and respectfully.

It's not easy being Christian. The New Testament does not offer us templates for how to negotiate living the Christian life in 21st-century Canada. But scripture over and over again does offer us the most critical assurance we need, namely that God is with us on that journey, strengthening us in that endeavour. I find that assurance best expressed in the letter of another New Testament figure, the apostle Paul, to the church in Rome, another early Christian congregation living in a place and time when their convictions made them seem like resident aliens. Paul wrote:

> No, in all these things we are more than conquerors through him who loved us. For I am convinced that neither death, nor life, nor angels, nor rulers, nor things present, nor things to come, nor powers, nor height, nor depth, nor anything else in all creation, will be able to separate us from the love of God in Christ Jesus our Lord. (Romans 8:37–39)

Amen and amen.

—*John H. Young*

This sermon is a revised version of one preached at a congregational anniversary in 2015.

Chapter 10
Ministry

Equipping the Saints

The Doctrinal Concept

The freedom to know where your heart and mind rest, the trust from congregants in the faith community, the witness of 2,000 years of faithful souls, the treasures in the nuances of the heresies, the vocation of life lived in constant reference to the purposes of God: such is the character of the pastoral life. Ministry is a calling. To feel a call from God is a fine thing. To have that call validated by a congregation is encouraging. To have the wider church—presbytery and Conference—test that call and find it true is a deep blessing. And to know that the call comes from God and is blessed by God is empowering and humbling. A person is in ministry because it is God's idea.

The pastoral ministry is a gift of God to the church. Service and love are God's before they are ours. "Do not neglect the gift that is in you," we hear from the writer of 1 Timothy, "which was given to you through prophecy with the laying on of hands by the council of elders" (4:14).

A word about the word *ministry*. We commonly use *ministry* to describe the work any of us do in the church, the work of Christ. Ministry is the work of all who are baptized. We place high value on the action that all of our church members offer in the life of the spiritual community, in engagement with the world, and in personal connections. In A Song of Faith we see the integration of ministry into the whole church:

> To embody God's love in the world,
> > the work of the church requires the ministry and
> > > discipleship
> > of all believers.

The word *ministry* is also used to speak about people upon whom the hands of the elders have been laid, people who have accepted the call to the pastoral life. This chapter is a discussion about the doctrine of ordered ministry. We could call it pastoral ministry. We could call it paid accountable ministry. We could speak of streams of ministry. We could also differentiate between diaconal and ordained ministry, but that has been done effectively in many other places. Our concern here is a broader scope. I am referring to the order of ministry, and I call it ministry.

Ministry is a calling. In Ephesians 4:11–12 we read, "The gifts he gave were that some would be apostles, some prophets, some evangelists, some pastors and teachers, to *equip the saints* for the work of ministry…" (italics mine). There is some quiet debate whether *ministry* in this passage refers to the apostolic ministry, a connection through the generations between current church leaders and the apostles of the early church. But the common reading of the passage is that some among us are set apart to prepare others to do Christ's work in the wider world. That is the inspiring message behind Martin Luther's famous phrase, "the priesthood of all believers."

The priesthood of all believers is a call to bring the sacred nature of God's presence to all we do, to everything that any of us does. Rather than bringing everyone *inside* the church to do what the priest does all day, it takes the blessing of vocation *outside* the church to the various responsibilities and opportunities for mission throughout the world. This distinction is significant as we consider the doctrine of ministry. It is important, because Luther didn't mean everyone should do what priests do. We don't all have to be priests or pastoral ministers.

That means we can focus on a theology of ministry apart from the theology of vocation. It means we can concentrate on ordination and diaconal ministry apart from the vocations of the laity. We can do this without in any way diminishing the ministry of members of the wider church.

Ministry is more than love and service. It is an identity. Ministry is theonomous—it is a life governed by God, in the sense of living a life in constant reference to the purposes of God. People in ministry listen for the call of the Spirit; it's not just figuring out what is the right or ethical thing to do, it's figuring out what the spiritual answer might be. It is a minister who will ask: "Where is the Spirit calling this church?" "How is it with your soul?" "How is your prayer life?" "Do you see God's hand in your life?" Lay people may ask those questions, but it is unequivocally the role of a minister to do so.

Ministry is a way of life. It is a perspective, a way of interpreting the world. Not that ministers don't get breaks, vacations, sabbaticals—of course. But the life of ministry is a life on the Way. It is public and it is reflective.

Ministry is more than a personal spirituality. Ministers carry the church's faith rather than merely their own. In this manner the heritage of faith can be brought to bear on contemporary issues. Decisions can be made carefully and with theological integrity: this integrity is not rigidity, it is precision. A solid understanding of the church's heritage gives one confidence to move constructively into new insights.

Ministry is a profession. A profession is a form of employment, but at root the word means to declare publicly. Ministers *profess* the faith of the church, acknowledge the hand of God in their lives, and accept the authorization and discipline of the church. Professing the faith is not a static event: it is an ongoing practice of developing faith, looking for God's grace and proclaiming it where it is seen, helping people think critically about their own faith, and making the witness of the church honest and constructive.

Ministry is relational. Pastoral care, work with children, weekly preaching, development of congregational leadership, choosing hymns with musicians, caring for the presbytery camp—all of these responsibilities involve dealing with people and developing deep and often long-standing relationships. A Christian model for relationships is the Trinity: the triune God in constant relationship, Creator, Christ, and Spirit. From that model comes our understanding that we are in relationship with God, and also that our human relationships are sacred. A doctrine of ministry can be based in a Trinitarian theology.

Despite different opinions about many theological issues among denominations, the World Council of Churches was able to come to ecumenical agreement in the early 1980s on some key and powerful definitions about ordained ministry. These statements were published in the document *Baptism, Eucharist and Ministry*. The statement speaks of the *necessity* of ministry, of people who are publicly and continually responsible for Christian guidance, who bring a multiplicity of gifts and nevertheless signify the church universal. Moreover, without ministers who since early times have been ordained, the church—and its work—is not complete.

It went on to say that the laity and the ordained are interrelated and mutually dependent: "the community needs ordained ministers," and "the ordained ministry has no existence apart from the community." [17]

Ministry always arises from the church and is part of the church. In The United Church of Canada, it is not a hierarchical relationship but a partnership. This partnership is with the lay members of the church. The detail-oriented governance of our Reformed heritage carefully outlines the responsibilities and relationships of each part of the church, and even in times of change, ministers are required not only to be familiar with them but also to ensure that they are respected. This indicates that the minister is to be committed to relationships, invested in the welfare of the church, and prepared to share the leadership. The theology of ministry here includes an element of discernment: looking for the presence of the Spirit, seeing the big picture, giving an honest and faithful account of that picture, and working with the lay people to develop the mission of Christ. It is Trinitarian.

There is also a mystical relationship with God, and with the heritage of faith, that is seen at commissioning to diaconal ministry and at ordination. The liturgical action is the laying on of hands. This act symbolizes the gift of the Holy Spirit. It also confers authority by those who carry the office, who have gone before—it is a connection through generations. The laying on of hands indicates the external call, validating the internal call the candidate received. Significantly, laying on of hands is also a gesture in baptism. In terms of a doctrine of ministry, this mystical connection speaks to the transcendent nature of God.

Ministry is a gift of God through the church and for the church. It is the setting apart—not setting over or against—of some members who have been called, and found called, by and to the church. The calling becomes a spiritual identity, not simply a line of work, that draws on mystical connections with the generations before us. At the same time it sets our face firmly toward the future and the coming fullness of God's realm.

Scripture for Preaching

Ephesians 4:11–16
The gifts he gave were that some would be apostles, some prophets, some evangelists, some pastors and teachers, to equip the saints for the work of ministry, for building up the body of Christ, until all of us come to the unity of the faith and of the knowledge of the Son of God, to maturity, to the measure of the full stature of Christ. We must no longer be children, tossed to and fro and blown about by every wind of doctrine, by people's trickery, by their craftiness in deceitful scheming. But speaking the truth in love, we must grow up in every way into him who is the head, into Christ, from whom the whole body, joined and knit together by every ligament with which it is equipped, as each part is working properly, promotes the body's growth in building itself up in love.

Jeremiah 20:9
If I say, "I will not mention [God],
    or speak any more in [God's] name,"
then within me there is something like a burning fire
    shut up in my bones;
I am weary with holding it in,
    and I cannot.

Why Is This Doctrine Important?

If all Christians are called, why do we need ordained or commissioned ministries? Careful consideration of the distinction between the vocation of all Christians through baptism, and the call of a relative few to serve in the church and its outreach ministries, reveals a different kind of call.

The priesthood of all believers is a call to serve the world, in the manner for which we each are talented and prepared, and in the places where we work, live, and play. The priesthood of all believers is intended to develop the mission of Christ and of the church outside the church.

Daniel Migliore presses the call of the relative few to serve the church. He distinguishes between missiology (the mission of the church—what we *do* for Christ) and ontology (the nature of being—who we *are*), sifting out the difference between ministry as function and ministry as vocational commitment. He writes:

> Ordination is properly understood *missiologically rather than ontologically.* That is, ordination is not a mysterious change of ontological status elevating the person ordained over other Christians. It is being commissioned and authorized to a particular task in the power of the Spirit. There is no basis in Scripture for thinking of ordination to the ministry of Word and sacrament as a "higher" or "fuller" ministry in comparison with other ministries of Christians. The clergy do not constitute a separate class of Christians. A hierarchical division between clergy and lay is a wound in the life of the church.
>
> This is not to say, however, that ministry can be reduced to mere function. The person of the minister cannot be simply divorced from the task of ministry. Ministry presupposes not only thorough educational preparation but also deep commitment to God and a sincere desire to serve Christ. Ordained ministry is a distinctive calling and not just a role one plays or a job one does.[18]

In the last few generations we have come to value the actions of our faith deeply. Perhaps we always did. Increasingly, though, we have come to take for granted phrases such as "actions speak louder than words" and "what I do is more important than what I believe." We have also come to make definitions by function rather than essence.

That is particularly true when we turn to a conversation about ministry. We speak easily about the tasks and responsibilities of ministry, but less so about the theology of ministry. We describe it by function, in the manner of a job description. Ministers visit the sick, lead the Sunday service, plan the youth retreat, guide the study group, recruit people for the Pride Parade, write prayers for a funeral, welcome the transient, break the bread, chair a presbytery committee, and so on. This is a list of tasks, and a checklist of tasks is easily managed. A person doesn't need to be a minister to accomplish any of these tasks. Indeed, lay people get a great deal of pleasure out of leading study groups, writing prayers, or offering pastoral care, any of these things and more—and are completely welcomed, appreciated, needed, and affirmed by the church.

A theology of ministry, however, brings an understanding that is different from the task list or the function of ministry. Ministry involves regular and responsible leadership in worship, preaching, and sacraments. It is a long-term commitment, a permanent vocation. It doesn't disappear at retirement. Retired ministers remain members of presbytery and are visited and cared for by the presbytery.

A theology of ministry acknowledges the relational element in ministry. That takes us beyond the vocabulary of function into the world of the Trinity, the relational foundation for the church, our faith, and in Christian terms for the world.

Many congregations have settled ministries that are flourishing. Some congregations, though, wonder about the merit of calling a minister when they might simply try to find people to offer occasional worship leadership, at a reduced cost. A deep awareness of the nature of ministry will help these pastoral charges understand why the presbytery insists they begin a Joint Needs Assessment process.

Ministers are representatives of something more than themselves, more than a congregation, and more than a denomination. Over and again the knowledge that we are in this calling because of God brings us the strength we need. The work can be difficult. It can be disturbing. It can hurt. To know that we go with God is a very fine thing. This knowledge is not a sense that because we go with God we are always right, and hence any challenger must be wrong, but rather that we trust we are on the right road. This faith can take the edge off disappointment or failure and transform it into learning or fresh possibility—or understandings of grace.

We are well aware of the dangers of pride, abuse, and clergy misconduct: how those have taken the shine off the apple! They are real. Our temptations, and the temptations of our clergy colleagues, require attention. A relational theology of ministry may help prevent the isolation that is so frequently part of misconduct, and would certainly help in the subsequent healing of people and collegial relationships.

In the United Church, for the most part, we assume a theology of ordained ministry that we don't lay out in as many words. In none of our statements, for instance, is there a delineated doctrine of ordered or ordained ministry. We find descriptive passages, but not a clearly articulated theology. Here are the most relevant passages:

> **Twenty Articles of Doctrine** [from 1925, edited over the years]
> **Article XVII. Of the Ministry.**
> We believe that Jesus Christ, as the Supreme Head of the Church, has appointed therein an ordained ministry of Word, Sacrament, and Pastoral Care and a diaconal ministry of Education, Service, and Pastoral Care, and calls men and women to these ministries; and that the Church, under the guidance of the Holy Spirit, recognizes and chooses those whom He calls, and should thereupon duly ordain or commission them to the work of the ministry.

> **A Statement of Faith, 1940**
> **VIII. The Ministry**
> We believe that God has appointed a Ministry in His Church for the preaching of the Word, the administration of the Sacraments, and the pastoral care of the people.
>
> We believe that the Church has authority to ordain to the Ministry by prayer and the laying on of hands those whom she finds, after due trial, to be called of God thereto.
>
> We believe that, for the due ordering of her life as a society, God has appointed a government in His Church, to be exercised, under Christ the head, by Ministers and representatives of the people.
>
> So we acknowledge the Holy Ministry appointed by God for the spread of the Gospel and the edification of His Church.

Here is the section from A Song of Faith (2006) more fully. It is a snapshot of the current expectations we have for ministry as a whole church.

> We are each given particular gifts of the Spirit.
> For the sake of the world,
> > God calls all followers of Jesus to Christian ministry.
> In the church,
> > some are called to specific ministries of leadership,
> > both lay and ordered;
> > some witness to the good news;
> > some uphold the art of worship;
> > some comfort the grieving and guide the wandering;
> > some build up the community of wisdom;
> > some stand with the oppressed and work for justice.
> To embody God's love in the world,
> > the work of the church requires the ministry and
> > > discipleship
> > of all believers.

Our dilemma is not for a lack of trying. Our denominational committees do struggle with definitions and roles in ministry, and with the nature of ministry itself. We simply have not arrived at an expressed doctrine yet. Theology is the umbrella that encompasses nature, purpose, and meaning; it would be the place for an articulation of the necessity of ministry.

Finally, consideration of doctrines associated with ministry will help the church into a clearer definition of ordained ministry, distinct from but alongside diaconal ministry and designated lay ministry. That will help untangle some of the confusion about roles, settlement, functions, wearing of stoles, use of the honorific "reverend," and other sources of tension between members of the order of ministry and in the wider church. Clarity truly helps. Clarity can smooth ruffled feathers, and that will help us be more effective overall. In his discussion of the nature of ordination in *Touchstone*, Rob Fennell writes:

> What I want to suggest is that we find ways to restate the dignity and worth of ordained ministry within The United Church of Canada.... *Dignity*...is not a matter of accruing to oneself a special set of powers. Rather, it is the recognition that there is an office within the Church of Jesus Christ that is distinctive and effective within the mission that God is enacting in the world. *Worth* is also a carefully chosen term; in the midst of much uneasiness and discouragement among our ordained ministers, we ought to assure them that they are needed, wanted, and have a unique place in our Church. We need to say aloud that their dedication and public commitment to serve Christ's mission has earned our respect and appreciation. This is not to suggest that other forms of ministry have lesser dignity and worth. It is simply to say that it is right and good for us to continue to welcome and value ordination.[19]

Priest, pastor, prophet: 1 Timothy echoes through the generations. Let us not neglect the gift that is in them, given to them with the laying on of hands by the council of elders (based on 1 Timothy 4:14). Robust discussions about the theology of ministry will help us sort out not what ministers do, but what ministry *is*.

How Does It Preach?

This theological concept is of particular interest to members of presbyteries because they have an acute awareness of roles in The United Church of Canada. Presbyteries, according to *The Manual* definition (C.1), consist of "members of the order of ministry and lay members of the United Church." Presbyteries carry oversight of congregations, and of ministers. If tensions related to the roles of lay people and clergy will surface anywhere, they are most likely to surface in presbytery gatherings.

Presbytery, then, is an important venue for this reflection; I would offer this sermon at a regular meeting, rather than an occasion such as a covenanting service where a particular minister and congregation are the focus.

The passage from Ephesians would come as no surprise in a reflection on ministry, but the Jeremiah passage, although it can be associated with call, would be unexpected. I suggest it to express the deep anguish many people have about their ministerial identity. Many ministers also would resonate with the powerful prophetic story, and with strong calls to mission and witness. I would read it twice: it's short, and it's important.

To preach this sermon in a Sunday morning worship service would not seem right. The focus is too finely tuned on the clergy. Although there are pastoral charges in which the local ministerial identity or theology of ministry are anxiety inducing, this sermon seems too distant from the congregation's pastoral needs to bring to the general worshipping public.

It would be a good idea to consult with the chair of the presbytery before offering the sermon. The chair might suggest a discussion period, or a guided study of a denominational document related to ministry.

The tone changes through the course of the sermon. It begins with an apologetic note at the loss of a church and the outcome for the minister. As I describe the nature of ministry, the tone becomes drier. Then with Jeremiah it becomes quite passionate, emotional even, as I describe why we need ministers. It settles down again as I talk about the priesthood of all believers, and toward the end I recreate an energetic tone with Trinitarian theology and the adventure into which we are called.

There is some repetition, which is a rhetorical tool, and I draw on the images of our hands, of a tree with lovers' initials, and of the necessity to be seen. Hands are part of ordination and commissioning. Luther loved God. And sometimes, in our frantic urge to look for function, we do not see the necessity of our order of ministry.

Sample Sermon

What's on Your Hands?

I'm glad to see you. You might think that's an aphorism: of course, I ought to begin a sermon with peers that way, and we have had quite a day. Truly, though, I am glad to see you. We need to be seen to each other. We need to be seen by each other.

This morning we sold one of our churches. We voted on the legal requirements to let one of our pastoral charges go ahead with a sale. We are partners. Our presbytery acknowledged that the forthcoming amalgamation brings fresh possibilities. But we didn't talk about my colleague, our friend in Christ, the minister in that congregation. We didn't, partly because we have processes that govern pastoral relations. Those processes have a private nature to them. We trust that those processes will be Spirit-led and helpful. We also didn't talk about my colleague, our friend in Christ, the minister in that congregation, Rose, because we are embarrassed. At least, I am. One among us is affected in a particular way, and we don't know what to say.

I want you to know I talked with Rose about this sermon. We collaborated a bit. I would never discuss someone's business out loud without permission, or tell a story that wasn't mine, or call out a colleague from the pulpit. I want you to know that so you can relax into a listening mode, and rest assured I'm not going to talk about you—unless I already asked!

We are fortunate to have ministers among us. We have some solid ministries in this presbytery, and we celebrate that. We are fortunate to have ministers among us—and yet the church cannot run without ministers. The church cannot run without ministers. I don't mean that the committees would fall apart, or the doors would stay shut on Sunday mornings, or the outreach work wouldn't go on. I don't mean the functioning of our mission, Christ's mission. I mean that in the nature of who we are as church, we cannot run without ministers.

It's not because those of us who are clergy are different—well, not any more than any one of us is different from another—but rather that the partnership we have, clergy and lay, requires both partners.

Our congregation made changes recently. I want to acknowledge that although every pastoral situation and every ministry person is different, I have some experience of change and loss, too. Rose, you are not alone. We are not alone. When our transition committee came to interview me for the changes they would propose, they asked about lay leadership. They expected me to say it's hard to recruit people. My answer was that we are a partnership. I value the leadership in the church and I think of them as partners. They get to come and go through the three-year terms they serve, and I get to work with different individuals during different terms.

The partnership we have, clergy and lay, requires both partners. The World Council of Churches puts it this way:

> In order to fulfill its mission, the Church needs persons who are publicly and continually responsible for pointing to its fundamental dependence on Jesus Christ, and thereby provide, within a multiplicity of gifts, a focus of its unity. The ministry of such persons, who since very early times have been ordained, is constitutive for the life and witness of the Church.

It goes on to say:

> All members of the believing community, ordained and lay, are interrelated. On the one hand, the community needs ordained ministers. Their presence reminds the community of the divine initiative, and of the dependence of the Church on Jesus Christ, who is the source of its mission and the foundation of its unity. They serve to build up the community in Christ and to strengthen its witness. In them the Church seeks an example of holiness and loving concern. On the other hand, the ordained ministry has no existence apart from the community. Ordained ministers can fulfill their calling only in and for the community. They cannot dispense with the recognition, the support and the encouragement of the community.[20]

Some of you have worked in the World Council of Churches. Several among us have attended General Assemblies. Many of us pray for sister churches globally because of the prayer roster the WCC makes available.

The writer of Ephesians has more poetic language. Rose read the full passage a moment ago. Here's the nugget: "The gifts [Christ] gave were that some would be apostles, some prophets, some evangelists, some pastors and teachers, to equip the saints for the work of ministry" (4:11). To equip the saints for the work of ministry—that's our part. Rose and I and the rest of your ordered friends sitting in these pews, resting assured that I'm not talking about them—that's our part.

We get to read scripture nearly every day to see what kind of situation *you're* in. We get to visit you in your homes and workplaces and coffee shops and inquire about the state of your soul. We get to hold the little ones at baptism and see their grandparents' eyes well up with tears. We get to bring the experience of the historic church to the issues of our day, even if it is to determine we need fresh tools. We are supposed to know the historic, orthodox, ecumenical faith as well as current concepts and invite you to explore them. We have the pleasure—yes, it's a pleasure—to write you monthly reports so you know how our part of the partnership is going and why what you are doing is vital. We get to do church administration and biblical interpretation, maintain the well-being of the congregation, and represent the congregation, too, as well as the church of Christ. And if this sounds heavy, we also absorb the wrongs and hurts done by our sisters and brothers whose misdemeanours affect the ministry we have, even beyond denomination and geography. Every time a minister is accused of sexual or financial misdemeanour, we take a hit.

And you know what? This partnership is so meaningful, so sacred, that we get to take it on for life. Even after I retire I'll be a member of presbytery. I'll be a member of presbytery till I die, and you send me singing across Jordan.

Look at your hands for a moment, your own hands in your lap. Two of those pairs of hands signed the sale of our church. Some of your hands are fresh from getting the dishes done, and they have that lovely lemon fragrance. Some of your hands are gnarled from pounding nails in church builds 50 years ago. One of you has purple nail polish from a Sunday school child. Somebody's hand put the water on that little one's head while the grandparents wept for joy. Somebody cleaned up the grape juice that stained the communion cloth last week. Two of you—you know who they are—two of you laid on hands last year at Conference when our candidate was ordained. I say "our candidate" because although he's from the other side of the presbytery, we're all in this together. We are inextricably twined together and we need each other. Specifically today, let me say we need our ministers; I mean in the nature of who we are as church, we need our ministers.

We need to be seen to each other. We need to be seen by each other. Here's a word:

> If I say, "I will not mention [God],
>   or speak any more in [God's] name,"
> then within me there is something like a burning fire
>   shut up in my bones;
> I am weary with holding it in,
>   and I cannot.

Here it is again:

> If I say, "I will not mention [God],
>   or speak any more in [God's] name,"
> then within me there is something like a burning fire
>   shut up in my bones;
> I am weary with holding it in,
>   and I cannot.

Yes, that's Jeremiah (20:9). He had a call, didn't he? Facing down the powers that were, speaking in the name of the God who is holy, a lonely voice calling out that this is no local god, no national god whose name burned in his bones like a fire. This was the God who created the alpenglow in the morning and the aurora borealis at night. This was the God who saw the tears in the grandparents' eyes and the bifida in the baby's spine. This was the God who heard the soldiers tear down the house, and who created even the stones that made up the walls of the prison cell in which Jeremiah sat.

Now look at your hands again. You've done that, haven't you? You've held those hands over your own lips so you wouldn't speak the truth, but the Spirit of God burned in your bones and you opened your lips and you spoke. If you are one of our ministers in this room, you did it because you had no choice. You had to show up at the surgery. You had to answer the nasty e-mail. You had to sing at the funeral, even though no one else would go; you went because you got to bury the man who had offended everybody else in his life, and you were the only one there, you and the undertaker. And you sang because if you didn't your bones would burn with fire.

This is why we need ministers. Ministers have to show up.

We are Protestants with a line in our family tree that comes from Luther, but what we see carved into the bark on that tree is not always accurate. We can carve initials on a tree and come back and remember an old flame, a lost lover, or a sunny day. We can look on the family tree and read *sola scriptura,* the authority of scripture, or *sole fide,* justification by faith alone. But likely we will also read "the priesthood of all believers" on that tree bark, and we may not remember what that lover of God really meant.

The priesthood of all believers is a call to bring the sacred nature of God's presence to all we do, to everything that any of us does. Rather than bringing everyone inside the church to do what the priest does all day, we use our hands to unlatch the door and take the blessing of vocation *outside* the church to the various responsibilities and opportunities for mission throughout the world. We use our hands with blessing to help the schoolchildren tie their shoes as they leave our classroom. We use our hands with blessing to keep the accounts in the business where we work. We use our blessed hands to get the garden in so the Brussels sprouts will be ready for market. Luther didn't mean everyone should do what priests do. We're not all priests, or pastoral ministers, and we shouldn't be. We need our ministers; I mean in the nature of who we are as church, we need our ministers.

I have to tell you, it's humbling to be about equipping the saints. I have to pay such close attention: I remember your names, I inquire after your families, I send a card with a prayer when your work takes you away for extended periods. It's humbling to know so much. That doesn't sound right: it's humbling to be *told* so much. It's not that I know so much as in I'm terrifically smart or an encyclopedic witness; we ministers among you get to receive you in pastoral care. We bring you confidence in that pastoral care, not a conviction that is arrogant or unquestioning, but confidence, an assurance that you are in the presence of Christ's minister. Holy Man, that is humbling.

And it makes me proud, proud in the good sense, that the ministry that is my job—but not my job, it's my life—is worth it for you. And that's a good thing, because it is difficult. Ministry is time consuming. We meet all kinds of people. I mean all kinds. We pray in ugly situations. Sometimes we are the only one remembering that Christ is in the room, and it may not be a welcome word we bring. Then like Jeremiah we decide how much fire we can take in our bones.

We need to be seen to each other. We need to be seen by each other. We are a partnership.

When I was in seminary one of the students with whom I shared the common kitchen was a rabbi. We often chatted together over steaming vegetables and open textbooks. He was chopping the ends off Brussels sprouts one day while talking about the deep pleasure of time to study. He spoke of it as a calling. "Catherine," he said, "when you're out there in the field, think of me occasionally. Remember that I told you, you should be a rabbi. Read the books. Teach the people. Get them to read the books, too."

So here I am, your resident rabbi, to tell you this, after all my reading, all my conversations with Rose, all my time carving initials into that tree with my hands: We need to be seen to each other. We are on an adventure together in this faith-filled life we share, and we need to be seen by each other. Amen.

—*Catherine Faith MacLean*

I wrote this sermon after a presbytery meeting, and changed the minister's name for publication. I wish I had offered to preach it then.

Chapter 11
Baptism

"We Want to Get Her Done"

The Doctrinal Concept

You are in the church office. The telephone rings.

"Is this the reverend?" asks a voice you do not recognize.

"Yes," you reply.

"My name is Sandra Smith. Harry and I have an 11-month-old daughter, Sasha. We want to get her done. My parents go to a church in Saint John, and they have been encouraging us to get her baptized. When can you do it for us?"

Most of us in ministry, maybe all of us who have served one or more congregations, have received some variation of that phone call. Likely we have had more than one. It light of that, why would one want to think about, and speak about, the doctrine of baptism?

To begin with, The United Church of Canada, in concert with most (though not all) Christian denominations, recognizes baptism as a sacrament.[21] "Visible signs [or forms] of an invisible grace" was how Augustine of Hippo described sacraments in general. John Calvin thought of sacraments as a way in which God used physical things to confirm God's grace toward us and love for us. God's promises were sure, Calvin asserted, but our human frailties required such signs to strengthen a faith that would otherwise be too weak.[22] Without agreeing with Calvin's more pessimistic view of human capacities, and with a strong emphasis on "the presence of the holy in the world," A Song of Faith captures this same sense when it calls the two sacraments the United Church recognizes—baptism and communion—"visible signs of the grace of God [in which…] ordinary things of life—water, bread, wine—point beyond themselves to God and God's love." The sacraments generally, in our denominational tradition, are a place where we see and celebrate God's love for us. Such is certainly the case for baptism.

Historically in the United Church, we have also seen baptism as the sacrament that, in a formal and outward way, makes one part of the Christian church. We share that view with many Christian denominations.

Different faith statements we have made, beginning with the

doctrinal statement adopted in 1925 as part of the original Basis of Union, have had different emphases in relation to baptism. Article XVI of the Twenty Articles of Doctrine highlighted the idea of baptism as that which "signified and sealed our union to Christ and participation in the blessings of the new covenant." The 1940 Statement of Faith, in section X. The Sacraments, noted of baptism that it made us "members of the Christian society" and that the use of water "signifies God's cleansing from sin and an initial participation in the gifts and graces of the new life." The United Church's most recent doctrinal statement, A Song of Faith (2006), emphasizes explicitly the initiating operation of God's grace in baptism, something implicitly understood in earlier faith statements. A Song of Faith also states clearly that baptism is the ritual by which an individual becomes part of the church. Finally, it picks up several other traditional emphases of the broad Christian community, namely, "our rebirth in faith" and God's cleansing power.

Nonetheless, in developing a theological explication that runs beyond short phrases and images from doctrinal statements, several issues arise. These issues face most Christian denominations, especially in Canada, the United States, and Western Europe. First, scripture offers a number of concepts or images related to baptism, but it does not put forward one main one. The different concepts and images in the United Church's doctrinal statements are all drawn from scripture. The New Testament does not contain a clear indication of what a baptism service or liturgy looked like in the first few generations of the church's life. In the passages that mention baptism, some features are present most of the time, but there is no uniformity.

Given the relative independence of early Christian congregations from one another, and the sometimes significant geographic distances between them, there was likely considerable variation. The 20th-century American liturgical scholar James F. White asserted that the New Testament contains five major themes or concepts related to baptism and acknowledged the existence of other themes or concepts, in his view more minor.[23] Other scholars, while agreeing about some of the five, would emphasize additional or different concepts in working out a New Testament understanding of baptism. In summary, scripture does not give us a clear, neat, and consistent picture of baptism, in terms of either theology or ritual. Baptismal understandings developed over time, and liturgies for baptism likewise became established over time.

Second, significant divisions exist in contemporary Christianity concerning the appropriate age for baptism. For some denominations, the only proper subjects for baptism are adults who can make a faith commitment for themselves; other denominations baptize people of any age, including infants. Within any United Church congregation of significant size, one will find congregational members who reject, for theological reasons, the baptism of infants and small children, and congregational members who support it. On this question, the New Testament again offers no guidance.

Most scholars agree that no definitive evidence exists for the baptism of infants and children prior to the early third century. Some argue that New Testament passages that speak of "households" being baptized indicate clearly that children were baptized. Other scholars, though, conclude from the requirement for people to "repent" of their sins prior to baptism (see, for example, Acts 2:38) and the fact that no passage makes it explicitly clear that anyone other than adults was baptized in New Testament times that children were not baptized until much later. On both sides of this question the notorious argument from silence is made. One group asserts that because one cannot find in the New Testament a prohibition against the baptism of children, obviously children were baptized. The other side argues that because one cannot find explicit reference to the baptism of children, children definitely were not baptized in the New Testament era.

More significant for this question, however, are historical developments and their accompanying theological understandings that have led different denominations to different practices. "Believers only" baptism arose among some of the Protestant groups as a result of the Reformation of the 16th century. That point of view was rejected by other Christian denominations. These developments have far more influence on current thinking and practice than anything one could find in the New Testament.

Third, while the United Church, in company with many other Protestant denominations, has been clear that people are encompassed fully by God's love with or without baptism, both "popular theology" and the formal theological understandings of some other Christian denominations have led a number of United Church members to believe that without baptism there is no possibility of a right or a saving relationship with God. Both of us, in asking people who have come to us seeking to have a child baptized why they wished to do so, have had some version of the following response: "So the baby won't go to hell if something happens."

There are conflicting theological understandings about baptism within the denomination, not to mention in the wider Christian community. How a person understands baptism, in relation to God's grace and an individual's eternal welfare, will influence that person's understanding of God and, quite likely, other aspects of their "personal creed"—the collection of "I believe" statements, positive or negative, that every active Christian holds.

Fourth, in an ever more secularized Canada, baptism is increasingly separated from the Christian church, at least in its institutional form. I still recall my astonishment in the late 1990s when a ministerial colleague recounted an advertisement in his local newspaper from a retired Baptist minister who was willing (for a fee) to come and do a home baptism for parents who wished to have one for their child. That said, these days, in at least some Canadian provinces, one can have marriages and baptisms presided over by officiants of the Church of All Seasons, an organization that appears to exist solely for the purpose of providing such services at a location of one's choice.

The separation of baptism from a close connection to the Christian church factors into the motivation of some people to have their children baptized. In addition to the scenario with which this chapter began, and more troubling, are those who seek to have their children baptized as an opportunity for a party with family and friends. Now, there is nothing wrong with having a large gathering to celebrate the baptism of a family member. The baptism of a child or of an adult is an event to celebrate. But for an increasing number of people, the baptismal ritual during a church service has become almost a thing to be endured in order to get to the important part of the day, the party that follows.

Scripture for Preaching

Galatians 3:23–29
Now before faith came, we were imprisoned and guarded under the law until faith would be revealed. Therefore the law was our disciplinarian until Christ came, so that we might be justified by faith. But now that faith has come, we are no longer subject to a disciplinarian, for in Christ Jesus you are all children of God through faith. As many of you as were baptized into Christ have clothed yourselves with Christ. There is no longer Jew or Greek, there is no longer slave or free, there is no longer male and female; for all of you are one in Christ Jesus. And if you belong to Christ, then you are Abraham's offspring, heirs according to the promise.

Why Is This Doctrine Important?

Baptism, accurately understood, exudes the grace of God. It would be hard to find a better, or briefer, expression of this conviction than in A Song of Faith:

> Before conscious thought or action on our part,
>   we are surrounded by God's redeeming love....
> Baptism signifies the nurturing, sustaining,
>   and transforming power of God's love
>   and our grateful response to that grace.

Baptism is not something that we "earn." It is not a reward for good conduct. It comes to us as grace. In the United Church's service book,

Celebrate God's Presence, the several options for an opening Statement of Purpose in the baptismal liturgy share an emphasis on understanding baptism as a celebration of God's grace.

In *What's Theology Got to Do with It?,* Anthony B. Robinson, an American theologian who taught for a while at Emmanuel College in Toronto, argues, correctly, that baptism is about both grace and response. He points out, though, that in the contemporary church the range of activities and tasks many of us take on mean that the "response" aspect of baptism is well covered. Indeed, we may fall into the trap, and experience the pitfalls, of believing that everything is up to us, an early-21-century form of "works righteousness." Response to the gift of God's grace in baptism ought not be avoided, let alone ignored. But Robinson asserts that our present context calls for a reminder that baptism is equally about grace, God's grace.[24] This message runs counter not only to tendencies in today's church but also to the wider culture of our society.

Baptism is the sacrament by which we formally recognize that a person becomes part of the Christian community. The importance of this doctrine goes beyond that, however. Because baptism comes to us as grace, the community that is the church should be one without distinctions of status. While our society makes distinctions on all sorts of bases, the church as the body of Christ should be a community to which we bring varieties of gifts, but not differences of valuing, whether concerning ourselves or others. Paul had much to say about the church as just such a place. The passage in 1 Corinthians 12—where Paul writes about the varieties of gifts the Spirit bestows and uses the human body as an analogy for the church to say that all parts or gifts are equally valuable and necessary—may come most quickly to mind. That said, a similar theme runs though Romans 12:1–8 and Ephesians 4:1–16. In Galatians 3:23–29, Paul speaks about the community of the baptized as one in which the traditional distinctions of his society were swept aside. Paul encouraged the church of his day to understand itself as a community radically different from its society; such an understanding of baptism would make us equally countercultural in our time.

Two themes of the early church's understanding of baptism were union in Christ and becoming part of the church. Our denomination's understanding of baptism has acknowledged these dimensions. Giving attention to them might strengthen the links, both to God and to one another, of contemporary members of our denomination.

Finally, we have this sacrament as part of our tradition. In our denomination, we place responsibility on congregational governing bodies to approve baptismal requests. Moreover, congregations are responsible for providing nurture and support for those baptized in their midst as these individuals grow in their understanding of, and commitment to, a life of Christian discipleship. But those aspects of our governance structure, and of the responsibility each of us takes on when someone is baptized in our midst, raise questions.

What understandings are present in the congregation, guiding it in its responsibilities toward those baptized? On what basis does the governing body respond to the requests for baptism the congregation's minister receives? Some wrestling with our theological understanding of baptism becomes crucial.

In addition, it is pastorally important to address this area. What theological understandings guide members of the congregation in their thinking about baptism? How does their theological view of baptism influence their understanding of, to name only a few areas, God, grace, and last things?

How Does It Preach?

The first question is what aspects of baptism to highlight in a "teaching sermon" about baptism. Each year on the first Sunday after Epiphany, a gospel passage recounting the baptism of Jesus occurs in the Revised Common Lectionary. That is one occasion to preach on baptism, and it is often suggested in lectionary-based worship resources. A focus on Jesus' baptism as the inauguration of his ministry would fit with seeing baptism as the beginning of the ministry of each Christian. Another theme is Jesus' acceptance of God's grace. I have preached on baptism on the first Sunday after Epiphany on more than one occasion, using one of the accounts of Jesus' baptism.

However, for a focus on the nature of the community created by baptism and a heavier emphasis on God's grace, other passages come to mind. I believe that Anthony Robinson is correct that most of us in the church are quite task-oriented and therefore have the "response" part of baptism quite clearly in mind. So the sermon that follows focuses on baptism as an example of God's grace, with attention to the nature of the community that is created. It also challenges the popular theology that sees baptism as necessary for salvation or a right relationship with God.

I have chosen Galatians 3:23-29 as the scripture lesson. Verse 28—"There is no longer Jew or Greek, there is no longer slave or free, there is no longer male and female; for all of you are one in Christ Jesus"—will likely be familiar to members of the congregation. A number of New Testament scholars believe Paul is quoting part of an early Christian baptismal liturgy in that verse.

I would begin with a baptism-related illustration that enables me to move on to focus on baptism as a place where God's grace is operative, or with a discussion of Galatians 3. In either case, I want the congregation to begin thinking about baptism as a time in which we experience genuine grace, a grace that then calls forth response on our part. If a baptism is taking place when one is preaching such a sermon, some strong connections can be made. God's grace comes to us in baptism not as a recognition of what we have done, nor as a reward for faithfulness, but simply because we are. In a society built on the concept that what we have we have earned by dint of our own hard work and abilities, the idea of grace, or gift—whether from God or from a human being—is a radical one. This idea, in our current context, needs to be stressed.

I would then use the Galatians 3 passage to have the congregation think about the kind of community that baptism, when we respond at our best, creates. It is a countercultural community in which the usual societal distinctions (and their accompanying "valuing") do not hold. Both historical examples and contemporary realities can be pointed to.

In reflecting on what it means to be a community created by baptism, I would also want the congregation to think about the kind of care they show for one another. Such care flows from the grace that we have received. If the sermon is being preached in the context of a baptism, the care for, and support of, the person being baptized could be noted. After all, baptismal liturgies in the United Church assume that baptism usually takes place in the context of communal worship. Those liturgies provide for members of the congregation to pledge aloud their support for those being baptized.

That support unquestionably includes helping in the Christian formation of those who have been baptized, but it is broader than that. Illustrations can be drawn from the life of the congregation or from Christian history showing church members exercising care toward other members of the congregation. These underline the sense that we always have such an obligation toward other members of the community. Stories drawn from the recent history of the congregation will particularly linger in your hearers' memories, and in many congregations, publicly known examples would come to mind. Be sensitive, though, to anything that would be confidential or potentially embarrassing.

I would conclude such a sermon with a reminder of who and whose we are.

Sample Sermon

Reflections on Baptizing Kittens

One Sunday when I was four years old, several babies were baptized during the Sunday morning service. The event made a significant impression on me. That evening, the minister and his family came to dinner at my grandmother's farm, where my family was also present. After dinner, the adults gathered in the parlour to talk. The minister's son, who was seven, and I quickly found that activity rather boring. So I asked my aunt, who lived on the farm, if I could take him to the kitchen to see Old Mother Cat and her three kittens. She smiled and said I could. We headed to the kitchen where, behind the wood stove, we found Old Mother Cat, as she was known, and her trio of four-day-old kittens. We picked up each one, tiny balls of incredibly soft fur, eyes still tightly shut.

I do not now recall which of us had the idea, but it occurred to one of us that if baptism was a good thing for babies, it must be an equally good and important thing for kittens. By what means I do not remember, though perhaps it was by virtue of his father's occupation, we agreed that the minister's son would baptize each kitten, while I would hold and present each one for baptism. So he climbed up on the kitchen counter, got a small bowl from the cupboard, and proceeded to fill it with water from the kitchen tap. It was agreed that I would get the kittens, one by one, from beside Old Mother Cat, since she knew me and always readily allowed me to pick up her kittens. I duly presented each kitten, stating the name that we had agreed upon. He then took the kitten from me and very carefully put a small bit of water on the kitten's head. I returned that kitten to Old Mother Cat and picked up the next one.

After we had finished baptizing all three, we emptied the water bowl into the sink and raced into the parlour to tell everyone what we had done. Upon hearing that we had "baptized the kittens," my aunt, for whom her cats were like children, headed speedily to the kitchen to check on Old Mother Cat and the kittens. I suspect she was somewhat unsure just what our ministrations might have entailed.

This story has a footnote I should share. We had chosen to name one kitten after each of us; the third one we called "Rings" for the pattern of rings in the fur on his tail. It did not occur to either of us to check on the sex of each kitten prior to baptizing them. Even if we had, to an unskilled eye, determining the sex of a four-day-old cat is not easy on the basis of a quick anatomical examination. Two cats—named after the minister's son and me. We had a fifty-fifty chance of being correct. We achieved those odds. The one named after the minister's son turned out to be male. But the kitten named John gave birth to a number of kittens during her lengthy life and was known around the farm as Johnny Girl.

So, what possessed the two of us to baptize kittens that evening? We could have just played with the kittens for a while before moving on to some other activity while the adults chatted away. From the perspective of many years later, I do not know what was going through my four-year-old mind or his seven-year-old one. But at some level I think, or at least I want to imagine, that we had understood the baptism that morning as an expression of God's love for the children who had been baptized. Since we had also been taught that God made and loved "all things large and small,"[25] it made sense that baptism was an appropriate means of demonstrating God's love for these three kittens.

I would like to think that that is how we thought about the baptism of the kittens. And I may be giving us a good deal more credit for theological thinking than I ought! But had we thought that way, it would have been good theology.

Why do we baptize in our denomination? When I speak here of baptizing, I do not just mean baptizing babies or small children. I mean baptizing, whether we are talking about a nine-week-old baby girl or a 90-year-old man. Whenever we baptize someone, we, as a church, are asserting a number of things.

First, we are saying that baptism is an act of grace, of God's grace, to us and for us. We may see this reality more clearly when the individual being baptized is an infant or a small child. We do not ask a child to do something or to be something in advance of being baptized. We baptize the child as a sign of God's all-encompassing and redeeming love, a love that, as the baptismal liturgy for children found in an earlier United Church service book put it, has surrounded each child from that child's beginning.[26] But whether the person being baptized is an infant, a young child, or an adult, we do not believe, as a denomination, that the love of God begins with the action of baptism or that the individual being baptized was "less loved" by God prior to baptism.

Baptism does make a difference in the lives of individuals if we all take seriously the promises we make at the time of a baptism, and I shall come to the difference baptism makes later in this sermon. But the difference does not arise because the person being baptized suddenly receives God's love and did not have it before. Baptism is, among other things, a recognition of the gift of God's love for the person being baptized, a love freely given, before we do anything to earn that love. It is grace. The United Church's most recent statement of faith, A Song of Faith, captures that sense with its claim that "Before conscious thought or action on our part, we are surrounded by God's redeeming love.... Baptism signifies the nurturing, sustaining, and transforming power of God's love and our grateful response to that grace." Yes, we do respond to that grace of God. And we should respond. But we respond to what we have first been given.

Second, like most Christian denominations, we understand baptism to be the means by which each of us becomes, in a formal way, a part of the church community. We certainly think that the people we baptize—whatever their age—were part of the church community before their baptism. But their baptism is the act by which we recognize and celebrate that reality. Baptism is the sacrament that marks the inclusion of the individual in our church community even if we have seen that child or that adult as part of our community for some time before they were baptized. It is through this ritual act that we understand a person to become, in a formal way, part of the body of Christ, for when we talk about the church, we are talking about the body of Christ.

This assertion that baptism makes us part of the body of Christ, or the church community, leads to a third dimension. When we speak about baptism as recognizing the individual as a part of the church community, we also believe it is a particular kind of community one joins via baptism. Here is where baptism should make an objective difference. When we take seriously the promises we make and the nature of the church community created by baptism, then being baptized does make a difference, an objective difference, in the lives of those who are baptized.

In his letter to the Galatians, Paul asserts that baptism was being "clothed...with Christ" or, to express the matter differently, becoming part of the body of Christ. For those who have thus put on Christ, or become part of the body of Christ via baptism, "there is no longer Jew or Greek, there is no longer slave or free, there is no longer male and female; for all of you are one in Christ Jesus."

Now that particular verse—Galatians 3:28—often gets quoted by itself, and we then lose the connection to the surrounding verses in which that one verse is set. This verse gets quoted because it makes such a strong claim for equality. In Paul's world, those three pairs of human identifiers represented the three major ways in which people were divided or classified—Jew or Greek (in other words, Jew or non-Jew, or Jew or Gentile, as one would find the terms in the Bible), slave or free, male or female. These groups had very different status levels. In the Jewish world in which Paul had grown up, Jew was superior to Greek, free was superior to slave, and male was superior to female. When I say "superior," I mean that in that society, the favoured or superior party had a higher status or value.

But in this passage, Paul makes a different assertion. He declares that for those who are baptized, these basic divisions of the ancient world no longer hold. The sense that baptism symbolized one's entry into a community where all had the same status did not hold beyond the confines of the early Christian community. However, even if one assumes that such a declaration had effect only in terms of the interaction within the Christian community, the claim is nonetheless a radical one. Becoming part of that community meant these societal distinctions no longer held. Wow!

Some biblical scholars think that Paul quotes here from an early Christian baptismal liturgy, that these words come from the baptismal service used in some early Christian churches. That may well be the case. Even if these words do not come from Paul himself, and he quotes here from something the Christians in Galatia would have heard when they were baptized, Paul clearly approves of this sentiment.

Paul holds up this vision, he might have said this reality, for the Christians in Galatia. His words speak to us all, however, about what it means to be part of the Christian community. This community of Christ's body, of the church, is one in which all societal distinctions that separate us into categories are swept away. It is a community we enter by faith, not by virtue of status or gifts or accomplishments, and our entry is symbolized by baptism. In Paul's reminder, he both affirmed a reality and also sought to see that reality lived out. It is such a community that we are called to be.

To stress the lack of distinction between members in societal terms is not, I need to say, an indication that we all possess the same gifts. I can assure you that you do not want me working on your car! I have gifts, but mechanical aptitude is definitely not one of them. Paul also had much to say elsewhere about varieties of gifts, and about the community's need to have varied gifts among its membership. Valuing everyone equally, and not maintaining the status differences of the surrounding society, does not mean that everyone can do everything. What we need to do is to recognize and to use in the life of the church the varieties of gifts found among the membership, but to avoid valuing some people more highly than others on the basis of their gifts.

When we baptize a child, the child's parents or guardians make statements about their faith and also pledge their intention to raise their child in this faith tradition. We, the members of the congregation who witness that baptism, promise to help them to do so. When adults are baptized in our midst, we similarly pledge to support them in their ongoing journey of faith. By supporting people, of whatever age, in their journey of faith, we are talking about a community that gives mindful intention to the formation of its membership. We are talking about equipping the saints, to use another term from Paul. The faith tradition is not an end in itself. It is a resource for living lives that are consistent with the faith we profess, a means for helping us make sense of our lives, and an anchor in times of trouble.

A community entered by baptism where there is neither Jew nor Greek, slave nor free, male nor female is a community whose members care for and about one another. It was that very quality, the care and love that members exercised one for another, that made early Christian communities stand out in the first several centuries of Christianity's existence. Non-Christians observed that care and love and commented positively upon it.[27] This feature proved an unintended recruiting tool, as non-Christians, curious about the care exercised especially for other members of the church but also for people outside it, wanted to know more. Sometimes, in learning more, they chose to join.

This area of mutual care, which ought to be a mark of the community, is one where I think most congregations do quite well. I know that my mother, whose health declined significantly over the final decade of her life, was able to stay in her own home until the last few weeks of her life because a number of people from her village congregation did things for her. That situation serves always for me as a lived experience of the church as a place where members care for one another. That situation is replicated in many congregations.

But in thinking about Paul's comments, and their wider ramifications in terms of the kind of community we create, I remember a situation from the pair of congregations I served in the late 1980s. It strikes me as more powerful and more revealing of an even deeper dimension of this sense of community. In the lead-up to, and aftermath of, the decision of the 1988 General Council on the ordination of self-declared gays and lesbians, the congregations I then served had sharp and deep divisions on the matter.

Congregational meetings in both congregations took place in the months after that General Council. Those people troubled by the General Council decision sought to make clear their opposition, even as I and other congregational members were supportive of the General Council's action. A meeting in one congregation drew not only those who were regularly in attendance at Sunday worship but also a number of people whose affiliation with the congregation was "historic" by virtue of family links rather than marked by any active personal presence.

I observed during that meeting a marked difference in behaviour by those troubled by the General Council's decision who were active participants in the congregation compared with those who were not. The active members listened genuinely and respectfully to arguments put forth by those who agreed with what the General Council had done. They sought to understand why others with whom they worshipped week by week saw the matter differently. The latter group, consisting of those who considered themselves part of the United Church though they rarely if ever darkened the church door, had little interest in listening to anyone, and they exhibited not much care toward those who saw things differently.

I was struck by the care and concern shown by those who attended church regularly for those who disagreed with them about the General Council's decision. There was strong disagreement, but also care and concern within the body. And so it should be. Being part of the body of Christ, part of a community formed by faith and celebrated by baptism, does not mean that we will always agree. But being part of such a body should influence how we relate to those with whom we disagree.

Such a community—where social distinctions carry no weight and where care for one another constitutes the yoke we wear—also witnesses to our wider world, even as such practices did to the world during the early generations of the church's life. Such practices were highly countercultural in Paul's day, and they are no less so in ours. As we baptize people as a sign of God's grace and celebrate their presence as part of the body of Christ, may we seek to live according to such an ideal. And to the God by whose grace we become part of the body of

Christ, to Jesus the Christ, the sign of that grace and love, and to the Holy Spirit, by whose presence that grace is active in our world, be all honour, glory, and praise. Amen.

—*John H. Young*

This version of the sermon was written for this book, although it borrows heavily from a sermon preached some time ago on baptism.

Chapter 12
Holy Communion

"What Should We Do with the Leftover Elements?"

The Doctrinal Concept

The elder's question to me was a simple one. "What should we do with the leftover elements?" I had just finished the morning service in one of the congregations I was serving and had only a few minutes before I needed to head away to the service at a second congregation. I hesitated. I had my own thoughts. I did not know whether my thoughts would mesh with hers. If they did not, explaining what I thought, and why, would take longer than the few minutes I had.

Perhaps sensing my anxiety about getting on the road, she said, "It is just that the Sunday school children came into the kitchen while we were cleaning up. They wanted to eat the cubes of bread. Some of us thought that was okay, but others were not so sure. And they did rush the plates of leftover bread. It was quite chaotic. Perhaps we could discuss the matter at the next session meeting."

I agreed with her suggestion, although I do not recall the session discussing the matter. I do remember subsequently taking about it with a small group of elders, a conversation in which I described the different ways congregational members might see the elements. Given the spectrum of viewpoints present in that congregation, I made a suggestion about what might be a good way to dispose of the leftover elements.

At the time, I realized that how one understood communion, or the Lord's Supper, or the eucharist—the first two terms being far more common in the United Church than the third—and in particular how one understood Christ to be, or not to be, present in the sacrament, went a long way to determining what you judged it appropriate to do with the leftover elements. From a greater distance, I now see that the elder's question involved that issue as well as several others related to communion.

What might we say about communion from the doctrinal perspective? Like baptism, we have seen it as a sacrament in our denomination (see the brief discussion of sacraments in general in chapter 11, Baptism). Aside from the obvious difference in the elements used in the two sacraments, another significant point of contrast is that baptism is a "once for all time" event, while communion is repeatable. Indeed, in some denominations, communion is a part of almost every worship service. While A New Creed does not address the matter of sacraments, our three other formal doctrinal statements do. All three view communion as a sacrament that nourishes and strengthens us for our Christian journey, although that emphasis is stronger and more explicit in the earlier statements than in A Song of Faith.

We have always stressed the concept of an "open table," sometimes with a little excessive pride, in comparison to denominations that restrict reception of the sacrament to their members. We have always wanted to emphasize that the table was not "ours"; it is Jesus Christ who invites us to "his Table."[28]

Both historic and contemporary issues arise regarding a doctrinal understanding of communion. Perhaps the most obvious one historically is the matter of what the elements are understood to mean and to represent. This "problem" did not exist until the ninth century. Earlier generations of Christians used language of this sacrament that at points sounded very "realistic" in their description of how the elements represented "the body of Christ"; at other times their language was highly symbolic. Augustine represents a case in point. Sometimes, when he speaks of communion, his language implies that he sees the elements as the literal body and blood of Jesus. At other points, it seems to reflect a notion that the elements represent Jesus' body and blood only in a symbolic way.[29]

Transubstantiation—the concept that the communion elements become, during the prayer of consecration, the literal body and blood of Jesus—first surfaced as an idea in the ninth century. Two centuries later it had become the only ecclesiastically permissible way to understand communion in the Christian West. That prescribed uniformity came apart during the Protestant Reformation. A variety of perspectives developed, which became associated with different denominational traditions.

A theological understanding shared by all key Protestant Reformers— that we are saved by grace, through faith—ensured that the previously existing uniformity would come apart. The Christian church in the West, in the late medieval period, had concluded that the sacraments had the power to bring about, or "to effect," the grace that they signified, or represented. No thoughtful medieval theologian would have suggested the rather mechanistic view of the sacraments, and especially of communion, that developed especially in the popular understanding, namely, that the sacraments could "save you." However, such a view was widely held by the general populace. The Protestant Reformers, with their emphasis on a "saving" grace coming as a result of faith, rejected both transubstantiation and the accompanying view of the sacraments as "instruments" of salvation. The sacraments could strengthen and nourish us, they believed. But only grace, accessed through faith, could save us.

When the Reformers thought about communion, they interpreted the elements in various ways. Ulrich Zwingli, a founder of the Reformed tradition, thought of the communion elements as memorial signs. They helped us to "remember" Jesus' life, death, and resurrection; they reminded us of what he did for us. However, the elements were always and only bread and wine, nothing more and nothing less. John Calvin, on the other hand, while rejecting transubstantiation, believed that the elements became, in a spiritual way, the body and blood of Christ for us. Exactly how this happened, Calvin confessed he did not know. Calvin regularly demonstrated remarkable honesty by pursuing a theological matter as far as his mind would take him and then acknowledging he could go no further in his reasoning. Communion, he wrote, was something he experienced rather than something whose process he could explain.[30]

Both Calvin's view that Christ was present in the communion elements in a spiritual manner, and Zwingli's view that the elements carried no additional meaning or presence beyond being aids to help us remember, have co-existed in the United Church. Article XVI of the Twenty Articles of Doctrine lays out Calvin's perspective explicitly, in its language that we receive Christ's body and blood "after a spiritual manner." However, the sermons I remember hearing in my late teens and early 20s about communion, sermons to which I paid attention because I was trying to figure out the sacrament, generally suggested what I later learned was Zwingli's perspective.

These days, in a typical United Church congregation, the views of members as to what the elements represent run the gamut from transubstantiation to Zwingli's "memorialist" understanding. I am in no way suggesting that this range is wrong or bad. Rather, acknowledging it is to recognize a reality that is perhaps not surprising in an era where people are free to move from one denomination to another. Strict interpretations of 16th-century positions are probably not helpful. Calvin's hesitation to go beyond a certain point has much to commend it. At the same time, to work out a doctrinal understanding of communion, we must think through what we believe the elements represent and how.

Another question, with very distinct pastoral implications, is who is eligible to receive communion, or to put it in less legalistic language, who is welcome at the table. The United Church prides itself on having an "open table." But what does that mean? There is not complete uniformity here. An earlier practice, explicitly outlined in Article XVI of the Twenty Articles of Doctrine and found also in earlier liturgies, made clear that all who "make a credible profession of their faith in the Lord Jesus" were welcome at the table.[31]

In practice this invitation to the table was usually understood to include only those who had been baptized and who had made a formal profession of faith (been confirmed). However, neither the words of Article XVI nor the liturgy expressly named those steps. Therefore, at least some ministers welcomed to the table people who could say in their hearts, in response to the spoken words of invitation in the liturgy, that they professed Jesus as their Saviour and that they were willing to follow in his way. These ministers judged that such a response to that invitation, rather than either baptism or confirmation, was what made a person welcome at the table. Indeed, when the movement to allow children to receive communion prior to making a formal profession of faith grew to an irresistible force in the 1970s and the 1980s, more than a few congregational governing bodies justified "opening the table to children" on just such grounds. They concluded that the entry of all people to the table, regardless of age, should be on the basis of the individual responding to that invitation in the liturgy.

While efforts across Christian bodies to reach consensus on the relationship between baptism and "first communion" has generally seen baptism as the entry point to eligibility to receive communion, our own denominational practice, at least in some congregations, would be different. In those congregations all who considered themselves Christian, baptized or not, would be welcomed at the table. Although I can imagine it happening, I have yet to be present at a United Church worship service when the presider has indicated that only those who have been baptized may receive. In fact, what I have seen in some communion services is an emphasis first and foremost on hospitality. In one instance, buttressed by the understanding that Jesus Christ is a gracious and welcoming host and perhaps also that authority over worship falls within the purview of the congregation's governing body, the presider stressed that everyone present—seemingly no matter even whether one was Christian—was welcome to receive the elements. This particular pattern would have implications for our relationship with other Christian churches. How and whom we welcome to the table is a significant question in relation to a doctrinal understanding of communion.

A third issue is how we choose to distribute the communion elements. Historically, there have been two patterns in the United Church. Some congregations, following Methodist tradition, invited those who wished to receive to come, to kneel at the communion rail, and to be served by the minister and an elder. Other congregations, following Presbyterian and Congregationalist practice, had lay members (usually called elders in an early time) distribute trays of bread and grape juice to the ends of the pews, while those sitting in the pews served one another. In the years after church union, serving communion through the pews become the dominant way, though some congregations, especially in Newfoundland and Labrador, continued the earlier Methodist pattern. A more recent variation on that Methodist pattern has been to serve communion by having people come to the front of the church to receive by intinction (dipping a piece of bread into a chalice filled with grape juice or wine), the bread and the grape juice or wine being held by the presider and a lay leader.

Both methods of distributing the elements carry good theological meaning. Coming forward suggests a physical response to the invitation and is, perhaps, a symbol of our Christian journey. Receiving from our neighbour in the pew emphasizes the equality of the members of the body, the sense that we do function as Christ to one another. While one person, for the sake of order, presides at the table, each of us shares in distributing communion to our neighbour. A thoughtful theological student remarked in my presence, "Personally, I like the symbolism of going forward to receive communion, but that method also is very clergy centred." Thinking about a doctrinal understanding of communion includes thinking about what theological message one wants to convey in how one distributes the elements.

A final issue: in the United Church and in many other mainstream Protestant denominations, communion often had a penitential quality, at least until the last 30 years or so. Earlier communion liturgies in our denomination reflected this. It may have flowed from an emphasis on communion as the remembrance of Jesus' life, death, and resurrection. Tied in with this penitential aspect, and supported by a particular understanding of Paul's words that one ought not to partake of the communion elements unworthily (1 Corinthians 11:27–32), there developed a notion that one needed not only to confess one's sins but also to be in a "good state," or even a "holy state," to be worthy to receive the elements.

The idea that a person's worthiness should be a factor in receiving communion runs counter to other theological values found in this sacrament, most especially the emphasis on this sacrament as a sign of God's grace to us. Doctrinal thinking about communion needs to challenge this understanding. Indeed, we come to the table not because we are worthy but because we are in need, in need of the grace that it signifies.

Scripture for Preaching

1 Corinthians 11:23–26
For I received from the Lord what I also handed on to you, that the Lord Jesus on the night when he was betrayed took a loaf of bread, and when he had given thanks, he broke it and said, "This is my body that is for you. Do this in remembrance of me." In the same way he took the cup also, after supper, saying, "This cup is the new covenant in my blood. Do this, as often as you drink it, in remembrance of me." For as often as you eat this bread and drink the cup, you proclaim the Lord's death until he comes.

Why Is This Doctrine Important?

Beyond the practical matter of how the leftover elements are to be treated, attention to this doctrine could remove a potentially divisive aspect of worship life and deepen the spiritual life of some congregational members. It can strengthen the sense of community in a congregation, and thereby its life and outreach.

Communion, as a part of our worship and congregational life, is deeply meaningful for some, while it leaves others unmoved. The former often want it to happen more often; the latter, less often. I do not mean that observation to criticize either group. Preaching feeds some of us more than the sacrament of communion. Others find their spiritual depths more touched by music or another of the arts. But I have found more than a few people in the United Church unsure about communion. Why do we do this? What exactly do we believe about communion?

These people do not find communion especially fulfilling. Some even wonder if something is wrong with them, because others do find the sacrament a meaningful aspect of their worship and spiritual life. Preaching about this sacrament may provide background and new ways of thinking about communion, and could deepen the sacrament's meaning for more members of the congregation.

This chapter opened with an elder's question about what to do with the leftover elements. The question may seem trivial, but I have found that what one person regards as the logical thing to do can strike another as preposterous. I have had people responsible for cleaning up after communion pour the leftover grape juice down the sink and dump the leftover bread in the garbage. Since they held a Zwinglian position—it was bread and wine, it was never anything other than bread and wine, and its only purpose was to remind us that Jesus died and rose again—their action had a certain logic to it. I found that practice troubling, given my sense of what the communion elements represent. But a member of the congregation whose view of their substance was transubstantiation (though they might not have used the term) was horrified.

In the congregations I have served, I have seen the full range of understandings of what the elements are. For example, I have noted the Zwinglian position above. It is still commonly found in the United Church, would be the view of many Baptist groups, and was certainly held by many in the congregations I have served. Others in those congregations interpreted the elements as being the "real" body of Jesus Christ, an identification that is the formal position of the Roman Catholic Church. In that denomination, via what is called "transubstantiation," the elements are understood to be changed during the prayer of consecration into the real or actual body of Jesus Christ. While some views are more common than others, the United Church does not have one formal interpretation as to what the communion elements represent. So a didactic sermon that provides some history and talks about different ways in which people in the United Church may view the communion elements can be useful. It can open up discussion on some other points, such as how to consider the understanding and sensibilities of others.

In the discussion I had with the elders concerning the communion elements, I talked about the range of views present in the congregation. We reached several resolutions. Given that some members saw the elements as Christ's body and blood, we determined that everyone involved in serving the elements needed to treat them with great respect.

Those who regarded the elements as "memory aids" obviously did not feel the same need, but they could understand the point of not offending others. Another resolution was that I would take the remaining elements home after each communion, put the bread out on the ground where the birds who hung around our backyard would later consume it, and pour the grape juice out on the ground. That solution was definitely not the preferred option for one individual, who believed in transubstantiation, but it did reflect an ancient tradition of pouring out a libation to God. It was a tolerable second best to this elder's preferred option of having me consume the remaining elements before the worship service was complete.

Finally, communion, like baptism, is a sign of God's grace. We do not come to receive communion because we have earned it. We come because it is a sign of the grace we have received from God, a grace that we need. Communion can, like baptism, raise questions about the kind of community we are. Do we practise the "equality of value" that communion suggests ought to be our reality? It can be a fruitful reflection about who we are as a congregation to think about communion, about what it means to "do this in remembrance of me," in the context of our collective life as the body of Christ.

How Does It Preach?

A service with communion offers a good opportunity for a reflection on some aspect of this sacrament. As the discussion above suggests, much teaching about communion could be profitable. The gospels of Matthew, Mark, and Luke all have accounts of Jesus' last meal with his friends, so any of those passages could work well for a sermon that explored aspects of this sacrament. The goals of the teaching sermon would determine the appropriate passage.

For the sermon that follows, I chose Paul's account of what we sometimes call the "Words of Institution" in a communion liturgy. This passage from 1 Corinthians 11 is the earliest written account we have of communion, and it allows for reflection on what the celebration of the sacrament represents.

In preaching, I would set the relatively short passage from 1 Corinthians in its larger context. Paul is concerned about what he has heard regarding celebrations of the Lord's Supper in Corinth. I could have read 1 Corinthians 11:17–34; the entire passage deals with issues around communion in Corinth. But I chose the shorter reading because, in the context of a congregational worship service, the sermon will need to be shorter, especially if one is serving more than one congregation. The longer reading introduces some other challenging themes that I would not want to introduce unless I was also going to address them in the sermon. In addition, the shorter reading allows for a focused consideration of the sacrament itself.

Having made that choice, I do judge it important to set this short reading in its larger context in 1 Corinthians 11. One needs to say something about the size and meeting options for a congregation in ancient Corinth. Contemporary congregational members hear the word *church*, and most assume if not a building at least some sort of dedicated space for the congregation's activities. That view is not accurate; no dedicated space existed. The congregation would have met at a member's home. A preacher should also explain something of the social customs of the day. Those customs help clarify how the situation that so troubled Paul could arise.

Having decided on a sermon examining the sacrament itself—the grace it represents and the kind of community it helps to create—I would spend some time analyzing the passage. What does one make of the repeated reference to remember Jesus, especially because it appears to mean that we need to remember Jesus' death? What does it mean that the celebration of the sacrament proclaims Jesus' death "until he comes"? I would then talk about why Paul gives such attention to remembering Jesus' death. For Paul, Jesus' willingness to give himself over to death is a sign of God's grace. I would conclude by talking about the kind of community, both local and worldwide, that communion can create and sustain.

Sample Sermon

Do This in Remembrance of Me

There was trouble in Corinth. The Christian community there had divisions, divisions that showed up when they gathered for worship and the Lord's Supper. In response, Paul shares the tradition about communion that he had received and had earlier handed on to them. It represents the earliest account we have of what we now call the sacrament of Holy Communion or the Lord's Supper. In it Paul touches on some important themes for us to contemplate as we share the sacrament of communion.

By way of background, Paul has heard of divisions in the church and of what he regards as the scandalous situation responsible for creating them. When the Corinthian church gathered for worship, some had much food with which they gorged themselves, while others went hungry. As biblical scholar Richard Hays points out, it is hard for us to imagine how this could happen. Think about going to a church potluck—we would want to ensure that everyone had enough. But, as Hays observes, Christians in Corinth did not have a building in which to gather. They met in a private home, a home almost certainly belonging to one of the more well-to-do members of the congregation. Hays makes the point that in such a home it is likely that, after the social customs of the day, the host would have invited the more prominent and prosperous members to join him in a dining area, a space that would have accommodated fewer than a dozen. The other congregational members probably gathered in an anteroom. In the custom of the day, the food would have been richer and more plentiful in the dining area.[32]

Paul is appalled and angry. His anger arises from what he sees as a complete lack of understanding of the nature of the community that has come together as a result of Jesus' death and resurrection, a community formed in response to God's generous grace. That situation provides the background for today's reading from 1 Corinthians, a passage that contains what we would call the heart of a communion service, the words and actions of Jesus at that last meal he had with his friends.

Paul's account is short. He makes clear that he has not invented this pattern for communion. He declares that this tradition has been handed down from the beginning in what is still a very young religious tradition. It is, he tells them, what he "received from the Lord." It's hard to say whether Paul, who never met Jesus, meant that literally or rather meant that he had passed on what early Christians who had known Jesus said happened at that last meal. What is safe to say is that Paul's account represents early Christian practice. Paul also makes clear that he reiterates something here that he had told the Corinthian Christians earlier.

Several things stand out in this brief account, quite apart from the details of bread and cup. The first is that Christians undertake this sacrament to remember Jesus. The words "in remembrance of me" follow the sharing of both the bread and the cup. The final verse of the passage suggests strongly that what we are to remember when we partake of the sacrament is Jesus' death; Paul writes: "For as often as you eat this bread and drink the cup, you proclaim the Lord's death until he comes" (1 Corinthians 11:26).

Why would we want to remember Jesus' death when we partake of communion? It seems to make more sense that this event might remind us of his life and his teachings, as well as his death and his resurrection. For Paul, however, Jesus' death is important. That death and his subsequent resurrection are a sign of God's grace. Remembering a death is probably not what we like doing, though much hymnody associated with Jesus' passion and Good Friday does just that. For Paul, however, it is Jesus' death and resurrection that reveal and represent God's grace. Paul is not unique in having this view. The early church heavily emphasized Jesus' death and resurrection for the same reason. Given the link between Jesus' death and resurrection and God's grace, Paul's stress on remembering Jesus' death makes sense. We want, and need, to remember God's grace.

Paul is deeply troubled by the divisions in the Corinthian community because such divisions ought not to persist in a community that has received such grace. In a community that has received such grace, undeservedly received such grace, a new attitude should be present. Baptism, at its best, creates a countercultural community where society's distinctions are not preserved and where genuine care for other members of the community prevails. If baptism creates such a community, then communion nourishes and sustains it. But Paul's criticism here is that the sacrament that ought to nourish and strengthen the community, that ought to lead the members to care for one another, has done nothing to challenge the distinctions already present in Corinthian society. By not challenging those distinctions, the celebration of communion has become almost a mockery.

So what might Paul's thoughts here mean for us? We, too, need to remember that this sacrament, as is always true of a sacrament, is about grace, God's grace to us. All who profess faith in Jesus and want to follow in his way are invited to this table. We are invited whether we are short or tall, rich or poor, young or old, retired or still farming, cis or trans, single or in relationship. We are invited. We are invited to come, not because we are worthy but because we have a need, a need to be nourished and strengthened for our Christian journey.

This sacrament also reminds us that we are part of one body. We all partake from this table at the front of the sanctuary. All of us. It is like a potluck we might hold in the church hall, except that there is a lot less food on this table. But in the symbol of a piece of bread and a small glass of grape juice we each take from this family table, we are reminded that we are one body. And we need to care for one another as a family at its best would. That was Paul's other point. The Corinthians had forgotten that when they partook of this sacrament, they were part of one body.

I want to push the one body piece just a little further. This sacrament symbolizes God's grace for each of us, a grace that reaches out to all of us through the life, death, and resurrection of Jesus Christ. We are one body, a body we entered via another act that symbolized God's grace. In this body, societal distinctions need to fade away. We need to become one body. But the body we join is not just the body of this congregation. It is Christ's worldwide body. It is a body that ought, within its life, to be a place where the hungry are fed, the stranger welcomed, the naked clothed, and the prisoner visited. It is a body that should mirror, insofar as possible, the justice and the peace we long for in our world and understand to be God's hope for the world.

> "This is my body that is for you. Do this in remembrance of me." In the same way he took the cup also, after supper, saying, "This cup is the new covenant in my blood. Do this, as often as you drink it, in remembrance of me." (1 Corinthians 11:24–26)

As we eat this bread and drink the cup, may we proclaim Jesus' death, and all it represents, until he comes. And to God, who offers us such grace, Jesus Christ, though whom we have come to know such grace, and the Holy Spirit, the divine presence with us today and in the days ahead, be all honour, glory, and praise. Amen.

—John H. Young

This sermon was written for this book.

Chapter 13
Last Things

The Destination and the Journey

The Doctrinal Concept

Winter nights in Yellowknife are long. The light begins to fade about two in the afternoon, and the sun doesn't rise again until well after nine in the morning. For people who are afraid of the dark, that can be an intimidating experience. And it can intensify the impact of any fear or anxiety.

In September 1992, nine miners were killed in an underground explosion. It quickly became apparent that the blast had been set deliberately, meaning that the men had been murdered. In this normally safe city, a wave of random petty crime ensued. Downtown, store windows were broken. Cars were damaged. I took my turn at the counselling centre and when my shift was finished in the evening, I went outside and found my station wagon window smashed in.

It was frightening. Normal life shattered with that broken glass. Later at the repair shop, another woman said to me, "It feels like the end of the world." No one knew why there had been an explosion or who had done it. As the fall turned to winter and there was no resolution, anxiety spread. As the darkness deepened, fear grew.

The end of a world: indeed, Yellowknife was changed irrevocably. People began locking their houses, certain individuals were treated with suspicion, speculation was rampant, and friends and neighbours were polarized by opinion and role. Community trust was shattered.

The doctrine of last things addresses the end of the world. *Eschatology* means the study (*ology*) of last things (*eschatos*). Eschatology is about final events, ultimate destiny, death, and the end of the world. It relates to the second coming, the resurrection of the dead, and the last judgment. These drastic events are not often the theme of Sunday worship in The United Church of Canada. There are occasions, however, when drastic events intrude inexorably, and it may be surprising to consider how frequently they do.

The doctrine of the last things appears near the end of A Song of Faith:

We place our hope in God.
We sing of a life beyond life
    and a future good beyond imagining:
    a new heaven and a new earth,
    the end of sorrow, pain, and tears,
    Christ's return and life with God,
    the making new of all things.
We yearn for the coming of that future,
even while participating in eternal life now.

The phrases echo the language of scripture. We hear Revelation 21:3-5 in particular ("And I heard a loud voice..."; see below.)

Our lives are precious. We matter, and we merit being treasured.

On the personal level, this doctrine draws into question what we hope for in our own future. In the big picture, the question is the purpose of existence, the end point of this world. Pastorally, the challenge is whether our faith makes us afraid or confident.

Scripture for Preaching

Revelation 21:1–7

Then I saw a new heaven and a new earth; for the first heaven and the first earth had passed away, and the sea was no more. And I saw the holy city, the new Jerusalem, coming down out of heaven from God, prepared as a bride adorned for her husband. And I heard a loud voice from the throne saying, "See, the home of God is among mortals. [God] will dwell with them; they will be [God's] peoples, and God...will be with them; [God] will wipe every tear from their eyes. Death will be no more; mourning and crying and pain will be no more, for the first things have passed away."

And the one who was seated on the throne said, "See, I am making all things new." Also [God] said, "Write this, for these words are trustworthy and true." Then [God] said to me, "It is done! I am the Alpha and the Omega, the beginning and the end. To the thirsty I will give water as a gift from the spring of the water of life. Those who conquer will inherit these things, and I will be their God and they will be my children."

Why Is This Doctrine Important?

The doctrine of last things is important when we consider war, cruelty, loss of species from our ecosystem, pollutants in our oceans, or a dogged sense that evil is strong around us. Questions arise about God's intentions. Some wonder if we are in a crucible where torment battles good, with torment winning. Others see a spiritual vacuum. Underlying it is doubt asking, Is that all there is? These are spiritual and religious concerns as well as existential problems.

Second, the doctrine of last things concerns death. At the time of a death, we are first confronted by the ending of a life. Later we entrust our loved one to God's eternal presence, and later still we have opportunity to reflect on the time of that person's life.

Third, there is the issue of popular culture. A neighbour may well lean over the fence at the cottage and ask what your United Church has to say about the rapture. It is part of a preacher's responsibility to prepare members of the congregation to take part in this conversation with confidence. The apocalyptic question is alive in our day: Margaret Atwood's *MaddAddam*, George Orwell's *1984* and other dystopian stories, Tim LaHaye and Jerry Jenkins's *Left Behind* series, the political use of the military, and triumphalist religion all echo the Book of Revelation.

Finally, there is the matter of human value and the worth of the efforts we offer to make this a better world, to bring about an end that is good. Imagine a two-sided weigh scale, holding in balance the present and the future: in our church we call this a *realized eschatology*. This is the primary matter discussed here. Realized eschatology is gnarly, fascinating, and deeply helpful. It rescues this scripture from right-wing theology. It is also an approach you may not easily find elsewhere.

Let's consider the familiar metaphor of journey. We often speak of our lives as a journey. "We are pilgrims on a journey." "She cared for me in my journey through cancer." "Their marriage was a journey of 50 years." "Moses never saw the Promised Land at the end of the journey." This metaphor of a pilgrimage, a road, a route is powerful. It drives our goals and fuels our plans. It is a relevant and dignified image. Our lives change through forward motion, developments, twists in the road, growth, experience, and death. Just as every minute of attentive automobile driving guarantees our safe arrival, every moment on our lifelong journey matters, and it is no different for our journey of faith. Events and relationships count. Remembering to value the growth is a spiritual practice.

Where does the journey take us? To a destination, a place we long for, home maybe or a new adventure. And the journey eventually leads us to death, of course. A focus on the spiritual destination is a vision of a hope of heaven, a promise of eternity. "I go to prepare a place for you," Jesus says in John 14:2. "When I tread the verge of Jordan / Bid my anxious fears subside," we sing ("Guide Me, O Thou Great Jehovah," *Voices United* 651). "Way over yonder that's where I'm bound," my 96-year-old friend declares. Confident of a destination, we get through the maze. With our eyes on the end of things, we are better able to endure present distress.

We acknowledge, then, that things do come to an end. Sometimes that ending is dramatic and life-changing, such as the explosions in Yellowknife. The doctrine of last things gives us understanding and vocabulary to find meaning in endings. It is a spiritual discipline to seek this understanding. Moreover, getting to the end is a journey. The journey counts. The doctrine of last things matters to us for two reasons: our journeys come to an end, and how we have spent that time matters.

So eschatology means that there will be an end. There will be a resolution. It is a promise offered frequently in scripture, and, I note for our purposes of investigating apocalyptic literature, in Revelation 21:5: "See, I am making all things new." All things will be refreshed, made holy, forgiven, renewed, and brought back to God. This is a promise and a hope. It is also a relief, because in the midst of anxiety we can assure ourselves there is meaning—even if meaning seems distant. Going deeper into this doctrine, we discover that we are released from the cycle of life or the circle of eternity. We have a destination, and it is good.

The doctrine of last things concerns the purpose of time. The Ancient Near East, the setting of the Old Testament, was dominated by religious and existential concepts from the empires that were in power. Our ancestors in faith developed ways of being faithful in spite of, or in opposition to, many of those concepts. The model of time that came from the Sumerian culture involved a wheel of time that spun ceaselessly. Days, seasons, years rotated in a circular pattern. Time was understood as an endless repetition of the same sequence of events. Walking away from that culture and into the desert, Abraham was called forward. He was given a future-oriented promise: descendants as many as the stars.

The shocker of Old Testament theology is this: we have a future good beyond imagining. Abraham is freed from living in a cyclical repetition of life, suffering, and experience. We—and all creation—are on a journey with a destination. The startling, liberating momentum of Hebrew scripture that breaks out of a ceaselessly spinning wheel of time is the beginning of eschatology. It is the dawn of a new understanding: the doctrine of last things.

Now let's bring that new understanding of a future-oriented promise into the biblical passage. The model of prophecy in Revelation is the Book of Daniel. Daniel referred to the Exile, when the faithful were captured and exiled by Babylon. The theology of this empire was one of gods playing with, tormenting, and destroying humankind. In the face of that, Daniel wrote about wind, beasts, a throne, the Ancient of Days—and deliverance.

It is noteworthy that while in captivity to the Babylonian Empire, our ancestors wrote the first creation story, in which God saw that creation—of which we were part—was good. The Revelation to John, modelled on Daniel, was also written at a time of disaster. The letters to the seven churches bring a message of hope, courage, and faith, a message that at the end the faithful would be rewarded.

God's intention of goodness, renewal, abundance, and the end of suffering can be understood as a promise that can really happen when we think of time moving on. We are not stuck in present circumstances. That is hope beyond mere human vision. It is a promise beyond the reality of our lives. The hope of "a future good beyond imagining" (A Song of Faith) furnishes theology with abundance.

In the doctrine of eschatology time is linear, not a circle or a wheel. We live in the past, inhabit the present, and expect the future. We matter: our timeline is a heritage of experience, present occurrence, and future expectation. Anticipating last things, we can learn from the past to inhabit a present that creates a future good beyond imagining.

This concept is a long way from using the Book of Revelation or the stories of Daniel to frighten. Judgment and punishment are found in passages of the Book of Revelation, but we are finding another way to understand this part of the Bible. That understanding is the spiritual purpose of time, a profound reason to preach the doctrine of eschatology.

A classical answer to the purpose of time has to do with reward and punishment. This version of the end times is part of our tradition. Here it is from the Twenty Articles of Faith in the Basis of Union, written in 1908 and adopted in 1925:

> **Article XIX. Of the Resurrection, the Last Judgement, and the Future Life.**
> We believe that there shall be a resurrection of the dead, both of the just and of the unjust, through the power of the Son of God, who shall come to judge the living and the dead; that the finally impenitent shall go away into eternal punishment and the righteous into life eternal.

Narratively, eternal punishment is no longer a large part of the United Church lexicon. How do we talk about that? Here's one way: In wrestling with the possibilities of hell, and the prospect that our neighbours or our loved ones or we ourselves would end up in eternal torment, many of us have resolved to align with hope. We stake our faith on future hope, not future devastation. We conclude that God's love is primary and unconditional.

It's quite all right to say you don't believe something. The church and the theologies that ring true for us have come through a hundred years since that statement of faith was written. Our beliefs have changed.

For that matter, people's opinions have always differed, and certainly eternal punishment was debated in lively terms in the early 20th century. As a preacher, you can model discernment for your listeners. You can state that there are some beliefs you don't hold. None of us can believe everything.

The crucial purpose of time is to bring meaning. Time brings perspective on the past. It makes room for value in "the meantime," between present and future, between now and then. In contemporary spiritual terms this perspective is important; meaning can be shaky ground in a postmodern world. Although the "circle of life" brings a connection among generations, it also folds us in upon ourselves again and again without release to a higher purpose. We know that life ends, that people die, that change of the most existential kind possible awaits each of us with a linear full stop. The doctrine of last things concerns the purpose of time.

A hopeful orientation toward the future lifts the pall of despair that covers much of our culture. We acknowledge that we face suffering, and we affirm that death doesn't have the final word. Understanding the future as a hope-filled, life-affirming, existential reality is a philosophical position that transforms lives. It can move us beyond the despair we hear in the grievance of the question, Is that all there is?

Time as the connection between last things and present things is made clear in A Song of Faith:

> Divine creation does not cease
>> until all things have found wholeness, union, and integration
>> with the common ground of all being.
> As children of the Timeless One,
>> our time-bound lives will find completion
>> in the all-embracing Creator.

Shame, worthlessness, isolation, and despair are rampant in our culture. Let's counter them by outlining the worth of the individual and God's love for creation as we find it in the doctrine of last things. We can do that by preaching from a vivid biblical passage.

How Does It Preach?

Biblical passages about last things may be unfamiliar or uncomfortable. People may be of the opinion that these texts belong to more evangelical churches. Others may say these texts are irrelevant. By taking people inside scripture that feels awkward, we can claim something that is ours. We have inherited scripture and it behooves us to open it and look inside. Actually, it is not so much that scripture belongs to us as that we belong to it.

The connection to contemporary life is what turns scholarship into a sermon. This doctrine is important because it can bring us hope. Pastorally, the challenge is whether our faith makes us afraid or confident. Crises bring up the big questions. Frankly, then, disaster is a superb time to preach about the doctrine of last things. Natural disaster, human-created disaster, climate-induced disaster: we ask big questions when big things happen. The point of the sermon is not to connect the coming of God's future with disaster, of course, but rather to engage a teaching moment. My point is for you to have a theology of last things in your pocket for when bad things happen. You will be ready when it is needed.

I set this sermon up with a hymn that uses the language of the scripture. I chose "Holy, Holy, Holy," which comes from Revelation 4:8 and 4:10. "Swing Low, Sweet Chariot" is another choice, and it's fun to sing. A little levity relaxes the congregation, which is a good thing if something difficult is about to follow. After the sermon we sang my words in *More Voices* 220, "Hope Shines as the Solitary Star":

> Hope shines as the solitary star.
> Faith is the inner light.
> You and I together mirror the Light of Lights,
> and illumine the pathway home.[33]

You could preach from Daniel or Ezekiel, but I chose Revelation because of the passages about judgment and because it is vivid. It was part of a series; if it were a stand-alone Sunday, I would add a passage with frightening images, such as 6:12–14. Always, one should consult a good commentary for a comprehensive background on the scripture.

Beginning in a playful mood can draw listeners in. If you are writing a similar sermon, I suggest you talk about oddities in agriculture or stargazing. Later in the sermon I use rhetorical questions. Sometimes I receive answers from the listening congregation that can make the preaching time more lively. Another device I employ is to continue the scripture passage mid-sermon. The meaning apparently shifts, and leaving this new passage until I had preached on the earlier parts meant listeners were not jumping ahead.

I also speak clearly about what I believe in this sermon, and about what I don't believe. In a sermon you *can* say, "I don't believe this." When you teach about various interpretations, you can't possibly hold them all in your own personal faith. With gnarly material that approach can bring clarity. And this time it was important to speak personally; I was aware that there were members of the congregation who really wanted to know what I thought. People want to know what you believe, not necessarily because they think you are right or want to follow you, but because you are modelling how to live in a postmodern world of conflicting truths.

A whole Sunday service could be crafted on Abraham breaking free of a cyclical understanding of time. Our ancestors in faith wrote the Abraham story about God's radical love that cherishes him, and us, and moved humankind away from a world view in which people didn't matter. For this Sunday, I simply made reference to it.

Last things is a difficult doctrine—although certainly not dull! Even though we face suffering, death doesn't have the last word. Faith-filled hope—not mere optimism, but rather thoughtful, considered, faith-filled hope—shines through like the sun scattering winter clouds, illuminating the whole landscape before us. Our faith makes us confident.

I close the sermon by quoting the last things section of A Song of Faith. In United Church ethos, we embrace the meantime because it creates the future. We have a holy destination, and the journey to get there is time well spent.

Sample Sermon

Last Things

The strains of "Holy, Holy, Holy" are fading away into the rafters. Music seems to get caught in the ceiling above us and held for a moment, as we absorb the power of singing.

On the first Sunday morning in my first pastoral charge as an ordained minister, I prayed with the choir and followed them into the sanctuary. I went to the pulpit, offered the call to worship, and proceeded to bow my head for the opening prayer. Immediately the organist played a loud chord, and the choir burst into that hymn. I nearly jumped out of my skin. I was startled! Verse 1 finished. The choir sat down and looked at me expectantly. I smiled, weakly, and began to pray.

"Holy, Holy, Holy" is one of our heritage hymns. Many congregations sang a verse by rote as an introit, a choral beginning to Sunday worship—so I learned! It has huge organ notes, and a descant, and the Book of Revelation sewn right into the verses. Saints throw their golden crowns along the sea, cherubim and seraphim fall down before holiness, and darkness hides God. It's magnificent. It's poetic. It's complex. The scripture it is based on is magnificent and poetic and complex, too. There are angels, dragons, catastrophes, and a big white horse. There are some truly odd occurrences.

The world we live in has some pretty strange occurrences, too. Sometimes calves are born with two heads. I tell you that on good authority: the Dean of Agriculture told me. Listen to this: for every 100,000 chickens that are bred at a time, there is always one missing an upper beak.[34] Again, this is true. These are odd things. This is not supermarket-checkout-line-magazine odd. Truly odd things, the stuff of apocalyptic literature or the last things in scripture, appear in the real world.

Last Halloween Katniss Everdeen came to my door several times, bow and arrows in hand. Do you remember the protagonist from the novel *The Hunger Games?* In my neighbourhood many girls dressed up as

Katniss. She takes on the authorities in her dystopian world, not because she wants to but because she volunteered as "tribute" in order to stand in for her sister, saving her from certain death. She fights other children in an intricate amphitheatre. She ends up fighting the empire.

I resisted reading *The Hunger Games* and I almost didn't go to the movie. I didn't want to support the glorification of child soldiers. Eventually I figured that I needed to learn the story in order to understand what many teens were absorbing. It has been described as a post-apocalyptic story, one that follows the end of the world.

The word "apocalypse" comes from ancient Greek language: *apo-kalupsis,* to uncover or reveal; *apo-kalupsis,* to peel away the veneer and see what is underneath. When we look under scary images, we will uncover something unexpected. Sometimes it's not scary at all. Sometimes it's just a little man in green, like the Wizard of Oz. Apocalyptic literature tells a story that runs deeper than the surface and reveals an unexpected truth.

I tell you this because the Book of Revelation is full of stories and images that are odd, calamitous, and sometimes frightening. I don't want you to think I'm leaving out those parts. For instance, here is chapter 6, verses 12 to 14:

> I looked, and there came a great earthquake; the sun became black as sackcloth, the full moon became like blood, and the stars of the sky fell to the earth as the fig tree drops its winter fruit when shaken by a gale. The sky vanished like a scroll rolling itself up, and every mountain and island was removed from its place.

I remember singing a song with those images at summer camp. Some of the leaders at that camp were convinced there would be a final destruction, and maybe even a rapture where the faithful would be saved and the rest of us perish. Why was I never frightened? I was never frightened because the preacher in my own church taught me about future hope, not future calamity.

The images of rapture have more recently arrived in the *Left Behind* books and movies. Their image of a triumphant Jesus is at once frightening, exclusive, and caricatured. Caricature is how apocalypse, rapture, last things, and eschatology are commonly illustrated in our culture: they are hard to take seriously. Perhaps that relegates them to the ridiculous—but we still have scripture to deal with, and I am unwilling to sit by and see scripture ridiculed.

Have you had neighbours ask you about how your church explains apocalypse? I have. I remember one of those camp friends coming up to me years later, at university, and confronting me. Clearly she knew I didn't believe I'd be raptured along with her. "What will you do?" she asked. "I don't know," I said. "God loves me."

There are alarming events around us that sound like the last things in the Book of Revelation. Ebola frightens people. Pirates near the Seychelles Islands intimidate. Rogue waves suck beachcombers into the ocean depths. We lose a loved one to death. Floods cover the town of High River, and the town doesn't recover for years. How do we process our spiritual responses? Are we afraid or confident? What can we find in our faith to guide us?

In a vivid and remarkable way, last things address what we hope for in our own future, the purpose of existence, and whether our faith makes us afraid or confident. Let's see how.

The writers of scripture knew life and fear and love and forgiveness, all the virtues and vices we do. The writer of the Book of Revelation knew the impact it makes to speak of the moon turning to blood and the stars falling. It is a small step in popular imagination from these images in Revelation to imagining a destructive cleansing of the world. But wait a minute! "Destructive cleansing" is an oxymoron: the words are contradictory! We don't clean something by destroying it.

The purpose of apocalyptic literature is to *uncover* and *reveal*. What I am remembering as I read this scripture is how much I love this world. I love the moon and the stars; I love the neighbours and the friends. And I believe God does love it all, us all, too.

Here is the essential bit: remember the repetitive phrase in the opening of the Book of Genesis? *And God saw that it was good.* Yes, I am asking scripture to speak to scripture. For although much of creation is destroyed in the Book of Revelation, I don't believe for a minute that God spitefully destroys anything. I believe *that* because of the first chapter of Genesis. We can't have it both ways. Does God love us, or not? I choose *yes*. I choose hope, goodness, and love.

Now I am going to tell you that I cut our first Revelation reading short. I stopped before verse 8. Verse 8 condemns the cowardly, the faithless, the polluted, murderers, fornicators, sorcerers, idolaters, and all liars to a lake that burns with fire and brimstone. Holy smoke! That sounds like popular apocalypse, *The Hunger Games* maybe. Oh dear, who among us is not on that list? We are all cowardly and faithless from time to time. It breaks my heart to think that my old camp friend thinks God might stop loving anybody. I simply don't believe it. From visiting with you, I know many of you don't believe God would stop loving anybody, either.

I want to tell you that I don't believe God condemns people. *We love this world, and we believe God does.* Whew. I mean that. A few minutes ago we prayed "thy kingdom come," yet we do not believe we will be the only ones to benefit by the coming of God's kingdom.

Okay, if you are with me this far, let's go a little further. *Thy kingdom come:* if we are going to address rapture and judgment we might as well address the second coming. Certainly my friend who was convinced she would be raptured would have asked me about the second coming, too. I want you to be prepared when she asks you. Here is how we speak about it: God is with us and *makes God's own home with us* rather than dropping in from elsewhere. The problem would be thinking God does not live here; the sadness would be living our own days and nights as though we are separate from God's Spirit. God is always with us; God doesn't need to return from anywhere!

All right, you are asking, if it isn't rapture or judgment or second coming, what do we learn from the doctrine of last things? Why read Revelation 21:1–7 at all? We hear it at graveside; what does it mean?

This is good news: *The doctrine of last things concerns the purpose of time.*

Let's explore that. The purpose of time is to live our lives, *to be*, to love, learn, grow, forgive, die. All this has holy value. Our lives are precious. The doctrine of last things ensures that this value is not lost.

Every morning that we get to open our eyes is an opportunity to rejoice: "See, I am making all things new." Every night when we shut out the light is a moment to remember that we matter: "See, the home of God is among mortals. God will dwell with them." In every situation when we are anxious there are words of reassurance: "To the thirsty I will give water as a gift from the spring of the water of life" (Revelation 21:7).

We measure a trajectory of past through present to future, and God's loving presence through it all. The doctrine of last things gives room for us to hope in our own future. It makes our treasured memory sacred. It makes the purpose of our current existence holy. These passages of apocalyptic literature peel back to reveal God's love. We can face the world unafraid and confident.

Even though we face suffering, death doesn't have the final word. We live with future hope, not future catastrophe. We are confident in hope because we do not believe it is God's purpose in time to destroy the earth, but rather God's purpose in time to renew it: "[God] will wipe every tear from their eyes" (Revelation 21:4).

The *meantime* creates the future. We have a holy destination, and the journey to get there is time well spent. Here is the meantime, our living, time well spent, from A Song of Faith:

> In the meantime, we embrace the present,
>   embodying hope, loving our enemies,
>   caring for the earth,
>   choosing life.

Amen.

—*Catherine Faith MacLean*

This sermon is edited from one given in a January series on the Book of Revelation at St. Paul's United Church in Edmonton. We wondered if studying difficult texts in the bleak midwinter would keep people engaged in church. It did.

For Further Reading

Graves, Mike, ed. *What's the Matter with Preaching Today?* Louisville: Westminster John Knox Press, 2004.

Hall, Douglas John. *Bound and Free: A Theologian's Journey.* Minneapolis: Fortress Press, 2005.

Hughes, Robert and Kysar, Robert. *Preaching Doctrine.* Minneapolis: Fortress Press, 1997.

Jones, Serene. *Feminist Theory and Christian Theology: Cartographies of Grace.* Minneapolis: Fortress Press, 2000.

Jones, Serene, and Lakeland, Paul, eds. *Constructive Theology: A Contemporary Approach to Classical Themes.* Minneapolis: Fortress Press, 2005.

Long, Thomas G. *The Witness of Preaching.* 2nd ed. Louisville: Westminster John Knox Press, 2005.

Mathers, Donald. *The Word and the Way.* Toronto: United Church Publishing House, 1962.

Migliore, Daniel L. *Faith Seeking Understanding.* 3rd ed. Grand Rapids: Eerdmans, 2014.

Placher, William C., ed. *Essentials of Christian Theology.* Louisville: Westminster John Knox Press, 2003.

Robinson, Anthony B. *What's Theology Got to Do with It?: Convictions, Vitality, and the Church.* Herndon, VA: Alban Institute, 2006.

Wilson, Paul Scott. *Preaching as Poetry: Beauty, Goodness, and Truth in Every Sermon.* Nashville: Abingdon Press, 2014.

Notes

Chapter 1

1   The four "subordinate standards" are the Twenty Articles of Doctrine; A Statement of Faith, 1940; A New Creed; and A Song of Faith. They are set out in sections 2.3–2.6 of The Basis of Union in *The Manual*. See *The Manual, 2013* (Toronto: United Church Publishing House, 2013), 11–28.

Chapter 2

2   Albert Schweitzer, *The Quest of the Historical Jesus,* trans. W. Montgomery (1906; repr. New York: Macmillan Publishing Company Limited, 1968).

3   Walter Brueggemann, *Genesis* (Atlanta: John Knox Press, 1982), 112. Indeed, the part of the paragraph from which these terms were taken is worth quoting in full. Brueggemann writes: "It is an assumption of the modern world (in which our exposition must be done) that there will be no genuine newness, no really independent gift yet to be given. Such ideologies press persons either *(a)* to *inordinate pride* which imagines the world has been completely entrusted to us and that we may construct our own future out of the present, or *(b)* to *deep despair* which believes the present world of inequity and oppression is forever and that there is no power in heaven or on earth that can make real change. Both the ideology of pride and the ideology of despair presume that the world is essentially a human artifact, that all possibilities are comprehended in human capacities for good or for ill."

4   To judge that the Farewell Discourse, in the form we have it, is a compilation of the editor(s) of John's gospel does not mean that the sayings found here do not reflect ancient material, or sayings of Jesus passed down in the Johannine community. For a good discussion of the Farewell Discourse and some of these questions, see Raymond Brown, *The Gospel of John, XIII–XXI* (Garden City, NY: Doubleday & Company Ltd., 1970), 581–604.

5   The concept of seeing John 14:6 as the "language of love" is not original to me. I first came across this concept when one of my professors in theological school shared with us having heard it in a lecture by the New Testament scholar Krister Stendahl. It has made good sense to me since I first heard about Stendahl's concept while doing my M.Div. degree.

Chapter 3

6   Donald M. Mathers, *The Word and the Way* (Toronto: United Church Publishing House, 1962), 118. Mathers's book was the first volume published in The New Curriculum, an ambitious Sunday school curriculum that sought to introduce students to contemporary biblical, theological, and historical scholarship. The curriculum, which included material for an adult Sunday school class or study group, had a three-year cycle corresponding to the then current "age divisions" in the denomination's Sunday school program.

Chapter 4

7   Daniel L. Migliore, *Faith Seeking Understanding,* 3rd ed. (Grand Rapids, MI: William B. Eerdmans Publishing Company, 2014), 46.

8   Mathers, *The Word and the Way,* 92–93.

9   Ibid., 95.

Chapter 6

10 John Calvin, *Institutes of the Christian Religion*, Book II, 1, 1–11, ed. John T. McNeill, trans. Ford Lewis Battles (Philadelphia: The Westminster Press, 1960), 241–55.

11 Serene Jones, *Feminist Theory and Christian Theology: Cartographies of Grace* (Minneapolis: Fortress Press, 2000), 94–125.

12 John Page Hopps, "Father, Lead Me Day by Day," in *The Hymnary of The United Church of Canada* (Toronto: United Church Publishing House, 1930), Hymn 596.

13 Migliore, *Faith Seeking Understanding*, 143.

14 See, for example, Joseph A. Fitzmyer, S.J., *Romans* (New York: Doubleday, 1992), 474–75.

Chapter 7

15 Mark Nicoll and Steve MacRae in Yellowknife United Church choir.

Chapter 9

16 A key leader, though probably not the apostle Peter. I accept the view of many New Testament scholars that this letter was written later than a Petrine authorship would make possible.

Chapter 10

17 *Baptism, Eucharist and Ministry*, Faith and Order Paper no. 111 (Geneva: World Council of Churches, 1982), 17, 18.

18 Migliore, *Faith Seeking Understanding*, 309.

19 Robert C. Fennell, "On Ordained Ministry," *Touchstone* 29, no. 1 (January 2011): 9. Used with permission.

20 *Baptism, Eucharist and Ministry*, 17, 18.

Chapter 11

21 The Society of Friends, or Quakers, for example, is a Christian denomination that does not have sacraments; baptism, therefore, is not a part of its tradition.

22 Calvin, *Institutes of the Christian Religion*, Book IV, xiv, 1–3, 1276–78.

23 See James F. White, *Introduction to Christian Worship*, 3rd ed. (Abingdon Press: Nashville, 2000), 217–20.

24 Anthony B. Robinson, *What's Theology Got to Do with It?: Convictions, Vitality, and the Church* (Herndon, VA: The Alban Institute, 2006), 179–183.

25 Maria Straub, "God Sees the Little Sparrow Fall," in *The Hymnary of The United Church of Canada* (Toronto: United Church Publishing House, 1930), Hymn 588.

26 *Service Book for the Use of Ministers Conducting Public Worship* (Toronto: The United Church of Canada by Ryerson Press, 1969), 43.

27 See Tertullian, *Apology*, Chap. 37, in vol. 3, *Ante-Nicene Fathers*, ed. Alexander Roberts and James Donaldson (1885–1896; repr., Peabody, MA: Hendrickson Publishers, Inc., 1995), 46.

Chapter 12

28 *Service Book for the Use of Ministers*, 8.

29 For a good discussion both of the language early church figures used and of how this early breadth of possibilities became reduced, see White, *Introduction to Christian Worship*, 248–59.

30 Calvin, *Institutes of the Christian Religion*, Book IV, xvii, 32, 1403–1404.

31 For this same sentiment expressed in earlier communion liturgies, see *Service Book for the Use of Ministers*, 8.

32 Richard B. Hays, *First Corinthians* (Louisville: John Knox Press, 1997), 195–97.

Chapter 13

33 *More Voices: Supplement to Voices United: The Hymn and Worship Book of The United Church of Canada* (Toronto and Kelowna: UCPH and Woodlake Books), 2007.

34 Frank Robinson, Associate Dean (Academic) and Professor, Poultry Production and Physiology, Faculty of Agricultural, Life and Environmental Sciences, University of Alberta, October 2008.

UNITED CHURCH
PUBLISHING HOUSE

We'd love to hear what you thought of this book.
Please add your review at UCRDstore.ca
or e-mail your comments to bookpub@united-church.ca